ActivePerl™ with ASP and ADO

ActivePerl™ with ASP and ADO

Tobias Martinsson

Wiley Computer Publishing

John Wiley & Sons, Inc.

NEW YORK • CHICHESTER • WEINHEIM • BRISBANE • SINGAPORE • TORONTO

Publisher: Robert Ipsen

Editor: Marjorie Spencer

Assistant Editor: Margaret Hendrey

Managing Editor: Frank Grazioli

Associate New Media Editor: Brian Snapp

Text Design & Composition: North Market Street Graphics

Designations used by companies to distinguish their products are often claimed as trademarks. In all instances where John Wiley & Sons, Inc., is aware of a claim, the product names appear in initial capital or ALL CAPITAL LETTERS. Readers, however, should contact the appropriate companies for more complete information regarding trademarks and registration.

ActiveState, ActivePerl, PerlScript, and Perl for Win32 are trademarks of ActiveState Tool Corp.

Published by John Wiley & Sons, Inc.

Published simultaneously in Canada.

This publication is designed to provide accurate and authoritative information in regard to the subject matter covered. It is sold with the understanding that the publisher is not engaged in professional services. If professional advice or other expert assistance is required, the services of a competent professional person should be sought.

Library of Congress Cataloging-in-Publication Data:

Martinsson, Tobias 1976–
ActivePerl with ASP and ADO / Tobias Martinsson.
  p.   cm.
  ISBN 0-471-38314-7 (paper/cd-rom : alk. paper)
  1. Perl (Computer program language)   2. Active server pages.   3. ActiveX.
I. Title.

QA76.73.P22 M33 2000
005.13'3—dc21

00-020737

Printed in the United States of America.

10 9 8 7 6 5 4 3 2 1

Dedicated to the reader; enjoy the material.

CONTENTS

Acknowledgments   xv

Introduction   xvii

Chapter 1   Active Server Pages   1

Getting Started with ASP   1
    To CGI or to ASP   2
    A Web Service's Nervous System   4
        The Application Object   4
        The ASPError Object   5
        The ObjectContext Object   5
        The Request Object   6
        The Response Object   6
        The Server Object   6
        The Session Object   7
        Writing Your Own COM Components   7

Installing Active Server Pages   7

The PerlScript Engine   8
    Installation   8
    Troubleshooting   8

Configuring the Scripting Language   9
    The Default Language   9
    Several Languages in One File   9
    Server-Side Configuration   10
        Windows 95 and 98   10
        Windows NT 4 and 2000   11

Server-Side Include Files   11
    Virtual File Names   12
    Relative File Name   12
    The Capacity of SSI   12

The Architecture of ASP   13
    Method   13
    Property   14
        Reading a Property   14
        Setting a Property   14
    Events   14

Collection 14
The Item() Method 15
The Count Property 16
The Remove() Method 17
The RemoveAll() Method 17

Summary 17

Chapter 2   Perl Programming Basics **19**

Getting a Head Start with Perl 20
In the Programmer's Toolbox . . . 20
The ActivePerl Documentation 20
Whenever You Need to Ask a Perl Question 21
The Perl Package Manager 23
Why Bother Installing Modules? 23
Installing Modules with PPM 23
Examples of Modules 26
The Standard Perl Modules 27

Introduction to Programming Perl 29
Programmatical Grammar 29
Scalar Variables 31
The Scalar Variable 33
Related Functions 35
The Array 36
Related Functions 38
The Associative Array 39
Related Functions 39
References and Nested Data Structures 43
File Handles 44
Special Variables 47

The Control Structures of Perl 47
Conditional Control Statements 49
Loop Control Statements 50
The For Loop 50
The Foreach Loop 50
The While Loop 51
The Until Loop 51
Labels 51

Regular Expressions 51
Beginning Regular Expressions 52
Pattern Matching 52
Modifiers 52
Metacharacters 53
Pattern Quantifiers 53
Predefined Character Classes 53
Matching Locations in a String 53
Extended Regular Expressions 54
Substitution 54
Translation 55

Modular Perl Programming   56
  Packages   56
  Subroutines   56
    Parameters   57
    Return Values   60
    Prototypes   61
    Further Reference   61
  The Symbol Table   61
    The Typeglob   62
  Modules   63
    Further Reference   63
  Object-Oriented Perl   63
Summary   67
  Further Reference   68

Chapter 3   Elevating the Stateless Internet   69

Introducing the Not-So-Visible ASP Objects   70
What You Need to Know about Applications   70
  The Events   71
Sharing Data on the Web   72
  Application Events in Global.asa   72
    Event: Application_OnStart   72
    Event: Application_OnEnd   73
  Adding Items to the Contents Collection   73
  Issues of Concurrency   73
  Cleaning Up the Application   75
The Session Object   75
  Session Events in Global.asa   76
    Event: Session_OnStart   76
    Event: Session_OnEnd   76
  The Session Object's Process   76
  Overview: The Application   78
  Overview: The Session   78
Summary   79

Chapter 4   Practical Active Server Pages   81

Levels of Communication   81
Taking Charge over the HTTP Stream   82
  An Old Recipe: Cookies   83
  When to Serve Cookies   83
  A New Cookie   84
  A Cookie with Subkeys   85
  Reading Cookies   85
Communicating with the Client   87
  Collecting Items in the Query String   87
  The Features of a Query String   87
  In-Memory Storage of Data   88

Storing the Items in a Hash   88
Storing the Variables in a Cookie   88
Example: Combining the Query String and the Session   90
Validate Submitted Data as Clean and Legal Entries   94
Checking the Form Fields   94
Checking for a Two-Letter State   96
Formatting Names   96
Checking a Five-Digit Zip Code   96
Checking a Phone Number in Format 888-888-8888   97
How to Respond to the Client   97
Sending a Status Header   97
Redirecting the Browser   97
The Form Collection   98
Example: Fetching a Remote Web Page   98
Client Certificates for Security   99
Server Variables   101
Example: Dumping All Server Variables   101
A Note for the COM Developer   102
Overview: The Response Object   103
Overview: The Request Object   103

Summary   105

Chapter 5   The Special Utility Objects   107

The Swiss Army Knife of ASP   107
The Server's Property   107
ScriptTimeout   108
The Utility Methods   108
The CreateObject() Method   108
The Execute() Method   108
The GetLastError() Method   109
The HTMLEncode() Method   109
The MapPath() Method   109
The Transfer() Method   111
URLEncode() Method   111
Overview: The Server Object   111

A Transactional Utility   111
Controlling Transactions   111
The ObjectContext Object   112
Everything about Errors   112
The ASPError Object   113

Summary   113

Chapter 6   Universal Data Access   115

Microsoft Data Access Components   115
The Medicine for Data Access   115
A and Ω of Relational Databases   118
The Structured Query Language   120

Data Manipulation Language	120
The Select Clause	121
BETWEEN	123
LIKE	123
IN	124
NOT	124
NULL	124
ALL, DISTINCT	125
Joining Tables	125
Data Definition Language	126
CREATE	126
DROP	126
ALTER	126
Data Control Language	127
ActiveX Data Objects for Data Access	127
Behind ADO	127
The OLE DB Data Provider	128
Dynamic Properties	129
Built-In Properties	130
The Data Source	130
The Native Provider	131
Universal Data Link	132
Data Source Name	132
Creating a System DSN	133
Creating a File DSN	133
No DSN or DSN-Less	133
Example with SQL Server and OLE DB	134
The OLE DB Consumer	134
The ADO Object Model	134
Connection	135
Recordset	135
Command	136
Parameter	136
Field	136
Error	136
Property	136
Record	136
Stream	136
System and Software Requirements	137
Database Requirements	137
Summary	137
Chapter 7 Database Programming in ADO	**139**
Introduction to the Connection	139
The Syntax	139
Making the Connection	141
Connecting without a DSN	141
Checking the Database Session for Errors	143

Executing an SQL Query	144
Making the Selection	144
Examining an Error	145
Performance Tweaking	147
Learning the Database Structure	150
Inserting New Records	156
Creating Database Tables	157
Deleting Database Tables	159
Database Transactions	159
Overview: The Connection	159
Summary	159

Chapter 8	**The Heart of ADO**	**163**
	Introduction to the Recordset	163
	The Syntax	163
	Perfecting the Recordset	164
	The Cursor Type Property	164
	The Right Type of Cursor	165
	The LockType Property	166
	The Right Type of Lock	166
	Rows and Columns	167
	How to Create the Recordset	169
	The Everyday Recordset	169
	A Better Recordset	171
	Examples of How To . . .	172
	Escape the While Loop and Catch Up on Speed	172
	Splitting the Recordset into Book Pages	174
	Using GetRows with CacheSize	180
	Searching for a Record	181
	Features You May Access	182
	A New Group of Records with Filter	183
	Ordering the Records	184
	Deleting Records	184
	Adding New Records	185
	ADO from Command Line Perl	186
	Back and Forth—Script Conversion	187
	Accessing ADO from Perl	187
	Splitting a Recordset with Perl	188
	The Disconnected Recordsets	194
	No Connections	194
	Hanging Up on the Data Source	195
	Creating the Recordset Programmatically	197
	Persisting a Recordset	199
	Saving It as a File	199
	As an XML Document	200
	In the Binary ADTG Format	201

Reading a Persisted Recordset from File   202
Persisting a Recordset to the ASP Response Object   202

Shaped Hierarchical Recordsets   203
The Shape Language   203
A Relation-Based Hierarchy   204
Parameterized Shape Statements   211
A Computed or Grouped Hierarchy   211
Disconnected Hierarchical Recordsets   215
Reshaping the Hierarchy   224
Overview: The Recordset   224

Summary   225

Chapter 9   Fast Queries with the Command Object   227

Introduction to the Command   227
Preparing a Fast Query   227
Parameters   229
Creating the Parameters   229
An Overview of the Parameter Object   232
Overview: The Command   232

Summary   234

Chapter 10   A Natural Systems Record   235

Introduction to the Record   235
Getting Your Hands on a Record   235
Moving, Deleting, and Copying   240
CopyRecord   240
DeleteRecord   241
MoveRecord   241
Overview: The Record   241

Summary   243

Chapter 11   Working the Stream of Data   245

Introduction to the Stream   245
Opening the Stream   245
Overview: The Stream   247

Summary   248

Appendix A: Bag of Scripts   251
Appendix B: What's on the CD-ROM   263
Appendix C: The HTTP Status Description   267
Appendix D: Content Types   269
Appendix E: ActivePerl Activity on the Web   271
Glossary   273
Index   279

First, I want to extend a great amount of gratitude to Doug Lankshear (http://www .activestate.com). Doug worked on the first port of Perl to Windows, and he is the cofounder of ActiveState Tools Corp.; thus, given his always-busy schedule developing next-generation Perl tools, it meant very much that he said yes to becoming the technical reviewer. Thank you, Doug. Titles aside, you are a very good person and friend— which is of much value regardless of circumstances.

Looking back, it means a lot that an experienced programmer by the name of Rene K. Mueller (http://the-labs.com) once said that Perl "is well worth learning." Built on words alone, Rene's personality and kindness in answering a multitude of questions from a beginning Perl programmer have caused a positive chain reaction. Rene, thank you for that and much more, and peace.

On the publishing side, thank you to Marjorie Spencer for being on the receiving end and the beginning of an e-mail that traveled in mysterious ways. Margaret Hendrey, I thank you for the confident work you have put into both the project and the research you have had to do. Now, let the wind blow our way since we're all aboard.

Rena, thank you for being by my side, being my warden while writing, always being on track knowing that "dollar sign, variable, dash, and greater than is the answer," flying like a cannonball in the metal coffin, howling at the moon. . . . It has an everlasting effect. . . .

Rising with the sun on the technological side, a thank you to J.T. for making this possible by "delivering the goods."

In terms of writing and direction, thank you to my brother, father, and mother for making this possible by many means, for many years.

Frank Grazioli, thank you very much, and my gratitude and best wishes to the people I never got to see, but who put their time and hands into getting this book in print.

Welcome to a book written for the Windows developer. It blends three powerful technologies, and you need not be experienced in any of these to find it easy to learn. Before we begin, however, I want to set the scene and present my point of view on the book that you are reading.

First, I wanted to make the book useful for the reader on the beginning to the intermediate level. Whether you had no experience or more experience, I wanted you to benefit from this book. In addition, the material had to make a good reference to keep on your desk. As I was writing, I pondered what I found lacking in books that I was unhappy with, what would have made these books better, and what I really wanted in a book that I bought myself. The answer was a book that explains jargon, buzzwords, or terms instead of assuming that you know them, and a book where code illustrates the ideas. Also, you should be able to find answers at any time without reading several pages, flipping through indexes, taking a guess, or resorting to searching the Internet. With that vision, time and effort were put into researching, making tables, and, of course, writing.

As a result, the first thing about the book is, simply put, Perl. The book does not assume or expect that you know Perl, so it gives an explanation of the language. It is focused on Perl as it relates to the topics treated because, personally and truthfully, I consider Perl to be one of the most suitable and powerful scripting languages available—an opinion shared by many other programmers. An ancient rumor, however, has it that only die-hard systems administrators on the UNIX operating system have use for Perl—and, if that weren't bad enough, that Perl is suitable only for an operating system as such and not for the Windows architecture. Well, the fact of the matter is that the rumor is simply not true, and it should be put to rest. On Windows, adapted and ported, Perl continues to be one of the most complete and powerful scripting languages for developers and systems administrators.

The breadth and depth of the Perl language has led to many books about it on various topics, including this one. This book focuses on Windows technologies of Active Server Pages and ActiveX Data Objects (ADO) of Microsoft Data Access Components. Compatible and accessible, Perl makes an excellent trio with these two technologies, paving the way for new and great Internet and database applications. I sincerely hope that you will enjoy the read and the reference.

How This Book Is Organized

In terms of presentation, a practical approach is used to illustrate theoretical concepts; code is used as the primary tool to show how to get something to work, whereas the text focuses on where, why, and how it works.

The book can be broken down into two major topics: Active Server Pages (ASP) and ActiveX Data Objects (ADO) (part of Microsoft Data Access Components). Each has an introductory chapter that covers ideas, concepts, and meanings, and a major topic that runs several chapters. There are also complementary sections for completeness so that you don't have to run to the historical library and dust off a book to get the background and full picture of something that is presented. Each topic is divided into chapters that treat a functionality of the topic, and at the end of each chapter there is an overview of what is exposed through the object that was presented.

Chapter 1 introduces Active Server Pages. It explains how to obtain, install, and configure the necessary software before getting started. It compares when, how, and why either ASP or the Common Gateway Interface (CGI) is best for development. It also takes a look on what needs Active Server Pages fulfill, what they may contain and how they work, what their object-oriented component structure is like, and the environment in which this structure works.

Chapter 2 is about ActivePerl. It looks at the tools included in the software bundle and how to use the ones that are most important for the perfect programming experience. The syntax, variables, built-in functions, control structures, and regular expressions of the scripting language are covered. An overview of the internal workings of Perl follows, and, finally, the approach of modular programming with subroutines and object-oriented programming is explained and illustrated.

Chapter 3 begins Active Server Pages programming with a discussion of storing global data on the server with the Application object and how to share it in the Web service. We also describe the Session object, which is associated with each unique client, and show how it can privatize and protect server-side data collected from the client and why it is useful. These objects, the events that trigger them, and how to program with the events are explained.

Chapter 4 continues with client and server interaction under Active Server Pages. In focus are the Response object and the Request object as we look at controlling the stream of data (such as HTML) to the client and collecting data (such as form data) from the client. In addition, form validation, cookies, digital certificates, and server variables are covered.

Chapter 5 ends the discussion of Active Server Pages with the interesting Special Utility objects. Included in this section are objects that control things on the server side, such as creating instances of external Component Object Model (COM) objects, handling transactions, and collecting data about an error that has occurred.

Chapter 6 introduces the database topics with the Universal Data Access strategy. The meanings behind the frequently used terms ODBC, OLE DB, and ADO are explained, as well as when, how, and where they work in an architectural structure. Relational databases and the Structured Query Language are explained and followed by instructions on how to connect the application to databases.

Chapter 7 explains database programming in ADO. It concerns the Connection object and shows how to make a connection, execute a query, and optimize a query. It also discusses how to extract the structure of a database, such as tables and columns, and how to create brand-new tables and columns from queries.

Chapter 8 continues with database programming on the important topic of the heart of ADO, namely the Recordset object. There is a discussion of how to create, configure, and optimize the Recordset, followed by a series of examples on uses of the Recordset both on the Internet and from the command line. More advanced topics are included, such as disconnecting Recordsets, creating a Recordset without an underlying database, saving Recordsets to files, and creating hierarchical Recordsets with the Shape language.

Chapter 9 focuses on the Command object, which helps to speed up queries. A Command object can represent a precompiled version of a command, whereas the database can store and reexecute the query without recompilation. As a result, the Command object can reduce compilation time in a commonly executed query, among other things.

Chapter 10 concentrates on Record objects. Instead of databases, the Record was made to work with natural hierarchy structures such as file systems and e-mail systems. Also covered is binding to URLs, where a URL pointing to a file can be connected, moved, deleted, or copied.

Chapter 11 discusses how to work the Stream object. A stream represents a stream of data such as textual or binary data.

Who Should Read This Book

A Windows developer who wants to develop powerful Active Server Pages and data access applications such as connecting databases to the Internet should read this book.

Whether this is your first encounter with Perl, Active Server Pages, or ActiveX Data Objects will not matter. Each topic is explained from the very beginning, and if you are a current programmer, there are several ways to look at this book. For current Perl programmers, a natural step on the Windows platform is to empower current knowledge by learning Active Server Pages and ActiveX Data Objects. ActiveX Data Objects paves the way for powerful offline database applications run from the command line and online databases on the Internet, and this book offers a wealth of information on it. An Active Server Pages programmer who feels limited in the current environment is guaranteed to enjoy the flexibility of PerlScript, and so is a beginner to Active Server.

In my personal experience, I've read books that were not related to Perl or PerlScript but that dealt with Active Server Pages and ActiveX Data Objects. With this in mind, whether you want to try a new scripting language or get a good reference that is not in your current language, jump into this book.

Tools You Will Need

In order to run the code presented in the book, you need the free software bundle ActivePerl, which is included on the accompanying CD-ROM, and a Web server that supports Active Server Pages—for example, the free Microsoft Personal Web Server or Microsoft Internet Information Services. Next, to connect to a database you need Microsoft Data Access Components. This includes ActiveX Data Objects (ADO). You can download these tools for free from the Internet and install them by following the instructions in the first chapter or by visiting the vendor's Web site.

What's on the CD-ROM/Disk/Web Site

The accompanying CD-ROM contains scripts as presented in the book and ActivePerl so that you can get started immediately. On the CD-ROM, one group of files is used on the Internet in Active Server Pages. The source code for those files is available in PerlScript, which is the scripting language used in Active Server Pages. A second group of files are related to ADO programming, which connects an application to data stores such as databases, spreadsheets, and files. These ADO files can be run both on and off the Internet. Where applicable—which is in the majority of cases—a PerlScript version of the script for the Active Server Pages plus an additional Perl version of the script, which is ready to be run from the command prompt, are available. A third group of scripts on the CD contains Active Server Pages PerlScript for common tasks such as sending e-mail, retrieving e-mail, drawing graphics on the fly, and finding the dimensions of an image. Furthermore, system administrative tasks are on the CD-ROM: for example, graphing the physical representation of the disk space on the local machine and graphing system usage of RAM and virtual memory plus the Windows services running on the machine.

Document Conventions

In terms of document conventions, there are only a few things that need to be noted, so let's cover those design considerations now.

Every table that contains enumerated constants will have a value field and a name field. Some values are in hexadecimal format, such as 0x00000100, and some are in integer format such as 4; Perl can handle either format. With the value, there will be a name, such as adHoldRecords, which can be used instead of the value and which is simply called by the name of the constant. The values of the constants are given so that if you want to use them directly instead of the names (which requires the loading of the constants), you can easily do so.

Every table at the end of a chapter will list methods of an object. When reading these, keep in mind that text in square brackets [ ] symbolizes something that is optional and need not be present for the method to work. When two or more items are separated by the pipe symbol (|), it means that only one of the two or more values should be used, but it can be any of the values listed. For example, a method named MoveAbroad is called and in the definition it says MoveAbroad(France|Italy). In this case you can choose either MoveAbroad(France) or MoveAbroad(Italy), but you have to choose one or the other.

## CHAPTER 1

Active Server Pages

M icrosoft's Active Server Pages (ASP) technology makes Internet development both easier to learn and more powerful to use. As a server-side technology, ASP introduces new and great scripting capabilities.

Getting Started with ASP

There are several similarities between documents in Hypertext Markup Language (HTML) and ASP. For example, both can contain plain text, HTML tags, and client-side scripting commands such as JavaScript. However, there are strong differences as well.

In contrast to HTML, which creates static documents, ASP enables your favorite scripting language to perform trivial to complex operations that otherwise are not possible without the use of Common Gateway Interface (CGI).

Either mixed with HTML or transparently run without output, script commands included in the ASP document are always processed on the server side. However, ASP differs from CGI, which runs or interprets an external program written in a programming or scripting language such as C or Perl. By cleverly integrating a scripting language instead, ASP prevents external process launch. The following types of content can be included when building an ASP document:

- Plain text
- HTML

- Client-side script commands
- Server-side script commands
- Dynamically included files such as ASP, HTML, or other documents

Each document with the file extension .asp—an Active Server page—is processed by a component (or unit of code) named the Active Server Pages engine. As the *scripting host*, it interfaces an ActiveX Scripting Engine—a specification of how to easily implement a scripting language into a host application—so that it can run script commands in the host application on the server side.

A number of scripting languages such as JScript, VBScript, REXX, and Python are available as ActiveX Scripting Engines. We will use none of the above, however. An ActiveX implementation of Perl, PerlScript provides server-side Perl scripting capabilities to scripting hosts such as an Active Server Pages–enabled Web server without need for Common Gateway Interface (CGI).

Additionally, the ActiveX Scripting Engines are used with technologies such as Windows Script Host and Microsoft Script Control, making them suitable for everything from Microsoft Word macros in PerlScript to distributed COM components for Active Server Pages.

In summary, on the Internet, Active Server Pages enables a scripting language to be implemented as a server-side ActiveX Scripting Engine. As a result, text, HTML, and other standard content types for Web documents can be combined into a single document—the ASP document—using server-side interpreted script commands. Because any script commands are run on the server side, and only the result is returned to the client, it is not possible to view the source code of the script. The result that is seen in the browser is the final product, and it is always HTML. The ActiveX Scripting Engine is not limited to Active Server Pages, but can also be embedded in other applications and utilized by other scripting languages, and all this with its natural language adapted for the ActiveX Scripting Host.

To CGI or to ASP

CGI, the interface for Internet scripting that has been around the longest, is widely known, respected, and deployed. Both its advantages and limitations are well known and in the majority of cases are very acceptable and suitable. However, a relatively new technology—Active Server Pages—is increasingly popular for scripting solutions. Let's look at why.

With many technologies available, the issue at hand is no longer using a technology because it works—even if it works wonders. On the contrary, for a given situation it is essential to know when to use which technology because it is the best. A great variety of Web servers, platforms, and scripting languages might be involved, and in some cases those factors might depend on a decision that is made outside of your jurisdiction. To bring part of the issue to light for Internet Information Services (IIS) on Windows, let's illustrate ASP with PerlScript and CGI with Perl. The comparison can be summarized as follows:

- No process launch occurs when using PerlScript or Perl for ISAPI. In contrast, CGI with the Perl interpreter (Perl.exe) does result in a process launch of the interpreter on the server. With increasing numbers of visitors, it will result in more process launches, and if that pressure is continued—as with a popular service—it will take its toll on the Web server's performance.

- Comparing PerlScript and PerlIS, the overhead from the Component Object Model (COM) increases the start-up of PerlScript. Therefore, simple CGI should use PerlIS.dll, but applications that are larger in scope should use Active Server Pages and PerlScript.

- Do you use Perl frequently or want to use it more often? Converting to PerlScript and Active Server Pages is recommended. Active Server Pages was designed to provide a complete Web service fully integrated with a scripting language. CGI, on the other hand, was designed as an interface that allows external programs to be run in an Internet environment. In short, when virtually integrating a scripting language by constantly executing CGI, choose instead the technology that has already integrated the language for you on the server side.

- For access to any of the IIS COM objects, such as the Session object, you need an ActiveX Scripting Engine.

In addition, Active Server Pages offers a way of maintaining the client's state. The phrase *maintaining state* is used more often than it is explained, but posing the following problem can summarize it:

On a Web service such as www.yourcompany.com, a single client can open numerous pages and travel between many links. For each requested page or newly opened page the client is to the server a new and unknown client just requesting a page located on the server. After the server has delivered the page, the server's "memory" of the client is erased. As a result, information that by script command was stored in variables on page 1 will not be available on page 2, so since the variables are not transferable between pages but lost with each new request, the state of the data is not maintained. When state is maintained, however, the variables are not lost between pages and are available by script command on any page during the client's visit.

In many cases, simple CGI maintains state by using cookies or passing the information to the next page as a part of the URL in the form www.somewhere.com?zipcode=21312, as you've probably seen many times on the Internet or specified in your own programming. Now, Active Server Pages provides a more elegant way of maintaining state on the server side: the Session object.

A unique Session object is created for and associated with each new client. By script command, data can be added, read, and removed from the Session object, which means that it basically serves as a data store. Everything in the object is stored and protected on the server side and does not maintain the state by classical means. If you want to use the Session object to maintain state, Active Server Pages must be used.

In summary, there is no universal answer to the question about when to use CGI and when to use ASP. It certainly will not hurt to know both technologies, to be able to get the best of both worlds and develop high-end applications within any environment on the Internet. What remains is the most important fact: You cannot foresee how everything will work in every situation, so you might have to experiment. What is presented here are general suggestions about where each technology has proven to be at its best; the industry is guaranteed to keep moving onward to higher ground.

A Web Service's Nervous System

Active Server Pages provides an application-level programming interface (API) through seven built-in objects. The API is the nervous system of the Web server, and it is used to provide more live content than static pages. Each built-in ASP object represents its own area of "expertise," and anywhere in the Web application, the ActiveX Scripting Engine can access the following built-in objects:

- Application
- ASPError
- ObjectContext
- Request
- Response
- Server
- Session

In addition to built-in objects, the applications can use external COM components on the server. Adding even more functionality to the Web, a component can be either handmade or premade. For example, with ActiveX Data Objects (ADO) from Microsoft, not only can you query a database such as SQL Server, Oracle, or MS Access from your Active Server pages, there is also support for managing remote file systems and e-mail systems. And if you want to build your own COM component for a proprietary service or to build upon an existing component, there is support for generating components in Perl, too.

The Application Object

The concept of the Application object is confusing to beginning programmers at first, so instead of diving right into it, let's begin by covering what *application* means to Internet Information Services, then summarize the Active Server Pages Application object.

In IIS contexts, an application comprises a directory and all its subdirectories. But first, a directory must be marked as an *application root* or else it will neither be an IIS application nor include subdirectories. A number of applications can be set and configured within the Web service. Examples are permissions, security, customized headers, and the default scripting engine for the IIS application, which are the *control centers* strategically put out on the Web service.

In ASP contexts, an Application (ASP) object is automatically assigned to an IIS application. The Application object is not like the other built-in objects because it maintains the state of its contents and makes them global and accessible to all users. Contents can be added, read, or removed by script command from the scripting engine. The Application object shares its server-side data within the users of a marked application and is designed to handle concurrency issues such as several clients wanting to modify the same value at the same time.

In general, the ASP Application object holds both trivial and advanced contents. For example, one everyday use of the Application object is storing a counter of the total number of visitors since the service was started or showing the number of concurrent visitors online at the moment. Types of advanced data that can be stored are disconnected record sets (see Chapter 8), connection information for a database, or advanced log information, to name a few.

The ASPError Object

Should something go wrong in a Web application, IIS will create an ASPError object that represents the error. It contains the error message regarding the incident, and the provided information can be used in a variety of ways.

At first, the client is by default redirected to a custom error page if trouble occurs. On the error page, a script reads the contents of the ASPError object. The error message may be output, automatically e-mailed to you, or written to the IIS log.

In terms of usage, both for programmers and administrators, the ASPError is a practical approach to finding out how, when, where, and why a script stopped working. Tracking down an error and improving the code is much easier with the facts at hand, and the Web service quickly becomes a more pleasant and bug-free experience.

The ObjectContext Object

In certain environments, it is necessary to deploy *transactions*. The use of a transaction is best illustrated by showing a potential flaw in a nontransactional environment. Consider the following: As a client, you enter an online store, select a few products, enter your credit card number, and submit the order. After a few seconds, an error is displayed.

One or two weeks pass, and a bank statement in the mail says your credit card has been debited by an Internet business. However, the products paid for never arrived. The initial cause is that the online store processed the order and charged the credit card, but generated an error before the order was entered into the current orders database. For a client, this is not a too horrible a situation, as a refund is due. For the business, however, it can be devastating.

Instead of allowing an error as described in the last paragraph, the order process can be run in a transactional environment. A transaction would require that the order be processed, the credit card be billed, and the order be entered in the database. Each operation must succeed, because if one operation fails, the transaction as a whole will be undone. For example, should the billing of the credit card fail, then the previous step—the order processing—will fail, too.

The ASP ObjectContext object is used in a transactional environment to either abort a transaction or commit a transaction—thus preventing the types of accidents described in the previous scenario.

The Request Object

The Request object gathers information sent from the client with a request to the Web server.

For example, the browser sends a command to the server when a Web page is requested. It is called a *simple request*, but if the client fills out an online form or uploads a file, or if the script must verify the client's identity in a database, it becomes more complex. The Request object can retrieve this additional data sent by the client. After the request has been processed, the values can be operated on, whether in a purchase order or an uploaded file. Furthermore, in business scenarios, encrypted sessions such as Secure Socket Layers (SSL) can require digital certificates from the client. The Request object can read the contents of a digital certificate.

In short, when data is passed from the client to the server, the Request object opens easy access to every variable.

The Response Object

The Request object operates on data that travels from client to server. However, the Request object often works with the Response object because the Response object controls the flow in the opposite direction, so the two are closely related in the ASP model.

When sent from the Response object, data goes from server to client. It can actually be used in a variety of ways. For example, the server can send a request to set a cookie on the client machine, control caching of Web pages, write to the log, and output HTML from script commands and raw binary content to the browser.

In short, script commands prepare how Web pages are treated, viewed, and presented to the client; then the Response object delivers. The commands are simple, but the effects are lasting.

The Server Object

With a wide variety of services at its disposal, the Server object is the Swiss army knife of Active Server Pages.

For example, you can create instances of COM objects in Active Server Pages. Or you can decode and encode strings, and transfer the client between pages while maintaining the state of the built-in objects like the Request object. The Server object also has the ability to execute separate ASP files like subroutines.

In short, the Server object got its name because it works exclusively on the server side. It provides some tools you might never use and others that you always use.

The Session Object

Maintaining state on the stateless HTTP protocol, the Session object will help you build more powerful applications.

In the same manner as the Application object, the Session object stores its data on the server and not on the client machine. It is very different from the Application object, however, because there is a unique Session object for each individual client that requests a Web page. And the data associated with that client is unique too.

Issued once for the client, the Session object stores variables added either by an event or by script command. The object then maintains state time as the client is visiting the Web site—its contents are available anywhere within the application even though a new request is generated for each Web page.

In short, this object is special to Active Server Pages because it uses no external means to store its Session variables, yet it enables the user's data to be individualized on the server.

Writing Your Own COM Components

Since the support for components is a part of the ASP architecture (and the foundation of Windows, for that matter), proprietary server components written in Delphi, Perl, Visual Basic, Visual C++, or any other language of choice can also be registered and accessed by your Web server and scripting engine.

Installing Active Server Pages

When installing Internet Information Services (IIS) on Windows NT 4.0 and Windows 2000, Active Server Pages installs with the Web server. On Windows 95/98, though, the support for Active Server Pages is in Personal Web Server (PWS)—formerly known as Peer Web Services.

Windows 98 has PWS available for installation on its CD-ROM. If the CD is not an option, PWS can be downloaded as a component of the NT Option Pack from http://www.microsoft.com—although it is not for Windows NT! Windows NT and Windows 2000 both include IIS on the CD as well.

In general, the Web server is often left as an additional component to install for Windows. Either run the installation program for NT Option Pack, if you downloaded it, or go to the Add/Remove Programs option in the control panel and add the Web server to your system. Alternatively, put the operating system CD in the CD-ROM drive and wait for autorun to launch the setup where you get to choose what components to install. The necessary components will be copied and installed from the operating system CD after you have located and selected them.

The PerlScript Engine

PerlScript (ActiveState Tool Corp.) is an ActiveX Scripting Engine that implements Perl for ActiveX Scripting Hosts. Not only will the engine work with a host as IIS Active Server Pages, it can also be embedded in environments such as Visual Basic applications by using Microsoft Script Control. In the same manner, external COM objects such as ActiveX Data Objects can be used in ordinary Perl applications, and Microsoft Script Control can interestingly embed other languages into Perl—for fun and not functionality.

Installation

To begin the installation, follow the next few steps:

1. Download the ActivePerl package from http://www.ActiveState.com.
2. Run the ActivePerl package.
3. Accept the agreement.
4. After reading and approving them, accept the installation options.
5. Choose the directory in which to install Perl.
6. Decide what components to install. At a minimum, install both Perl and PerlScript in order to use Active Server Pages, and please install the documentation. If unsure, install all components.
7. Select the options you want to apply. In general, it looks fine out of the box.
8. Wait for the installation to finish.
9. Restart the computer if prompted.

Troubleshooting

If PerlScript does not seem to work after the ActivePerl installation, this is normally fixed by reinstalling the package. However, to assure yourself that PerlScript was in fact not installed properly, follow these simple steps:

1. Enter command prompt.
2. Type perl -v.
3. If the version number of Perl is printed, move on to step 5.
4. Enter the bin subdirectory of your Perl installation.
5. Type perl -e "use Win32::OLE; new Win32::OLE('PerlScript') || die;"
6. If the output is Died, the PerlScript engine could not be found. Ensure that PerlSE.dll is in the same directory as PerlCore.dll.
7. If all else fails, reinstall ActivePerl.

Configuring the Scripting Language

When the Web server is installed and is ready to process an ASP page for the first time, there are a few things to notice. First, the engine knows that VBScript and JScript install with ASP, and therefore has VBScript as the registered default language. What that means is that a script command in another language will not work until either the configuration or a page command is told what language to use. The next sections show the different methods of setting the default language to PerlScript—or any other scripting language, for that matter. Second, the various ways to set a new scripting language are presented, as well as how to set it up within the document for page scope and how to configure a more concrete solution toward effective Active Server pages.

The Default Language

When the default scripting language for Active Server Pages is set by a page command, the setting will last only during the processing of the script commands in the current page.

A page command is always prefixed by the at sign (@), and because it is in effect for the current page, it must be reissued in subsequent documents. For the scripting language option, the command <%@Language=PerlScript%> is issued within the .asp document to instruct the engine to interpret the script commands as PerlScript. Don't worry about the syntax of the following example if you are unfamiliar with ASP or Perl; in the rest of the book, there will be plentiful explanation regarding syntax.

```
<%@ Language=PerlScript %>
<TITLE> PerlScript As The Default Language For The Page
</TITLE>
<HTML>
  <BODY>
   <%
    $Response->Write("Hello From PerlScript");
   %>
   <BR>Processed By Active Server Pages<BR>
  </BODY>
</HTML>
```

First, if the <%@ Language=PerlScript %> command is omitted, the VBScript Engine will try to interpret the PerlScript as if it were VBScript. As a result, an error is generated and outputted in a message. The next important point regarding script commands is the special notation <% %>. In the Active Server Pages engine, code inside that notation is always to be interpreted by the current default scripting language—PerlScript.

Several Languages in One File

When you need to use small blocks of code for several scripting languages in your Active Server pages, or when for some reason it is not appropriate to issue the page command within your document, the following programmatical grammar is correct:

```
<HTML>
<BODY>
 <TITLE> How To Use Several Scripting Languages </TITLE>
  <SCRIPT LANGUAGE="PerlScript" RUNAT="Server">
  $Response->Write("Hello From PerlScript");
  </SCRIPT>

  <SCRIPT LANGUAGE="VBScript" RUNAT="Server">
  Response.Write "Hello From VBScript"
  </SCRIPT>

  <BR>Hello From HTML</BR>
</BODY>
</HTML>
```

In this example, the script tags are used to tell the ASP engine what language to use for the code within its delimiters—no default language notations. Furthermore, in the language tag, it is stipulated that the processing should be done on the server side because that is where the scripting engine is installed. No limit applies to how many scripting languages can be used in the same document, and the syntax might vary greatly between languages.

Server-Side Configuration

When page commands are getting old, the default scripting language can be set on the server side by an administrative operation. The alternative to specifying the default scripting language within the .asp documents is modifying either the registry or the metabase configuration.

Windows 95 and 98

In Microsoft Internet Information Server 3.0 or earlier, the default scripting language can be set in the following registry key:

```
\\HKEY_LOCAL_MACHINE\System\CurrentControlSet\Services\W3SVC\ASP\Parame-
ters\DefaultScriptingLanguage
```

To navigate onto this registry key, follow these easy steps:

1. Click on Start in the bottom left corner.
2. Choose Run.
3. Type Regedit in the input box, then click OK.
4. Click HKEY_LOCAL_MACHINE.
5. Next, follow the way to the registry key in the previous paragraph.
6. Right-click on the key and choose Modify.
7. Enter the default language to use.

The next section describes a more permanent setting that applies to the configuration defined in the metabase.

Windows NT 4 and 2000

With IIS 4.0, the default language setting was moved to the metabase, so for IIS 4.0 and later it will need to be set in the metabase either via the management console or by other means. On Windows 2000, the following steps will set the default language.

1. Open the control panel.
2. Choose Administrative Tools.
3. Choose Internet Services Manager.
4. Right-click on the Web service or Web application and choose Properties.
5. If a Web service was chosen, click on the Home Directory tab, and if a Web application was chosen, start under the Virtual Directory tab.
6. Click on Configuration.
7. Choose the App Options tab.
8. In Default ASP Language, type PerlScript.

In the location where the default scripting language is set, there are several other options that can be modified as well, such as how long a script can run before it generates an error (the script time-out) and whether or not to output a custom error message in case of an error. A custom error is preferred for a Web application that is a public service since it will prevent detailed error messages from being displayed.

Server-Side Include Files

An Active Server Pages document is not limited to its current document. On the contrary, on its behalf PerlScript can use its native programming libraries and import modules as normal. But as an added functionality for Active Server Pages, external files (HTML, ASP, or other) on the server can be imported into the current document by using server-side includes.

Server-side includes are a useful way of storing either code or global content. A common scenario is when your Web pages may have a header that includes your logo, links, and a randomly displayed banner, and then a footer with a copyright notice and a search engine. Server-side includes can be utilized in this scenario so that, instead of writing the code for the header and footer in each document and spending a day updating the Web site when it is time to redesign, you can store the header and footer in separate files on your server, thus allowing them to be imported as server-side includes and changed only once to become globally effective.

Server-side includes are imported using what looks like an HTML comment. In general, include files have the file extension .inc, since this is descriptive and a good decision for design. However, an include file can, for example, have an .asp extension and still be included with no problem.

Virtual File Names

Although it sounds abstract, a virtual file is simply the location of a file the way the Web server maps it. For example, you may have installed a Web server locally and given it the domain http://www.domain.com. The virtual directory /Files/ might exist within the domain, so to direct the browser there, the URL should point to http://www.domain.com/Files/.

On the physical drive, the location might be something completely different than what is seen in the URL—for example, C:\Inetpub\Includes\. But we are only concerned with the virtual path.

```
<!--#INCLUDE VIRTUAL="/Files/Header.inc"  -->
 <HTML>
    This is static text between server-side includes
 </HTML>
<!--#INCLUDE VIRTUAL="/Files/Footer.inc"  -->
```

In the previous example, the virtual path, which is a path related to how your Web site is structured, points to the virtual location Files, where both the header and footer are located as .inc files. On the other hand, the relative path to the server-side include files can be used by exchanging VIRTUAL for FILE.

Relative File Name

While the virtual file name maps by virtual directories, the relative file name is mapped from the current location of the script that includes the file. For example, if your script is executing in the directory Files, the following will map the file with Files as the top-level directory. The full path then looks like Files\Relative\Path\Header.inc.

```
<!--#INCLUDE FILE="\Relative\Path\Header.inc"  -->

<HTML>
   This is static text between server-side includes
</HTML>

<!--#INCLUDE FILE="\Relative\Path\Footer.inc"  -->
```

The Capacity of SSI

Although an include file is useful, it should be noted that there is one limitation. The following will not work:

```
<!--#include virtual="/<%=$username%>"-->
```

However, the following will work since it is encapsulated within PerlScript:

```
<%
if($username eq 'administrator') {
%>
    <!--#INCLUDE VIRTUAL="/ADMIN/webmanager.inc"-->
```

```
<%
}
else {
%>

    <!--#INCLUDE VIRTUAL="/JOEUSER/webmanager.inc"-->

<%
}
%>
```

Furthermore, when a file is included, the file itself can include other files, which in turn can include more files. In essence, this is a very useful technology for global design across Web pages.

The Architecture of ASP

Although the term *object-oriented programming* may be somewhat unfamiliar, the foundation of ASP is based on it. An object provides a service, and each object is created to rule its own little section of the IIS Web service. Consequently, the only knowledge needed to use an object is:

- The methods of the object, because they give access to operations on data
- The properties of the object, because they give access to important data
- The events certain actions may result in

In the next sections, these individual parts that make up an ASP object will be explained. You might be especially interested in these if this is your first encounter with object-oriented programming; otherwise they can be safely skipped provided that an understanding of methods, properties, and collections is in place.

Method

A *method* is a block of code that is protected in a class. It performs operations on data related to its object, and can both be given data to work with and return data. A method is only accessed through an object that is an instance of the class where the method belongs. Don't worry about classes if this is the first time you have heard about them, as we will get back to them in the next chapter.

```
class Graphics

method drawLine {
block of code
}

end class
```

The class is named Graphics and the method is called drawLine. drawLine cannot be called at any time, however. In order to gain access to that method, a class instance of Graphics must be created.

```
myObject = new Graphics

myObject::drawLine
```

The built-in objects of Active Server Pages are already instantiated when the scripting engine goes to work, so it is never necessary to create a class instance.

Property

A *property* defines the attributes of the object that you are working with. For example, if the object is a rectangle, its attributes are its dimensions, color, and so forth.

In terms of an object, the properties can be read and written to examine an object or to define or redefine its attributes or behavior.

Reading a Property

In Perl and PerlScript, the curly brackets around its name identify a property. As seen in the example of methods, no such identifiers surround a method, and this is how methods and properties are distinguished.

```
# Property
$Object->{Property};

# Not a property
$Object->Method;
```

Setting a Property

There is more than one way to set a property, but choose one approach for consistency.

```
$Object->{Property} = 'Value';
$Object->SetProperty('PropertyName', 'Value');
```

In this book, the curly braces approach is the preferred way of setting the value of a property.

Events

An *event* is a block of code that is executed upon an event. Not all objects have events, but, for example, when ADO opens a database, an event is run. Similarly, when a database is closed, another event is run. The events are not random at all, but are specified for each action that relates to the object.

Collection

When studying the built-in objects, it is apparent that most of them have collections. Although collections dynamically resize themselves when an item is either added or removed, in most cases the items are already defined when the scripting engine accesses them. In either case, the collection solves the issue of grouping a set of

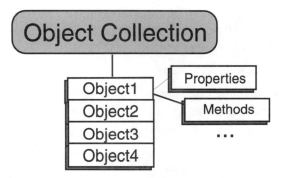

Figure 1.1   Simplified view of the collection.

related variables such as text, numbers, or objects into one easy and accessible data structure (Figure 1.1).

In most instances, the object-provided collections contain data such as cookies, form data, and server variables, to name a few examples. For instance, if a form is filled out online and it contains 10 text fields that were filled out, the collection that stores the form data will have 10 items in its collection that can be accessed either by their unique names or by an index number. Data can be added by script command, but it can only be added to the application and session's special collection named Contents. With the Contents collection, variables can be dynamically added, read, and removed from the collection while its values are defined by the program.

The Item() Method

The Item() method is used when you want to retrieve the value of an item in a collection. First, when specifying the item to get, it can be referenced either by key name or index as a part of the collection.

In most collections, a default method has been assigned to each collection, and in most cases that is the Item() method. However, in cases where the call to Item is left out, a reference to where the value is located in memory is provided. In contrast, when Item is specified in the call, the value is returned as Item() will do the dereferencing.

The Item() method returns the value, and the following example shows how to return the value of an item by key and by index:

```
$Object->Collection('Name')->Item();
$Object->Collection(1)->Item();
```

As mentioned, many collections have Item() set as the default method to be called in case no method is specified. The following is valid syntax as well; however, a reference is being returned.

```
$Object->Collection('Name')
```

It is very possible for an item to contain subitems. What this means is essentially that the item contains another item. However, in raw data, the items and subitems are generally comma-separated. If the item to fetch is not specified by name or index, a comma-separated list of all the values is provided. The next example is an illustration of how it can look when a subitem is requested from a collection.

```
$Object->Collection($index)->Item($subIndex);
```

When a subitem is present, a way to detect subitems is present as well. Every collection provides a Count property that will return the number of items in a collection or the number of subitems of an item.

The Count Property

The Count property is used to count the number of objects in a collection or the number of subitems in an item; therefore, it is the only way to detect whether or not more values are to be read.

The use of the Count property is best illustrated with an example. Let's say that a database is queried to return all columns from a certain table. In the Web application that fetches the result from the database, it is impossible to know how many columns will be returned. For example, there can be an unknown number of columns, such as first name, last name, address, and phone, in addition to eight more columns. Now, by design everything returned from a relational database in columns is placed in a collection named the Fields collection; to retrieve the number of items in the collection, the Count property can be used. With that number in hand, a loop can be used to display all items. Feel free to skip this if you are familiar with the syntax; it is mainly for back-reference purposes.

The syntax for reading the Count property for the Fields collection is as follows:

```
$Object->Fields->{Count};
```

When the number of items has been fetched, a simple way of looping the collection is by using a for loop that ranges from the index of the first item to the index of the last.

```
$maxItems = $Object->Fields->{Count};

for(my $index=0; $index<=$maxItems; $index++) {
    $Response->Write( 'Item $index: ' );
    $Response->Write( $Object->Fields($index)->{Value} );
    $Response->Write( '<BR>' );
    }
```

In this example, the first item starts at 0. Please notice, however, that not every collection will start at 0. Yet another way of displaying the items of the Fields collection is to iterate the collection. That method does not require any use of Count or knowledge of which index is the first. The syntax for iterating through a collection is the following.

```
use Win32::OLE qw(in)

foreach my $item (in($Object->Fields)) {
    $Response->Write( $item->{Name});
```

```
$Response->Write( '=' );
$Response->Write( $item->{Value} );
$Response->Write( '<BR>' );
}
```

In addition to this example, the first line imports the method for iterating the collection, and the method is available in the Win32::OLE module. However, the following alternative syntax works just as well as the one in the preceding example:

```
foreach my $item (Win32::OLE::in($Object->Fields)) { … }
```

The Remove() Method

Active Server Pages provides an effective method for removing items of a collection that were added by script command—the Remove() method.

As mentioned, the method will only remove the items that were added by script command. This limits the Remove() method to the items available in the Contents collection. In essence, the items you are able to remove by this method are solely the items you were able to add by script command to either the Application or the Session object. Logically there is no reason to remove any other items as they are only temporary for the current page being processed.

The Remove() method will take a key name or an index as its parameter for locating the object in the Contents collection. When a key name is used, the Contents collection will be searched until the Remove() method finds the key name, as it cannot know in which order the keys were added. If the index is used, it will count up until the item represented by the index from the first item in the collection. It can look as follows:

```
$object->Contents->Remove("Keyname");
$object->Contents->Remove(1);
```

The RemoveAll() Method

When you want to clean up the complete Contents collection, instead of removing items one at a time in a loop, the RemoveAll() method will remove every single object in the collection.

```
$object->Contents->RemoveAll();
```

Summary

In this chapter we have introduced Active Server Pages (ASP). An application-level programming interface, ASP consists of seven built-in objects that can be used to empower a Web service in various ways. These objects are the Application, ASPError, Request, Response, Object Context, Server, and Session objects. Each built-in ASP object exposes an interface to a certain type of functionality through its collections, events, methods, and properties, and allows the programmer to use the functionality. To manifest itself, ASP provides its own file extension (.asp). ASP documents reside on the Web server and can not only contain everything that an HTML document can contain but can also utilize the built-in ASP objects and external COM objects. Programming in ASP is done by embedding server-side script commands in a familiar scripting language within the HTML. The commands will be executed on the server side by an ActiveX Scripting Engine such as PerlScript. Compared to the Common Gateway Interface (CGI), which relies on an external program to perform a certain task, ASP is integrated into the Component Object Model (COM); thus ASP does not call any external programs. As a result, when Perl is used, no external process launch of the Perl interpreter occurs when executing script commands through ASP as opposed to the process launch that occurs when using Perl and CGI. ASP and PerlScript are easy to install, and they require very little or no configuration. Simply download the free software from the Internet or locate ActivePerl on the CD accompanying this book, and run the installer on your system. Configuring the server to use PerlScript can either take place per executed ASP document by a special page command in the document, or it can be easily configured on the server side. Like many other Web servers, ASP allows server-side include (SSI) files. The most important thing to know about SSIs is that they can contain anything that an ordinary Active Server Pages document can. For example, you can use SSIs for HTML layout purposes, executing script commands, or including other include files. In short, ASP provides complete functionality for powerful Web applications.

Up next is a chapter on the basics of programming Perl. It will be the final stop before we start programming Active Server Pages; however, if you know Perl, you may safely skip Chapter 2 without a loss of continuity.

Perl Programming Basics

The Practical Extraction and Report Language (Perl) has collected some of the most powerful features of several languages. Its functions are very wide in spectrum, and the features have grown since the first release of Perl and turned into features for which programmers look to Perl. While many of the built-in functions provide optimized routines for common programming tasks instead of forcing the programmer to reinvent the wheel, others lend supreme yet simple functionality for the simple tasks. In addition to all this, Perl supports both a classic model and an object-oriented model of programming. Whereas both computer science today and a number of programming languages are devoted to object-oriented programming, Perl does not make one school of programming prevalent.

Before getting started, you should be aware that because Perl is a rather free-form language, learning the basics becomes only the beginning. There are many different ways of writing Perl code that acts the same but certainly does not look the same; thus the approach, style, and structure of writing the code quickly become a personal preference. The free-form approach of programming Perl, however, does not mean that the language in itself is a quick hack (although it can be used to write quick hacks). Instead, the freedom to write code that is either simplistic or complex is one of its major features.

In any case, whether the Perl code is short and cryptic or long and well described, this is an introduction to the functions and methodologies of Perl and how they can be applied to describe the language. How you use it is between you and Perl—very negotiable—but you must start with the Perl programming basics.

Getting a Head Start with Perl

In this section, we begin the journey into Perl by exploring the components included in the ActivePerl software package. It is important to first learn a few simple basics on what you can do with the tools provided with ActivePerl, because they come in handy when you encounter potential problems in a programming project. These tools greatly enhance the first few weeks of the Perl experience and speed up the process of learning while providing a solid foundation for the future.

In addition to how these tools are used to leverage the surroundings of Perl, the basics of programming Perl will be covered with discussion and examples. No familiarity with Perl or any other programming language is assumed—although it doesn't hurt—for anything that is presented, so please take your time, read things over, and try everything out on your local installation if this is your first experience with Perl.

In the Programmer's Toolbox . . .

A number of components are installed with ActivePerl, and quite a few of them quickly become familiar. Whether you need to turn to these tools for programming advice, development of skills, or means of extending Perl, we will concentrate on getting the two most important tools surrounding Perl going. They provide all of these functions, and they are:

- The Perl documentation
- Perl Package Manager

The ActivePerl documentation contains the core Perl documentation, a priceless set of documents that cover absolutely all earthly knowledge about Perl. It is *the tool* for actual programming problems and finding answers to questions on the scale from trivial to tough. The second tool is Perl Package Manager, a package management application. Perl Package Manager makes it more than easy to install additional functionality for Perl by downloading packages, or prebuilt libraries of code, from remote locations by automating the task of package management.

The ActivePerl Documentation

A giant collection of documents, the ActivePerl documentation contains important contributions from several authors. Each document generally provides advice and instructions on a specific set of topics, and the documentation is divided into the following sections:

- **Getting Started** includes the welcome page, installation instructions, and some history on the evolution of Perl through time.
- **ActivePerl Components** discusses, among other things, the various components that can be installed with ActivePerl and what their uses are.

- **ActivePerl FAQ** contains frequently asked questions (FAQ) about Perl on Win32, how-to examples, and information on embedding Perl in applications written in other languages and extending Perl. It also covers automation of items such as Microsoft Office Excel spreadsheets.

- **Core Perl FAQ** is the number one–ranked spot for finding quick answers on the problems that occur when programming, and it has plenty of how-to documentation. It is quite extensive, so give it a chance in case of a problem because there is most likely documentation there. In addition, this section also includes comparisons between scripting languages, and the history and story behind Perl.

- **Core Perl Docs** includes everything you need to become a Perl expert. It is a huge amount of documentation on literally everything about Perl.

- **Module Docs** is the information about the installed root modules for Perl and how to use them. In addition, documentation for modules installed with Perl Package Manager will automatically be added to the same index. Each paper describes how to use the module that was added to the Perl installation.

Whenever You Need to Ask a Perl Question

When looking for answers to your Perl questions, it is not always easy to sift through the documentation by hand and find exactly the right paper. Simply opening the right window, finding the right window, or finding the right section can become somewhat time consuming. The remedy is a command-line tool named *Perldoc* (file name: perl-doc.bat), which is available to make it first easier but most importantly quicker to look up topics in the documentation. The following example illustrates how Perldoc provides information about a built-in Perl function:

1. Enter the command prompt.
2. Enter Perldoc and you will see an index of available commands.
3. Enter Perldoc -h and you will get more extensive information on how to use the program.
4. Enter Perldoc -f my and a listing about the my function will be printed to the screen.

Without overly long searching, this approach rapidly provides, on the screen, the answer about what the my( ) function is meant for, including description, syntax, and further references.

While built-in functions provide definitive facts, this might not always be satisfying. In this case, when further information becomes necessary, Perldoc can be told how and where to search for your keywords. Specifying either one of the options at the command line uses this feature. For example, previously, the -f switch was used to declare that what we were looking for was a function. The available options are presented in Table 2.1.

Although its appearance is not very elegant and has no windows and buttons, Perldoc is really useful. It is advantageous not to have such controls as clickable buttons because the program executes faster, crashes less often than a browser, and provides

Table 2.1 Command Line Options

OPTION	MEANING
-h	Shows the help message.
-r	Performs a recursive search.
-i	Ignores case sensitivity.
-t	Defaults on Win32. Displays using Pod2Text. (Pod is a format.)
-u	Does not allow the Pod text to be formatted.
-m	Displays the full file when a module is requested.
-l	Prints the module's file name so that it can be located.
-F	Provides the file name.
-v	Displays detailed output during search.
-X	Uses the index if available.
-q	Searches the questions in Perlfaq 1–9.
-f	Looks up a function.

quicker answers. In addition, it suits the preference of working against a black background in a dark room without the sun glaring at the monitor.

One word of notice, however: It is advisable to become familiar with the Perl documentation before using Perldoc. Browse around the papers on the local installation, and in that way you will quickly learn what documents it will search. There is a naming convention used for the documents that is worth getting friendly with:

- Documents in the core Perl documentation begin with the letters perl, followed by an abbreviation that describes the topic of the document. For example perldoc, perldata will pull up the core documentation about data types in Perl.

- Perl frequently asked questions are named with a number, so that perldoc perlfaq6 will retrieve the sixth FAQ.

- The module docs are pulled up by entering perldoc *modulename*, thus the following commands are valid: perldoc Benchmark, perldoc attrs, and perldoc English.

- The built-in functions of Perl are browsed by using the -f option, as previously seen, thus the following commands are valid: perldoc -f my, perldoc -f local, perldoc -f print.

All of this gives a general idea of what the Perl documentation includes, and makes it much easier to search the known territory.

In short, Perldoc is a powerful tool for finding quick, elaborate, and exact answers about Perl. It is superior to manually browsing the documentation by hand. However, it is necessary to become familiar with the documentation in order to use the full potential of Perldoc.

The Perl Package Manager

Not so long ago, extending the functionality of Perl was somewhat of a problem. For example, Perl could be extended to drawing graphics, sending e-mail, and managing Windows services, and understandably this made Perl the language of choice. As many experienced, though, it was an inconvenience to install modules to extend Perl's tool-box because it involved a lot of work.

For our convenience, ActiveState released Perl Package Manager (PPM). This solved the problems that many found with installing and managing modules, plus made module procedures very easy. Instead of being downloaded, upgraded, removed, or created by hand, a module is prepackaged for Perl Package Manager. After a module is completed for download, Perl Package Manager automates all the tasks so that virtually everyone can install the desired modules.

Why Bother Installing Modules?

In general, a module is installed for several reasons. Normally the reason is because a module gives some functionality, not provided by Perl's built-in functions, that you need for your script. There are two types of modules:

- Modules that provide reusable code built on Perl functionality: For example, Perl scripts written to send e-mail and check e-mail are bundled into the Libnet package for this reason.
- Modules that extend Perl with functionality written in C/C++ or a mixture between C/C++ and Perl: For example, the GD graphics library is a Perl port of a C graphics library that enables Perl to generate graphics on the fly.

A module has a number of characteristics and conventions. First, the file extension for a Perl module is always .pm. The .pm file may optionally autoload dynamically linked executables that it uses to extend its capacity.

Installing Modules with PPM

Perl Package Manager downloads modules that are located in a repository. The ActiveState repository is the default, and it is the location where the most popular modules are made available. It is pretty much configurable to suit your own needs, but let's first follow the next example either mentally or on the computer to see how it can be used.

1. Enter the command prompt.
2. Type ppm and hit enter.
3. A PPM shell opens, so enter help to see the available commands.

When asking PPM to bring up the help menu, the commands in Table 2.2 are the listed commands for PPM:

Table 2.2   Perl Package Manager Commands

COMMAND	MEANING
exit	Quits the program.
genconfig	Prints a valid PPM configuration file to the screen.
info PACKAGE	Prints the summary of either the installed PACKAGE or all installed packages.
install PACKAGE	Installs the specified package on the computer.
quit	Quits the program.
query	Prints the names of all installed packages.
remove PACKAGE	Removes the installation of PACKAGE.
search	Prints all packages available for installation from the repository.
summary PACKAGE	Prints a summary of PACKAGE.
set	Sets an option in PPM.
verify	Verifies that all installed packages on the computer are up to date.

In the table, the commands are in their most simplistic form. Most can be extended, as will be shown, but let's begin with an example of how to install a package from the ActiveState repository.

When installing a package, you can (1) know the name of the package; (2) search for text that you know is in the name or is part of the abstract description of a package; or (3) list all available packages. In the example, the package named Libnet will be searched, found, and installed. Assuming that you are still in a PPM prompt, continue from the example.

1. Type search and wait for the result.

    After action 1, a whole list of packages flashes by on the screen. Did you catch any of it? Don't expect to. Depending on the version of Windows that you use, you might be fortunate enough to have the command prompt windows scrollable. If that is the case, you can easily scroll up the lines and see what all the available packages were. However, when you can't do that, you can specify the number of names to show and then pause the program until you press a key.

2. Type set more 3 and issue search once more.

    Action 2 will force the program to pause every third line. This is one way to locate the Libnet package successfully. Next, do the following:

3. Enter help query for options on how to retrieve information about packages.

4. Bring up the description for Libnet by typing query /abstract libnet, and it will tell you about the package, which is an application programming interface to a variety

of Internet protocols. Essentially, the same information can be extracted by typing summary libnet.

5. Enter install libnet.

Installing a package with PPM is very easy and straightforward. The one thing to note, however, is that you will not be notified about the status of the installation until the package has been downloaded. The exception to this rule is if the package cannot be found, in which case PPM will notify you.

In order to customize some features of PPM, the set command has a number of variables that it is able to modify. The outcome is that some behavior in PPM is changed. Table 2.3 shows the arguments for the set command:

Table 2.3 Options for the Set Command

OPTION	MEANING
build DIRECTORY	Makes DIRECTORY the package build directory.
case [Yes | No]	Whether the search performed is case sensitive or case insensitive is specified insensitive is specified with a string that has a value of either yes or no. When no argument is given, the current setting is reversed: For example, yes becomes no.
clean [Yes | No]	Normally, temporary files will be removed after a package has been built. This option can be used to change that.
confirm [Yes | No]	A detailed confirmation of an install, remove, or upgrade operation is printed upon completion.
force_install [Yes | No]	A package will normally continue installing even if a dependency of the package cannot be installed. Use this option to change that if desired.
more N	Sets PPM to scroll N lines, then pause and wait for a key to be hit. The default setting is 0, which means it does not pause at all.
repository /remove Name	Removes repository name from the available repositories.
repository Name Location	Adds repository name located at the URL or directory defined in Location.
root Directory	Accesses the install root directory for the current session.
save	Saves the options.
trace	A number between 0 and 4 that indicates the tracing of the session.
tracefile	Displays the file to which the tracing information is written.

In general, Perl Package Manager will be installed with the best settings for your system. But, with all this in mind, what else is there to know about it? Table 2.4 gives more commands that can be used.

Examples of Modules

There are lots of modules. Following is a list of a few of them and what they are used for:

Libnet. Application programming interface to the most popular Internet protocols. Libnet enables you to send e-mail, check e-mail, use newsgroups, transfer files, and write software that uses any of the classes.

GD: graphics library. Generate graphics on the fly in Active Server Pages or other applications. Full support for graphics primitives, fonts, brushes, color palettes, and loading and saving of the images.

LWP: library for WWW access in Perl. Application programming interface to the World Wide Web. The classes and functions help you build WWW clients with support for most protocols, including HTTP, HTTPS, Gopher, news, and FTP, to name a few.

Table 2.4   Further Use of PPM

COMMAND	DESCRIPTION
install /location LOCATION PACKAGE	The location option tells PPM to look for PACKAGE at the URL or directory LOCATION.
query /option [PATTERN]	PATTERN is an optional Perl regular expression for filtering what packages to display. Otherwise, the local packages will be printed. Option can be either /abstract, /author, or /title, if specified. Abstract provides a description of the package, and author and title are exactly what they sound like.
search /option [PATTERN] search /location LOCATION[PATTERN]	The search command takes the same options as the query. LOCATION can be used to set the URL or directory for where to look for packages.
summary [PACKAGE] summary ./location LOCATION [PACKAGE]	Provides a summary, which includes name, version, and an abstract description of a package in the repository or the repository specified in LOCATION.
verify [PACKAGE] upgrade [PACKAGE] verify /location LOCATION [PACKAGE]	Verifies that either a specified PACKAGE or all packages are up to date compared with the version in the repository. Upgrade is used to upgrade a package, and LOCATION is used to get the upgrade from the specified LOCATION.

Win32 modules. Win32::Internet implements the Win32 Internet APIs and provides object-oriented access to HTTP, FTP, and Gopher.

Many modules also give very powerful features at hand that are, if not fun, at least useful when developing client applications.

- **Win32::OLE** supports automation. It makes it easy to use Microsoft Office by automating Word, Excel, Access, and other products from Perl. It is also used by PerlScript, and its methods are well worth checking out.

- **Win32::GUI** makes the familiar windows graphical user interface (GUI) controls available for Perl. Full-blown GUI client applications can be written in Perl for Windows. The Tk module provides a non-Windows-look GUI.

- **Win32::NetAdmin** can be used by administrators who want to manage network groups and users with a few lines of Perl.

The Standard Perl Modules

The standard Perl modules (Table 2.5) are those that are installed with ActivePerl. The table of these modules contains a summary of each one. To learn more about a given

Table 2.5 The Standard Perl Modules

MODULE	SUMMARY
AnyDBM_File	Provides framework for multiple DBMs.
attrs	Allows you to set and get attributes of a subroutine.
AutoLoader	Loads subroutines only when they are needed.
AutoSplit	Splits a package into files that the AutoLoader can use.
autouse	Does not load a module until a function/method of it is called.
base	Simplifies setting up @ISA at compile time.
Benchmark	Benchmarks scripts and code snippets by timing and comparing them.
blib	Lets you test programs against an uninstalled package.
Carp	Provides everything you need for generating better error messages.
Config	Provides access to Perl configuration information.
constant	Declares constants at compile time.
Cwd	Returns the path name of current working directory.
diagnostics	Provides descriptive error messages from the Perl compiler and interpreter.
DirHandle	Provides an object-oriented interface to directory handling functions.
Dumpvalue	Performs screen dump of Perl data.
DynaLoader	Provides an interface to dynamic linking mechanisms.
English	Provides detailed names for the short special Perl variables.

Continues

Table 2.5   The Standard Perl Modules *(Continued)*

MODULE	SUMMARY
Env	Imports environment variables as ordinary variables.
Errno	Defines and conditionally exports system error constants defined in errno.h.
Exporter	Provides a default import method for modules to inherit.
Fatal	Exchanges a return value of false to a script that stops executing and reports the error so that you don't have to check the return value.
Fcntl	Loads the C Fcntl.h defines and make its routines available.
fields	Enables compile-time class fields.
FileCache	Allows you to keep more files open than the system normally permits.
FileHandle	Provides an object-oriented interface for working with file handles.
FindBin	Locates the bin directory the current Perl script is run in.
integer	Tells the Perl compiler to use integer arithmetic instead of floating point from here to the end of the block of code.
lib	Provides simple manipulation of @INC at compile time.
locale	Enables or disables POSIX locales for built-in functions by use locale; and no locale.
O	Provides a generic interface to Perl compiler back ends.
Opcode	Lets you disable opcodes when compiling Perl code.
ops	Disables unsafe opcodes at compile time.
overload	Lets you set Perl functions as your own subroutines.
POSIX	Gives access to the majority of POSIX 1003.1 identifiers.
re	Allows alterations to the behavior of regular expressions.
Safe	Provides compartments in which Perl code can be evaluated.
SDBM_File	Provides tired access to SDBM database files.
SelectSaver	For file handles, this module can save and restore a file handle when you need to work with a different one temporarily.
SelfLoader	Loads functions only on demand.
Shell	Runs shell commands from within Perl.
sigtrap	Provides simple signal handling.
Socket	Translates socket.h, which provides socket programming support.
strict	Prevents unsafe constructs.
subs	Predeclares subroutines.
Symbol	Manipulates Perl symbols and their names.
UNIVERSAL	Is the base class for all classes.
vars	Predeclares global variable names.

functionality, enter perldoc *modulename* at the command prompt or browse in the online documentation.

Introduction to Programming Perl

Every introduction to a computer programming or scripting language must begin somewhere. Since most parts of a programming language are interconnected, it is very difficult to structure a tutorial perfectly. However, this chapter begins at one end and moves step by step to the other. A word of advice, however, is to skip sections that don't make sense—because they will make sense later—and read back over them when you know what you have learned.

Programmatical Grammar

In programming, the grammatical rules of a language are its syntax. The conventions of programming with Perl are simple:

1. A comment is indicated by a pound sign (#). It always runs to the end of the current line and it is always ignored by the Perl interpreter. The comments are used to describe the workings of the code, such as what information a variable holds or what a subroutine does, and also other items such as author, description, or product name. It is also a helpful inclusion for the next programmer who will look at or work with your code—even if that programmer is you!

2. A line that starts with an equal sign (=) signals the start of a section of Plain Old Documentation (POD), which is a documentation format that can be embedded in code. Perl modules are generally documented in POD.

3. A simple statement, such as a call to a built-in function, ends with a semicolon (;). A simple statement normally executes a command, and the semicolon is the separator between statements. As a parallel, Visual Basic uses the new line metacharacter, which means that you hit the Enter key between statements, and C/C++, like Perl, uses a semicolon for the purpose of separating simple statements.

4. A compound statement, or grouped series of instructions or commands—also called a *block*—is enclosed within curly braces ({}). A compound statement is a series of instructions, and it can also include other compound statements. In essence, compound statements are executed by a controlling statement that, for example, executes the block of code 10 times, executes it only if the given password was correct, or prints the contents of a file until the file has reached its end.

Scalar Variables

By means of in-memory storage of information, Perl provides the scalar variables to store information. *Scalar variables* are used to hold values and can be set at one point in the program and then retrieved, edited, or deleted at a later point. Moreover, there are three types of scalar variables that you can work with in Perl:

- The scalar variable
- The array of scalar variables
- The associative array of scalar variables

When declaring a variable, it must be provided with its own identifier, which predicates what context it is stored in. Although every single variable in Perl is a scalar variable, the context determines what data type a given variable is and what operations can be performed on it. For example, a list of related scalar variables is commonly stored in an array, while a single value is held in a scalar variable. The data type identifier is a special character ($, @, or %), and following it is an identifier name that may contain letters, digits, and underscores up to a total of 251 characters. Keep in mind, though, that a name is case sensitive, so if a variable was named in all uppercase letters, it will not be found if the script tries to locate it by means of all lowercase letters. The same is true for any combination of upper- and lowercase letters that is used for naming and locating a variable. In general, it is common to begin a variable name with a letter or an underscore as the first character after the identifier, then follow this with any character. It is not, however, valid to follow a variable whose first character is a digit with characters other than digits. Variables that are not of the same type can share the same name without being mixed up, since the identifier type in the call for the variable will let Perl know which variable to get. Notice, however, that there are predefined variables for Perl's behavior whose names you do not want to use by mistake. Normally these special scalar variables are followed by special characters such as /, !, and [, so it is best to avoid using similar names when declaring variables.

In terms of identifier types, $ is the identifier for a scalar variable, @ for the array, and % for the associative array. The identifier type and identifier name are used when Perl locates the variable when it is called or when an operation is performed on the variable in the program. In addition, while some programming languages may require you to define the type of data and amount of the data that you want the variable to contain, Perl does not have such a requirement for its variables to work as expected. It simply has the scalar variable, and it can hold practically all data types. In this sense, Perl is somewhat different than many languages, but also much more simple to manage because it does not make you think about what data types you are using.

Finally, a scope can be used to define where the variable is accessed after it has been declared. In general, a variable that is declared without a scope is essentially accessible anywhere in the code, but as the code grows and is divided into subroutines, it becomes less and less practical not to declare it as private to one or several blocks of code. (A block of code is the commands that are enclosed by curly braces.) There are two kinds of scope:

Dynamic scope. A dynamically scoped variable is declared by the local() function and to begin with it is accessible within the block of code where it was declared. Moreover, if a subroutine (which is another block of code) is called from within its scope, the locally declared variable can be accessed in the called subroutine.

Lexical scope. The lexically scoped variable is declared with the my() function and can be used to keep a private variable. In Perl, most declared variables are declared with lexical scope. Its restriction is that it can only be accessed within the block of code in which it was declared.

In summary, when a variable is declared as just described, the type of variable is set by the type identifier that describes its context, and then it is followed by the name assigned to the variable. The name of the variable normally starts with a letter or an underscore, and then is followed by any combination of valid characters. However, a variable cannot be followed by anything but digits if the first character is a digit. When declared, the initial value of a declared variable is nothing, which in Perl is equal to undef. A variable, however, can have its value initialized at any point, including upon declaration, by following it with an equal sign (=) and the value to set. All of this is true for variables whose scope has been defined. Dynamic and lexical scope are used to make variables more accessible or less accessible to the right parts of the program. Later in the program, both the type identifier and the identifier name are used in the script to locate the variable and its value, provided that it is in the right scope when called.

The Scalar Variable

As the cornerstone of Perl, the scalar variable is the underlying placeholder of all entities. The scalar variable refers to a single value that either is numeric, a string of text, or a reference to another value. Thanks to this interoperability, numbers and strings are interchangeable and can transparently converse with each other.

You can declare the scalar variable anywhere in your program. It can be initialized with a value on the spot or assigned a value later in the program. Until it is assigned a value, however, it will be equal to "undef" or better known as a null value. In order to define a variable as a scalar, put the identifier type $ before the identifier name. Next, to assign a value, separate the value and variable with an equal sign. The following are all valid scalar variables with different types of values:

```
my $MyDoubleQuotedText = "Stuff";
my $MySingleQuotedText = 'Stuff';
my $MyNumber = 100;
my $MyFloat = 100.99;
my $MyReadableMillion = 1_000_000;
```

In the previous example, a variety of values were put into scalar variables, such as strings, integers, floating-point values, and a way of explicitly writing a large number readably by using the underscore (which by the way will not affect calculations). There is an upper limit to the size of the numbers a scalar is capable of storing (which few general scripts reach); the strings can be as long as the memory on the machine can handle. You can declare and assign values to more than one scalar on the same line by enclosing them within parentheses.

```
my ($text, $twodigitnumber, $digit);
my ($Text, $TwoDigitNumber, $Digit) = ('Hello', 34, 5);
```

As seen in the first example, strings can be enclosed within double quotes and single quotes. When you work with strings, whether you use double or single quotes for scalar values will matter.

In terms of text, the double-quoted string has many characteristics. It first of all allows you to embed white space such as new line characters, spaces, and tab characters into the string, which can be used for formatting the output. Second and more interestingly, enclosing a scalar value in double quotes will cause scalar variables to be interpreted as scalar values instead of text. If you include a variable within a double-quoted string, either deliberately or by mistake, it will register a value of what is represented instead of treating the variable name as plain text.

```
###############################################################
# The following example demonstrates what is called variable #
# interpolation - The two scalar variables within the double-#
# quoted string are treated as scalar values.                 #
###############################################################

my $What = "Ask";
my $Who = "Bob";
my $SayWhat = "$What $Who \n"; # Prints "Ask Bob" and a newline
```

There are some things to beware of when using double-quoted strings. Data type identifiers, for example, are interpreted in double-quoted strings since you can use scalar variables. Moreover, control characters, which include all the data type identifiers, cannot be represented as literal characters if they are not escaped by explicitly telling the interpreter to treat them as characters without a meaning. The following is an occasion where a variable will not print the expected result:

```
my $EndResult = "$1,000"; # This will output ",000"
```

As a remedy, the proper way to escape a control character or any other character is to put a backslash in front of it. Backslashing a character causes it to be treated as the plain character or text. On some common occasions, it is important to remember to escape the control characters. For example, when opening a file on the file system, each backslash in the file path must be escaped or else the file will not be found. The next example shows how to backslash by correcting the previous mistake:

```
my $EndResult = "\$1,000"; # This will output "$1,000"
```

In contrast to the flexibility of the double-quoted strings, the single-quoted string is much stricter. In a single-quoted string everything is treated as a pure textual representation, so neither white space nor scalar values will be treated as anything but pure textual characters. This eliminates the need for escaping characters, and provides a practical way of embedding double quotes, for example, within a string without making it unreadable by escaping every double quote.

```
my $SayHi = '$Greet $Name \n'; #Outputs "$Greet $Name \n"
```

On the topic of strings, it quite often becomes necessary to concatenate two or more strings—in other words, to join the strings together into one single string. The dot operator is used to concatenate string values. For example:

```
###############################################################
# The following example demonstrates concatenation where two #
# scalars are combined into one new scalar variable          #
###############################################################
```

```
my ($Say, $Who) = ("Take me to", "your leader");

my $MyMessage = $Say." ".$Who.".";  # "Take me to your leader";
```

However, recall that double quotes are allowed within single quotes. This is perfect for writing HTML in Active Server Pages or another application, but it does not allow scalar values to be interpolated. The solution is to concatenate these strings (or use single quotes in the HTML, although it would not serve this example):

```
print '<TD ALIGN="LEFT"
BGCOLOR="#FFFFFF">'.$scalarString.'</TD>';
```

versus

```
print "<TD ALIGN=\"LEFT\"
BGCOLOR=\"#FFFFFF\">$scalarString</TD>";
```

Related Functions

uc(string)

Converts a string into a string of all uppercase letters.

```
$allLower = "hello";
$allUpper = uc($allLower);
```

ucfirst(string)

Converts the first character of a string into an uppercase character.

```
$myName = "andreas";
$newName = ucfirst($myName);
```

substr(string, offset [,length] [,replacement])

Returns a substring from *string* that is *length* long in characters and starts at the position *offset*. Offset is 0 by default, but if a negative number is used, then it starts from the right end and moves to the left. *Replacement* can be specified as the value with which to replace the extracted substring. Copy text from the original string:

```
$string = "abcdef";
$substring = substr($string, 0, 3);

print $string, "=", $substring;
```

To remove the substring from the original, one minor change is made:

```
$string = "abcdef";

$substring = substr($string, 0, 3, undef);

print $string, "=", $substring;
```

index(string, substring [,start])

Returns the index of the first *substring* found in *string*. *Start* is 0 by default, and the method returns −1 if the *substring* is not found.

```
$string = "abcdefghi";

$index = index($string, "efg", 0);

print $index;
```

rindex(string, substring [,start])

Same as the index function, except that it returns the last index of the string to match.

```
$string = "x_x_x_x_x_x";

$index = rindex($string, "_x");

print $index;
```

ord(character)

Returns the character value of the first character in the given string, in this case *a* (although *b* and *c* are there):

```
$string = "abc";

print ord($string);
```

length(string)

Returns the length in characters of the value of EXPR, or $_ if EXPR is not specified.

```
$string = "abc";

print length($string);
```

lcfirst(string)

Returns a string of EXPR where the first letter is lowercase, or returns a string of $_ if EXPR is not specified where the first letter is lowercase.

```
$string = "Hello";

$string = lcfirst($string);

print $string;
```

lc(string)

Returns an all-lowercase string of EXPR, or returns a lowercase string of $_ if EXPR is not specified.

```
$string = "HELLO";

$string = lc($string);

print $string;
```

hex(hexadecimal)

Returns the value of the hexadecimal EXPR. $_ is assumed as EXPR if no other value is specified.

```
print hex('ff'), "\t", hex('ee'), "\t", hex('ee');
```

chr(number)

Returns the character represented by *N*, or the value in $_ if *N* is not used.

```
print chr(97); # Prints "a"
```

chop(value)

If used with a scalar value, removes the last character and returns the new string. When used in list context, removes the last character of all elements. The value of $_ is assumed if nothing else is specified.

```
$str = "Hello";

chop($str);

print $str;        # Prints "Hello"
```

chomp(value)

Same as chop, with one important exception. It removes the last character only if it is the same value as in $/, which in Windows is the new line character.

The Array

When putting a group of related scalar variables in one place, the array is the data structure that you will use in Perl. Its identifier type is the at sign (@), and as a placeholder the array contains ordinary scalar variables that are called *elements* because of the array context. The data structure is fully dynamic, so it will expand and contract as new elements are added or removed from the list, and there are several built-in functions for its management.

As elements are placed in the array, they are in an ordered list that when illustrated looks like a stack (Figure 2.1). The last element is always put on top of the stack; thus added items are placed there, too. However, this would be of little use if it were the only way of manipulating the array. Elements can be put anywhere in the array, although stack operations provides a natural flow of operations. First, however, to access the elements, you need to know that the list's index and first element start at 0. So if there are three elements, as in the preceding example, then the last element is accessed with 2. There are two more ways of accessing the last element of the array; the preferred way is by using the index −1. However, a cryptic-looking $#arrayname can be used as the element index when accessing the last element in the list.

In the array, the scalar variables are often related in some sense. For example, the array French_Cities could contain all cities in France, and Ford_Models could contain all models of the Ford car that are available. The array can be declared either as empty or with elements. In an ordinary array elements are enclosed within parentheses.

```
my @array = ();                         # Empty Array
my @secondarray = ("John", "Doe", 12);  # Array with three
elements
```

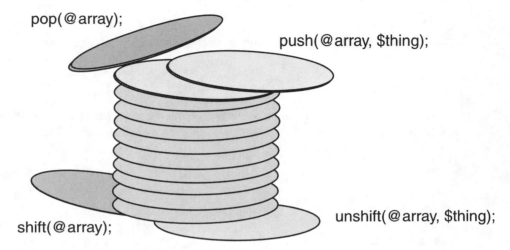

pop(@array);

push(@array, $thing);

shift(@array);

unshift(@array, $thing);

Figure 2.1 The stack of items in the array.

```
print $array[0], "\n", $array[1], "\n";  # Print element no 1 and 2
print $array[-1], "\t", $array[$#array]; # Print the last element
```

When you want to save yourself some time, the qw function provides generalized quotes as you enter the elements into the array. It allows you to omit both quotation marks and comma signs. And on top of the qw function, there are a number of other built-in functions that relate to the array directly.

Related Functions

pop(@array)

Removes and returns the last element of @array, and always uses the special variable @_ in subroutines and in every other case in which @array is not specified.

```
my @a = qw(John Doe 12);  # Three-element array
$Age = pop(@array);       # Pop the last element
```

push(@array, list)

Appends the elements of list to @array, and returns the new number of elements in the @array.

```
my @a = qw(John Doe 12);          # Three element array "a"
my @b = qw(1 2 3 4 5);            # Five element array "b"

my $NumElements = push(@a, @b); # Push "b" onto "a"
```

shift(@array)

Removes and returns the first element of ARRAY. Uses @_ in subroutines if ARRAY is not specified.

```
my @a = qw(John Doe 12);  # Three element array

my $FirstName = shift @a; # Remove the first element
```

unshift(@array, list)

Appends a list of elements to the beginning of an existing array, then returns the number of new elements.

```
my @a = qw(John Doe 12); # Three element array
my @b = qw(1 2 3 4 5);   # Five element array

unshift(@a, @b);         # Unishift "b" in front of "a"
```

splice(@array, offset [,length] [,list])

Removes and returns the LENGTH number of elements from the ARRAY starting at 0. Alternatively specifies an OFFSET at which to start in the array index, and replaces the removed elements with LIST.

```
my @thislist = qw(1 2 3 4 5);  # Five element array
my @replace = qw(a b c);       # Three element array
# Return and replace three elements
#
my @thatlist = splice(@thislist, 0, 3, @replace);

# Print both arrays
#
print @thatlist, "\n", @thislist;
```

reverse(list)

When LIST are scalars in list context, reverses their order. When the returned value is forced to a scalar, it comes back reverted.

```
@order = qw(1 2 3 4 5 6 7 8 9 10); # The array to revert
$String = "Perl";                   # The string to revert

@order = reverse @order;           # Reverse the array
print @order;                      # Print the array

# The following forces reverse $string to be evaluated in
# scalar context - contrary to list-context
#
print scalar(reverse($string));
```

map (EXPR, LIST)

map {BLOCK}, LIST

Map evaluates either the block or the expression it specifies for each element in the list used with it. Then it returns the list of the values that match the result.

The following example uses a block when mapping, and this is the first time the special variable $_ is introduced in this book. Essentially, in most list operations the value of each element in the list is assumed in the funny-looking $_ variable. This example multiplies the value of the array by itself.

```
my @list = qw(1 2 3 4 5)
my @newlist = map { $_ * $_ } @list
print @newlist;
```

sort([SUBNAME\BLOCK], list)

sort(list)

It is pretty common to want to sort an array. Here are a few examples of numeric sorting:

```
@numbers = qw(45 3 4 56 5 2 34 5);

# Sort numerically min to max
#
@listA = sort{$a <=> $b} @numbers;

# Sort numerically max to min
#
@listB = sort{$b <=> $a} @numbers;
```

And the same thing, but with characters:

```
@names = qw("Bob", "Ron", "John", "Seb");

# Sort numerically min to max
#
@listA = sort{$a cmp $b} @names;

# Sort numerically max to min
#
@listB = sort{$b cmp $a} @names;
```

The first method does this by default, which you can see if you do the following:

```
print sort @names;
```

split(/PATTERN/, EXPR [,LIMIT])

A regularly used function. Returns a list of every value in EXPR that was separated by PATTERN, or the original EXPR if no separation was made. LIMIT can restrict the number of scalars to return. If no parameters are specified, it will split $_ by white space.

The following will split a string by the comma character, which is escaped by a back-slash—just in case—and the result is that each word is returned into an array:

```
$String = "Joe,Blow,Hwy 24 S,Degas,Las Vegas";
@a = split(/\,/, $String);
```

join(EXPR, LIST)

This one does the opposite of what the previous function did:

```
@list = ('Joe Blow', 'Hwy 24 S, 'Degas', 'Las Vegas');
$String = join(",", @list);
```

The Associative Array

The associative array—also known as the *hash*—is an array, but it indexes its elements in a different manner. The type identifier is the percent sign (%), and the index is by key instead of integer. The hash table keys are strings that are associated with each value. The hash also expands and contracts dynamically.

```
my %hash = ('ColorA' => 'Blue',
            'ColorB' => 'Red',
            'ColorC' => 'Green');
```

And, indexed by key and accessed as a scalar variable.

```
print $hash{'ColorC'};
```

Related Functions

delete(key)

The delete function deletes a key and its value from the hash. It returns the value of the key or under if there is no such key.

```
delete($hash{key});
```

each(hash)

Returns the key and value of the next element in the hash.

```
my ($key, $value) = each %Hash;
```

exists(key)

Returns true if the key exists in the given hash.

```
print exists($hash{$key});
```

keys(hash)

Returns a list of all the keys in the hash or the number of keys if evaluated in a scalar context. Can also be used to preallocate the number of keys in the hash instead of letting this be done dynamically.

```
print keys(%HASH), "\n", scalar(keys(%HASH));
```

values(hash)

Returns a list of all the values in the hash or the number of values if evaluated in a scalar context.

```
print keys(%HASH), "\n", scalar(keys(%HASH))
```

References and Nested Data Structures

A reference does not classify exactly as a variable. However, as just seen, the variables that have been presented only hold scalar values, and lack the ability to hold arrays and hashes. The reference solves that issue.

A reference points to an existing variable rather than representing its value. It knows how to locate the variable, but it does not hold the variable's value. In order to retrieve the value of the variable that the reference points to, it must be dereferenced. A reference that is dereferenced returns the actual variable so that its value can be directly accessed.

The most common way to create a reference is to use the backslash operator. This entails preceeding any other variable, subroutine, or value with the backslash, such as:

```
# Makes a reference to a scalar variable
#
$reference1 = \$someScalar;

# Makes a reference to array
#
$reference2 = \@someArray;
```

The dereferencing of these is done as follows:

```
print $$reference1;
print @$reference2;
```

Placing the variable type being pointed to in front of the reference variable dereferences a reference. A reference can also point to another reference, and in that case, every reference that it points to must be dereferenced in its logical order. For example:

```
# A regular scalar
#
$scalar = "Hello World";

# Reference it in six steps
#
$refToScalar = \\\\\\$scalar;

# This will print the location to its next reference and not "Hello
# World"
#
print $$refToScalar, "\n";

# This, however, will print "Hello World" since it is dereferenced
# in six steps. Not one, five or seven..
#
print $$$$$$$refToScalar, "\n";
```

It is very common to make the dereferencing more readable—or quite possibly the opposite—by enclosing the reference within curly braces:

```
# The array
#
@someArray = qw(1 2 3 4 5);

# The hash
#
%someHash = ('a' => 'Anderson',
             'b' => 'Bob');

# Reference the array
#
$reference1 = \@someArray;
```

```
# Reference the hash
#
$reference2 = \%someHash;

# Dereference the array
#
print @{$reference1};

# Dereference the hash
#
print %{$reference2};
```

This would yield the expected and unwanted result of printing out all the elements within both list context variables. Why is it the expected behavior? First, a single element in a list is a scalar and must be accessed by a scalar, which means that neither @ nor % are valid for accessing single elements—$ must be used. Next, there is no index for the array or key for the hash to specify which element to retrieve. The following syntax is a clean way of accessing a scalar through the reference:

```
# Access the first element in the referenced array
#
print $reference1->[0];

# Access the value for key "a" in the referenced hash
#
print $reference2->{'a'};
```

This code is equivalent to the following dereferencing, which is commonly used when accessing list values in an object:

```
# Same as in previous example
#
print ${$reference1}[0];

# Same as in previous example
#
print ${$reference2}{'a'};
```

In either system of dereferencing, the syntax is descriptive in its own way. The former is a bit more explicit than the clean use of arrow notation. The final note about the basics of references involves a function and an alternative but ordinary way of creating references.

Whether you know that you need to verify that a variable is a reference or find out what type of data it is referencing, the built-in ref() function will return a value if the variable is a reference and false (a null value) if it is not a reference. Its true value will be a string of text that describes the type of data the reference is pointing to. In addition to this feature, a reference can point to an anonymous storage, which is a set of values not associated with a variable. For anonymous arrays, square brackets are used to enclose the elements instead of parentheses. For hashes, curly braces to show anonymous storage replace the parentheses.

```perl
# An anonymous array - notice the brackets because they symbolize it
# is anonymous and the $-prefix for someArray to show the reference
#
$someArray = [1, 2, 3, 4, 5];

# An anonymous hash - notice curly braces and $-prefix for someHash
#
$someHash = {'a' => 'Anderson',
             'b' => 'Bob'};

# The following will print ARRAY
#
print ref($someArray), "\n";

# The following will print HASH
#
print ref($someHash), "\n";

# Print the first element
#
print $someArray->[0], "\n";

# Print the 'a' key's value
#
print $someHash->{'a'};
```

With all of this discussion about references, let's look at how to create some complex data structures. The first one is an anonymous array that will contain arrays—a list of lists.

```perl
# Create the reference to the anonymous array
#
$anonArray = [Text, [1,2,3]];

# This prints "Text"
#
print $anonArray->[0];

# This prints 2
#
print $anonArray->[1][1];
```

This declaration will produce the same output as the following one:

```perl
$MyText = "Text"

@MyNumbers = (1,2,3);

@references = (\$MyText, \@MyNumbers);

# Is equivalent to
# @references = \($MyText, @MyNumbers);
```

A further example:

```perl
# Reference to anonymous array
#
```

```
$a = ["Text", [1,2,3], {"Hello"=>"World"}];

# Prints "World"
#
print $a->[2]->{'Hello'};
```

As seen, the references can hold many different values and are useful when building nested data structures. This can be elaborated on further. To read more about it, the following resources are recommended:

- See "Perl Referenced and Nested Data Structures" by Larry Wall et al. It is in the core Perl documentation, and it is a long and complete tutorial on references. Read it by issuing perldoc perlref from the command prompt.

- See "Mark's Very Short Tutorial about References" by Mark-Jason Dominus. It was originally written for and published in *The Perl Journal 3*, #2, but has with permission been reprinted in the core Perl documentation. The document is a tutorial on references that, as the title says, is shorter than perlref, but delivers according to its introductory paragraph the 10 percent of perlref that is needed for 90 percent of the benefit. Run it from the command prompt by issuing perldoc perlreftut.

- See "Manipulating Lists of Lists in Perl" by Tom Christiansen. It is in the core Perl documentation as the perllol page, and it describes everything known about arrays of arrays. It can be viewed by issuing perldoc perllol.

- See "Perl Data Structures Cookbook" by Tom Christiansen. This document is a part of the core documentation, and can be read by issuing perldoc perldst.

File Handles

A file handle is an input/output (I/O) channel between your program and the operating system. In the operating system, there are three file handles already open for the program: STDIN (standard input), STDOUT (standard output), STDERR (standard error). But Perl is far from limited to these file handles as the only channels. You can open your own file handles to files on the system or use them for sending and receiving data from remote servers.

By default, the print and write functions will write to STDOUT, STDIN will wait for input to the program from the client, and STDERR is where an error message is channeled before being put into the special variable $!, which contains error messages. If you want a file handle that is not routed to either of the default channels, such as an I/O connection to a file, you will need to open it explicitly by using the open() function.

```
open(FILE, "C:\\file.txt");
```

This creates the file handle FILE, which can coexist with any other variables of the same name. The specified file is opened for reading only, and it will be read one line at a time or placed into an array by using the < > operator. Always close an open file handle when you don't need it any longer. For example:

```
open(FILE, "c:\\file.txt");
@fileContents = <FILE>;
close(FILE);
```

When opening a file handle, there are four different modes that can be used, as seen in Table 2.6.

When you want to send data through the channel, you use the print function. For example, to append a line to a file, the following is correct:

```
open(FILE, ">>c:\\file.txt");
print FILE "Append mode\n";
close(FILE);
```

By default, any file opened by a file handle is opened as an ASCII (plain text) file. When the file you want to open is a binary file, you must specify that you are reading binary data with the command binmode (FILE); a binary file does not have lines in the sense ASCII files do.

- See "Perlfaq 5" by Tom Christiansen and Nathan Torkington in the core Perl documentation. It contains information on files and formats, and among other practical things how to count the number of lines, delete a line, insert a line in the middle of a file, and read a file in by paragraphs, for example. Issue perldoc perlfaq5 from the command prompt.

- See "Tutorial on Opening Things in Perl" by Tom Christiansen in the core Perl documentation. It has everything you need to know about binary files, file locking, and more.

Special Variables

In the Perl language, there are predefined variables that have special meaning to Perl. These variables are available to the programmer, and can be examined to obtain further information about what is going on or set some options for how Perl behaves in certain situations. For every special variable, there are one default name and one name that is defined when using the English module (Table 2.7).

Table 2.8 contains arrays, hashes, file handles, and constants that are special to Perl.

Table 2.6 Opening a File Handle

SYNTAX	MODE
open(FILE, "<$file");	Read only.
open(FILE, "$file");	
open(FILE, ">$file");	Erases existing contents. Write only.
open(FILE, "+<$file");	Read/write.
open(FILE, "+>$file");	Erases existing content. Read/write.
open(FILE, ">>$file");	Appends to the end of the file.

Table 2.7 Special Variables

VARIABLE	ENGLISH	MEANING
$_	$ARG	Default variable to which Perl assigns an input value in situations such as pattern matching or other input operations such as looping a list or reading from a file handle. In such events, print(); and print($_); are equivalent.
$.	$INPUT_LINE_NUMBER $NR	Position of the input line number of last read file handle. Closing the file handle resets this value.
$/	$INPUT_RECORD_SEPARATOR $RS	Input record separator, which is the new line metacharacter by default. Setting this value to undef or localizing the variable is common in order to read the full contents of a file without a line separator. One example is a binary file, which has no concept of lines that text files use.
$|	$OUTPUT_AUTOFLUSH	Tells Perl whether to flush the buffer immediately after each write() or print(). Zero, which is default, does not flush immediately.
$, $OFS	$OUTPUT_FIELD_SEPARATOR	Output field separator for the print()operator
$\ $"	$OUTPUT_RECORD_SEPARATOR $LIST_SEPARATOR	Output record separator for the print() operator $, for list values. When a list is interpolated into a double-quoted string or similar element, the $" will separate the elements. For example: print "@array" will use $" as separator. Space by default.
$;	$SUBSCRIPT_SEPARATOR	Subscript separator for emulated multidimensional $SUBSEP arrays. "\034" is default.
$?	$CHILD_ERROR	Status value returned from a system() command.
$!	$OS_ERROR $ERRNO	In case of a failed function call, this variable will contain either an error code or a string describing the error.

Continues

Table 2.7 Special Variables *(Continued)*

VARIABLE	ENGLISH	MEANING
$^E	$EXTENDED_OS_ERROR	Operating system–specific error code.
$@	$EVAL_ERROR	If an eval( ) command fails, this variable contains the Perl syntax error message.
$$	$PROCESS_ID $PID	Process ID number, a unique number that identifies the process among the other processes run on the machine.
$0	$PROGRAM_NAME	Name of the program that is executed. Index at which an array should start, and the first character in a substring.
$]	$PERL_VERSION	Perl version plus patch level divided by 1000.
$^D	$DEBUGGING	Current value of the debugging flags in Perl.
$^O	$OSNAME	Name of the current operating system for which the version of Perl being run was compiled.
$^T	$BASETIME	Time the current script began running, in number of seconds since 1970.
$^X	$EXECUTABLE_NAME	The name Perl.exe was executed as.
$n		Special variable used with regular expressions that contain the text matched by the set of parentheses associated with the number *n.* For example, $1 returns the result from the match of the expression in the first parenthesis, $2 the second, and so forth.
$&	$MATCH	String that was matched by the last successful pattern match. Read only.
$`	$PREMATCH	String preceding $MATCH. Read only.
$'	$POSTMATCH	String following $MATCH. Read only.
$+	$LAST_PAREN_MATCH	Last bracket that was matched by the last search pattern. Read only.

Table 2.8 More Global, Special Variables

VARIABLE	MEANING
@ARGV	Keeps the command line arguments passed to the script when it was executed.
@INC	Keeps the locations to look for files that will incorporated by *do*, *require*, or *use*.
%INC	Keeps the file name of each file included by *do* or *require*.
%ENV	Keeps the current environment variables.
%SIG	Sets signal handlers for certain signals.
ARGV	File handle iterating over command line filenames in @ARGV.
STDERR	File handle for standard error.
STDIN	File handle for standard input.
STDOUT	File handle for standard output.
DATA	File handle referring to anything after the _END_ token.
END	Logical end. Nothing is read past this point unless read by the DATA file handle.
FILE	File name being used.
LINE	Current line number in the script.
PACKAGE	Name of the current package.

The Control Structures of Perl

The control structures of a programming language are used to direct the flow of the program by determining when to execute a block of code or reexecute the same block, and at what point to stop executing a block of code. There are three types of control structures:

- Conditional control statements
- Loop control statement
- Labels

Conditional Control Statements

The conditional control statement determines whether or not a block of code will be executed. It is either an if statement or an unless statement. The if statement will execute its associated block of code if the expression it poses is true.

```
if(Expression) {Block of code}
```

Should the expression not be true, the code within curly braces is safely ignored. Mathematical operators that can be used for conditional expression are shown in Table 2.9.

An if statement can, provided that its expression is false, be continued by further conditional control statements as elsif and else. The else statement will execute its block of code without testing an expression. It only requires that its preceding if has failed. The elsif, on the other hand, will test an expression if the control statement prior to it has failed.

Table 2.9 Mathematical Operators in Perl

OPERATOR	MEANING
++	Increment
—	Decrement
**	Power of
+	Addition
–	Subtraction
*	Multiplication
/	Division
%	Modulus
>	Greater than
<	Less than
>=	Greater than or equal to
<=	Less than or equal to
==	Equal to
!=	Not equal to
<=>	Comparison
¦	Bitwise OR
&	Bitwise AND
eq	Stringwise equal to
ne	Stringwise not equal to
cmp	Stringwise comparison
gt	Stringwise greater than
lt	Stringwise less than
ge	Stringwise greater than or equal to
le	Stringwise less than or equal to

Table 2.10 Logical Operators in Perl

OPERATOR	MEANING
&&	Logical and operator. The left and right expressions must both return true.
||	Logical or operator. Either one of the expressions, evaluated from left to the right, must return true. If the expression on the left side is false, the right expression is evaluated. Otherwise the right expression is not evaluated at all.
!	Logical not operator that tells the expression to return true if the expression is false.
and	Low-priority and operator.
or	Low-priority or operator.
xor	Low-priority xor operator.

```perl
my $name = 'Rena';

if($name eq 'Bob') {
    print "Your name is Bob!";
    }
    elsif($name eq 'John') {
        print "Your name is John!";
        }
        else {
            print "Your name is $name!"
            }
```

In contrast, the unless statement does prevent execution of the command on its left side provided that its expression is true.

```perl
my $number=9;

print "$number is less than or equal to five"
unless($number>=5);
```

The construct for the unless statement can be adapted by the if statement, too, in order to perform the operation to the left if the expression is true.

In addition to simple conditional expressions, a series of expressions can be stated by separating them with logical operators (Table 2.10).

```perl
if(LeftExpression && RightExpression) {
...
}
```

Loop Control Statements

A loop control statement is used to execute code a repeated number of times within the program.

The For Loop

The for loop has many different constructs, but one of the most common includes three steps:

- An index value is initialized.
- A conditional expression compares the index value to a maximum value to determine whether the block of code should be reexecuted or exited.
- A mathematical expression defines how the index value is changed per loop to get close to the maximum value.

The most basic for loop initializes its index to 0 or 1 and increments the index by adding 1 to it per each loop for as long as the index is less than or equal to the maximum value.

```
for($i=1; $i <= 15; $i++) {
    print "Loop $i", "\n";
    }
```

After having looped 15 times, it exits. A different kind of construct for the same loop is to use the range operator and numerically tell it how many times to loop the block of code.

```
for(1..15) {
    print "Loop $_", "\n";
    }
```

The Foreach Loop

The foreach loop is similar to the for loop but is used in list context. It takes an array as its only expression and assigns the current element in the array to a defined variable, loops the code, then moves to the next element in the array and repeats until there are no more elements.

```
my @friends = qw('Mike', 'Rena', 'Andy');

foreach my $friend (@friends) {
    print "$friend ", "\n";
    }
```

The While Loop

The while loop tests a conditional statement before it begins the loop. It is very often used in a context where you loop something until it reaches its end, such as a file or a result returned from a database query.

```
while($i <= 15) {
print "Loop $i", "\n"
$i++;
}
```

It can be used with mathematical expressions, as just shown. A more common use, however, is to open a file and print each line of the file until the end of the file is reached.

```
open(F, "somefile.txt");

    while($line = <F>) {
    print $line;
    }

close(F);
```

The Until Loop

The until loop is the complete contrast of the while loop. It executes the code it controls until its conditional statement is true. It is a very natural construct.

```
print $i++ until($i==10);
```

Labels

Labels mark up control structures, which makes it easier to refer to a block of code in detail. In the block context, next, last, and redo can be used to continue a block of code, exit by breaking out of it, or restart the loop.

```
GUESS: while(1)
    {
    print "Concentrate on a number between 0 and 10: ";

    $input = <STDIN>;
    $a = int rand(0,11);

    print "The number is $a\n";

    next GUESS if ($input!=$a);
    last GUESS if ($input==$a);
    }

print "Great!";
```

The next, last, and redo functions can also be applied in a block of code that is not labeled. In such loops the function will apply to the innermost enclosing loop.

Regular Expressions

Regular expressions provide text matching and text manipulation capabilities. Perl has a set of the most powerful regular expressions available, and this is enough material to fill a book in itself.

Beginning Regular Expressions

Regular expressions can be made very simple or immensely complicated. First, Perl has pattern binding operators that indicate whether a regular expression should return success when it matches a pattern or when a pattern is not found. These operators are =~ and !~. The expression follows.

```
$text =~ operator/pattern/modifier
```

The operator indicates the type of operation—matching, substitution, or translation—to perform on the pattern.

Pattern Matching

The matching operator m is the default operator and is used to search for patterns in a string of text. In the expression, the pattern represents the text to match.

```
$text =~ m/Hello/; # Match "Hello" in $text
```

You can omit the m operator since Perl defaults to using the pattern matching operator.

Modifiers

A modifier (Table 2.11) is used to tell the regular expressions how to treat the text used for matching and the pattern it matches.

```
$text = "hello world";

print $text=~m/(HELLO)/i;
```

Metacharacters

When expanding the regular expressions, certain characters with special meanings are used to steer the matching in the right direction. These characters, called *metacharacters*, are displayed in Table 2.12.

You can match an expression either at the beginning or the end of a string by using the ^ and $ metacharacters.

```
$text =~ /^Hello/; # Match "Hello" at the beginning of $text
$text =~ /Hello$/; # Match "Hello" at the end of $text
```

Several expressions can be matched by enclosing each expression within parentheses; this will result in their matches being loaded into the special variables $n where n is a number for the match in the order it occurred.

Table 2.11   Modifiers for Regular Expressions

MODIFIER	FUNCTION
i	Case-insensitive match.
m	Treats string as multiple lines.
s	Treats string as a single line.
x	Extended regular expressions. Allows white space formatting.

Table 2.12 Metacharacters for Regular Expressions

METACHARACTER	FUNCTION
\	Escapes the character following it
.	Matches any single character except for a new line
^	Matches at the beginning of the string
$	Matches at the end of the string
[. . .]	Matches the character class within square brackets
(. . .)	Groups regular expressions
|	Matches either the expression preceding it or the expression following it

```
$text = "Hello From Perl";
print $1, $2 if $text=~/(Hello) From (Perl)/; # $1="Hello",
$2="Perl"
```

A minus sign can be used to indicate a group of letters from beginning to end on which the operation should occur (Table 2.13).

Pattern Quantifiers

The pattern quantifier (Table 2.14) simplifies the task of matching a certain pattern a number of times.

Predefined Character Classes

There are a number of predefined character classes with their own codes that can be used in regular expressions (Table 2.15).

Matching Locations in a String

Anchors are used in regular expressions to match at certain locations within a string. You have already seen ^ and $. Table 2.16 shows other anchors.

Extended Regular Expressions

Perl enables extended regular expressions to be embedded. Extensions are identified by a string enclosed within parentheses that begins with a question mark and then a function character (Table 2.17).

Table 2.13 Grouped Series to Match

GROUP	CHARACTERS
[a–z]	Matches all lowercase characters from a through z
[A–Z]	Matches all uppercase characters from A through Z
[a–zA–Z]	Matches both lowercase and uppercase characters
[0–9]	Matches all digits

Table 2.14 Quantifiers for How Many Times a Pattern Is Matched

QUANTIFIER	FUNCTION
*	Matches the element preceding it 0 or more times
+	Matches the element preceding it 0 or more times
?	Matches the element preceding it 0 times or 1 time
{n}	Matches the preceding element n times
{n,}	Matches the preceding element at least n times
{n,m}	Matches the preceding element n times but not more than m times

Substitution

The operator for substitution is used when matching and substituting a pattern. The pattern specifies what to look for, and then the replacement pattern tells what to replace it with.

```
# Does a case-insensitive match for January and replaces the first
# occurrence of January with February
#
$text =~ s/january/February/i;

# Removes all HTML-tags in a string
#
$text =~ s/<.*?>//g;

# Substitutes a name in the form Firstname Lastname to Lastname,
# Firstname
#
$text =~ s/(\w+)\s(\w+)/$2, $1/g;
```

When the substitution is completed, the operator returns the number of substitutions made, including zero if none were made.

Table 2.15 Predefined Character Classes

CODE	MATCHES
\w	An alphanumeric character, including underscore and period
\W	A nonalphanumeric character
\s	A white space character
\S	A non-white space character
\d	A digit
\D	A non digit

Table 2.16   Anchors

ANCHOR	MATCHES
\b	A word boundary
\B	A nonword boundary
\A	At beginning of string
\Z	At end of string or before a new line
\z	At end of string only
\G	Matches where previous m//g left off

Translation

The translation operator is used to translate characters one by one. No modifiers are necessary due to the fact that characters are translated individually. For example:

```
# Convert all lower-case characters into upper-case
#
$text=~tr/[a-z]/[A-Z]/;
```

Table 2.17   Extended Regular Expressions

EXTENSION	MEANING
(?#text)	Serves as a comment.
(?:pattern)	Groups patterns without making back references such as $1 .. $n.
(?=pattern)	Matches the result of (?=pattern) without including (?=pattern) in the final product. Called zero-width positive look-ahead assertion.
(?!pattern)	Matches the pattern that is not followed by the expression from (?!pattern). Called zero-width negative look-ahead assertion.
(?<=pattern)	Matches the pattern that follows the expression (?<=pattern) without including (?<=pattern). Called zero-width positive look-behind assertion.
(?<!=pattern)	Matches any occurrence of the expression that follows (<!=pattern) without including (<!=pattern). Called zero-width negative look-behind assertion.
(?>pattern)	Matches the substring that the stand-alone pattern would match if it were anchored at the given position.
(?(condition)true | false)	The condition determines the pattern to match. Either the condition is an (?(condition)true) integer or a look-ahead, look-behind, or evaluate zero-width assertion.

Modular Perl Programming

To some degree, modular programming applies to most every written application and modern programming language today. First, what modular programming promotes is essentially a simple way of structuring a program by dividing its working parts into modules. Then, each module performs its own task, and as long as it only returns the projected result and works with the application, the module is doing its job to the fullest. Some examples of modules in an application are ones that print text, calculate sums, read the contents of a file, or put an interface for drawing graphics in the hands of the programmer. On its lowest level, when modularizing you hide away some data in a module and keep it protected until you call it from the program because you need it to perform its operation. And if you need to redo the operation, you can always call it again later in the program instead of it being lost forever. Also, modular programming expands its scope because code that was written to perform a task in one application should be reused in another application if it has the same needs, and therefore the modules become little packages of services. On its many levels, modular programming has been applied in forms such as subroutines in programs, packages in Perl, and object-oriented programming. Even programming models such as the Component Object Model encourage everything, including the parts of an operating system, to be completely modular.

Packages

A *package* is the foundation for modular programming in Perl, and it designates a new name space where the names of the parts of your program, such as variables, are located. It is an easy way to hide data away, and when something is declared outside of a package, it is put into the main name space, which is where all scripts in the book so far have resided—although this is not explicitly declared. The following shows how to place a variable in a package and in the main package:

```
package myPackage;
$var = "Hello World";
1;

package main;
$var = "Main Package";

print $main::var;
print $myPackage::var;
1;
```

You could have skipped the main declaration and still have accessed your main variable as a part of that package. As just seen, when accessing something that belongs to an outside package, there are two colons separating the package name and the variable name.

Subroutines

A car is not just one big welded chunk of metal. When something breaks on the car, you get a new part to replace the old one. It is natural, practical, and clever to build a car from parts instead of making it as one single thing. Programming methodology is the same. You would not want to make everything into one big welded chunk because it is not natural, practical, or clever. Just as parts of a car can be improved and replaced, parts of code must undergo this process too. This is where modular programming comes into the picture. An application is a set of operations being performed, sometimes once and sometimes repeatedly, and it can often be divided into parts. From the beginning to the end of the program, you pick out every group of commands that perform an operation and modularize them by placing them into a subroutine. Next, the subroutine is given a name that describes its function.

```
sub NameOfSub
{
    #...Some code to be executed...
```

A program can result in four subroutines. For example, sub A logs you onto your mail account, sub B receives e-mail, sub C sends e-mail, and sub D disconnects you from the mail server. The logical order of operation is to first execute sub A, then sub B, sub C, and sub D. In modular programming, you add a subroutine that acts as a controlling subroutine, whose only function is calling the other subroutines of the program.

```
sub ControlSub
{
    A();
    B();
    C();
    D();
}

sub A
{
    # Logs onto mail account
}

sub B
{
    # Receives mail
}

sub C
{
    # Sends mail
}

sub D
{
    # Disconnects from mailserver
}
```

Parameters

It would be difficult to send mail, for example, if no e-mail text or address to send to were passed to sub C. For this purpose there are parameters. The parameters are passed to a subroutine inside the parentheses that follow the name of the subroutine.

When programming Perl, it is at first difficult to get used to the rule that all parameters to a subroutine are automatically placed in the special variable @_ and therefore they must be either read or extracted from this special variable.

```perl
############################################################
# Calling the sub printString with a value as parameter
############################################################

PrintString("Hello From Perl!");

############################################################
# PrintString: Prints the parameter passed to it to
#              demonstrate a simple parameter
############################################################
sub PrintString
{
    my ($param) = shift;

    print $param;
}
```

The subroutine PrintString essentially encapsulates a call to a print function by which it prints out the value of the parameter sent. The former example simply outputs "Hello From Perl!" as a string. Admittedly, it is not a very useful thing to encapsulate as a subroutine, and especially not when all the functionality for printing a string is already in the print() function. It will probably create more of a headache than a function. Instead, a subroutine that can perform a calculation would be far more efficient than one that prints a simple statement to the standard output. So let's make the subroutine CalcAvg and pass a couple of numbers to it.

```perl
############################################################
# Call CalcAvg with the numbers to calculate average
############################################################

CalcAvg(1,5,6);
CalcAvg(431,25,236,12,23,3);

############################################################
# CalcAvg: Read the parameters-array into one where the
#          numbers are stored. Extract the number of elem-
#          ents into $elements and set the total sum of
#          their values to zero. Then loop each element of
#          the array, add up the total, and divide it by
#          the number of elements to get the average.
############################################################

sub CalcAvg
{
    my (@numbers) = @_;
    my ($elements) = scalar(@numbers);
    my ($total) = 0;

    foreach my $number (@numbers) {
        $total+=$number;
```

```
        }

        my $avg = ($total/$elements);

        print "The average is: $avg", "\n";
}
```

Performing calculations such as this is a much more useful task for a subroutine. It now encloses a group of commands that perform a joint operation and produce an expected result. Moreover, the routine can be reused in other applications. If you want to pass several arrays or hash tables to a subroutine, it is not possible the ordinary way. The reason is because the problem arises when you make a script as follows and attempt to read the parameters:

```
###########################################################
# Pass one hash, array, and scalar to the subroutine
# GetParams
###########################################################
my %param1 = ('a'=>'Hello',
              'b'=>'World');

my @param2 = (1,2,3,4,5,6,7,8,9,10);

my $param3 = "Good morning";

GetParams(%param1, @param2, $param3);

###########################################################
# GetParams: Shows how to fail getting the right values
#            because the parameters were not passed by
#            reference
#
###########################################################

sub GetParams
{
    my (%param1, @param2, $param3) = @_;

    print %param1, "\n";

    print @param2, "\n";

    print $param3, "\n";
}
```

First, %param1 will have all variables passed to the subroutine loaded into it, including every single element of the arrays plus the scalar. And it is also the only value that will print, so in the end it produces a corrupted result. The result is to use references that are passed as scalars and extracted as scalars, but on the inside point to the original data structure they represent. Now the script can be rewritten.

```
###########################################################
# Pass one hash, array, and scalar by reference to the
# subroutine GetParams
###########################################################
```

```perl
my %param1 = ('a'=>'Hello',
              'b'=>'World');

my @param2 = (1,2,3,4,5,6,7,8,9,10);

my $param3 = "Wednesday";

GetParams(\%param1, \@param2, \$param3);

############################################################
# GetParams: Receives a hash, array, and scalar that are
#            passed by reference. Outputs them all.
############################################################

sub GetParams
{
    my ($param1, $param2, $param3) = @_;

    print %$param1, "\n";

    print @$param2, "\n";

    print $$param3, "\n";
}
```

Return Values

Whether an array, hash table, or single scalar is returned from a subroutine, there is only one way to return a value but two ways to write it. An expression can stand by itself at the end of the subroutine and it will return its value or result or the subroutine can be explicitly ended by the return function followed by the value to return.

```perl
############################################################
# retVal_One: Returns the value of $c
############################################################

sub retVal_One
{
    my ($a, $b) = @_;

    my $c = ($a*$b);

    return $c;
}

############################################################
# retVal_Two: Returns the value of expression $a*$b
############################################################

sub retVal_Two
{
    my ($a, $b) = @_;

    ($a*$b);
}
```

In both cases, it is simply a matter of personal taste which one you like the best. In Perl, code can be written with very few lines. Returning two arrays from a subroutine can be a little trickier. It requires the use of references, again:

```perl
my ($a, $b) = RetArrays();

print @{$a}, "\n\n\n", @{$b};

sub RetArrays
{
    my @arrayOne = qw(a b c);
    my @arrayTwo = qw(d e f);

    return(\@arrayOne, \@arrayTwo);
}
```

Prototypes

Prototypes allow you to specify the types of variables that are sent in the parameter list to the subroutine (Table 2.18).

Certain control characters can be applied to the prototypes as well. Putting a backslash before one of the symbols will force a parameter to be of that exact type. A semicolon is used to include optional parameters in the parameter prototypes to the right of the semicolon.

Further Reference

See "Perl Subroutines" in the core Perl documentation, which provides a thorough description on most topics related to subroutines, such as scope and subroutines, persistent private variables, prototypes, pass by reference, and much more. Read it from the command prompt by entering perldoc perlsub.

The Symbol Table

For every package, Perl keeps an internal hash table that is known as the symbol table. It points to named data in the package, such as variables, but since a hash table cannot accept duplicate names, the variables $myvar, @myvar, and %myvar cannot

Table 2.18 Prototype Representations

SYMBOL	DATA
$	Scalar
@	Array
%	Hash
&	Anonymous subroutine
*	Type glob

coexist. The solution is to point to these variables by name instead of identifier. What holds this name between the symbol table and the actual data is called a typeglob.

The Typeglob

The typeglob an internal data type that holds a symbol table entry. Identified and accessed by script with the *name syntax, the typeglob is what the symbol table uses when accessing a variable.

```
$name = "Bob";
@name = ("Bob", "Mary", "Joe");

%name = ("2000" => 1_234_243);

*newName = *name;

print $newName, "\n";
print @newName, "\n";
print %newName, "\n";
```

One caveat exists, though. Lexical variables are not listed in the symbol table, so they cannot be accessed by typeglobbing, and that is something to keep in mind. It has its areas of usage, though, such as when passing a file handle to a subroutine.

```
###########################################################
# Example of opening a filehandle and passing it as a
# parameter to a filehandle, then trying to print the
# contents of it after the subroutine has manipulated
# the file - in this case, the subroutine reads a part
# from the filehandle, and then the calling point does
# the same after the subroutine has finished
###########################################################

open(FILE, "D:\\c.pl");

GetParams(FILE);

print while(<FILE>);

###########################################################
# GetParamFile: Localizes a filehandle, reads 50 characters
#               and then prints the contents to the screen
#               between delimiters that show that it was
#               output within the subroutine
###########################################################

sub GetParamFile
{
    local(*FILE) = @_;

    print "-GetParamFile--\n\n".

    read(FILE, $file, 50);

    print $file;
    print "-End GetParamFile--\n\n";
}
```

Modules

One level higher up than the subroutine, the module is separate from the program until imported. Modules are used because they already contain the code needed for an application or they extend the functionality of Perl. In its simplest form, a module is a package that is saved to a file with the same name as the package and the file extension .pm (Perl module). Not only is this one step further in modularizing code than what subroutines and packages do, it also handles the name space better than an ordinary package in terms of the junk it contributes.

The module is imported into a program by the use keyword followed by its name. For example, a module named StringThing is imported the following way:

```
use StringThing;
```

In the creation of a module, its name is normally nested so that it can be both descriptive and accurate for the task the module was written to perform. A name and then two colons before its module name normally precede the name of the module. The first name describes the type of functionality the module is specific for, or which group of modules it is fit for. For example, Windows-specific modules normally follow the convention Win32::Modulename, while a module that handles some functionality related to images would be called Image::Modulename. This is a nested module name, and although no such module as Image may exist, it is common to describe the functionality of modules so that both modules and the files they are packed into can be neatly organized and structured, not only in Perl.

Further Reference

- See "Perl Modules" in the core Perl documentation for a description of how Perl modules work. Read it from the command prompt by entering perldoc perlmod.

- See "Constructing New Perl Modules and Finding Existing Ones" in the core Perl documentation for exactly what the title says. Read it from the command prompt by entering perldoc perlmodlib.

Object-Oriented Perl

With Perl 5, the support for an object-oriented model of programming (OOP) was introduced. OOP is essentially a direct structure of programming for protecting and giving access to items such as variables and subroutines through a simple interface.

In OOP, the class is at the base level and contains a set of related variables and subroutines. The class belongs to the literal source code; thus the author decides the freedom or limitation of the contents that a class provides the programmer. In Perl, a class is simply a package, and the contents that belong to the package are known as methods and attributes instead of subroutines and variables. However, before data in a class can be accessed, an instance of the class must be created, and that instance is what is called an object.

In object-oriented programming, the class is the underlying source of the attributes and methods that can be accessed through the objects. In Perl, a class is simply a package that understands how to return objects. At least one of the subroutines in the class returns an object as a blessed reference. The blessing tells the object what package it belongs to, or gives it a sense of identity, so when a method is called through an object, Perl looks in the class the object refers to for the method to run.

After a class is constructed, it needs to be supplied with the method that returns the blessed reference as the class instance. In OOP terms, the method that fits the bill is called a *constructor*, and not only does it return the object, it is also a natural place to initialize any attributes with their values. In the constructor, normally the attributes are stored within an associative array because it provides a natural interface for the programmer. However, other data types such as an ordinary array are allowed, and what the blessed reference really cares about and returns is a reference of the decided-upon data type, but with a sense of identify. An object is freed from memory when the last reference to an object no longer exists, and although some languages require a destructor (as opposed to constructor) for this task, Perl automates it (although Perl gives the option of using explicit destructors).

```perl
package Computer;

sub new
{
    my $package = shift;
    my ($processor, $mhz, $ram) = @_;

    my $class = ref($package) || $package;

    my $self = {
                "Processor" => $processor,
                "Mhz" => $mhz,
                "RAM" => $ram
                };

    bless ($self, $class);
    return $self;
}
1;

$box1 = new Computer("Intel", "666", "128");
$box2 = new Computer("Intel", "266", "64");

print $box1->{Processor}, "\t";
print $box1->{Mhz}, " Mhz","\t";
print $box1->{RAM}, " Mb RAM","\n";

print $box2->{Processor}, "\t";
print $box2->{Mhz}, " Mhz", "\t";
print $box2->{RAM}, " Mb RAM\n";
```

The big thing about classes is that they can inherit. When you inherit a class, you embed new functionality by utilizing the existing functionality of the inherited class.

This is called *software reuse*, since the child class can both use existing methods and provide its own functionality built upon the parent class. When it is desired to have one class inherit from another, the class name must be put in a class array named @ISA. The @ISA contains names of the parent class for the child, and next we let the parent class do the blessing of the reference.

```perl
package Thing;

sub new

{
    my $package = shift;

    my ($name, $born, $weight, $height, $color) = @_;

    my $class = ref($package) || $package;

    my $self = {'Name'      => $name,
                'Born'      => $born,
                'Height'    => $weight,
                'Weight'    => $height,
                'Color'     => $color
            };

    bless($self, $class);
    return $self;
}
1;

package Fruit;

@Fruit::ISA = (Thing);

sub new
{
    my $package = shift;
    my $class = ref($package) || $package;

    my $self = new Thing(@_);

    bless($self, $class);
    return $self;
}

sub set
{
    my $self = shift;
    my ($property, $value) = @_;
    $self->{$property} = $value;
}
1;

package Human;

@Human::ISA = (Thing);
```

```
sub new
{
    my $package = shift;
    my ($name, $born, $height, $weight,
        $race, $country, $city, $occupation) = @_;
    my $self = new Thing($name, $born, $height, $weight, $race);

    $self->{Country} = $country;
    $self->{City} = $city;
    $self->{Occupation} = $occupation;

    return $self;
}
1;

my $apple = new Fruit('Apple', 'Fall 2001', '2', '5', 'Green');
my $human = new Human('D. Thorne', 'Jul 15, 1975',
                      '5,6', '180', 'Caucasian', 'France',
                      'Paris', 'Student');

print $human->{Occupation};
print $apple->{Color};

$apple->set('Quantity', '350');
print $apple->{Quantity};
```

Thing is a general-purpose description we apply to objects in the world. A thing always has certain characteristics that we use to describe it: for example, a name (or, in the worst case, we call it *unknown*), the birthdate of the thing (or the date it was discovered), and physical characteristics such as height, weight, and color. Many items can be elaborated on from being a thing, which makes this an excellent parent class. In the code examples, the child classes Fruit and Human inherit from Thing. The fruit can be an apple, orange, pear, plum, and so forth because all of the class properties apply to it, so we make the fruit Apple, which was "born" or harvested in fall 2001. Its height and weight are given, and so is its color—which describes the apple as either red or green, by which we can guess what the apple tastes like. In addition, Perl has a special-purpose method for creating new properties or setting existing properties. The method is named *Set*. A human can be categorized as a "thing," too. We know there is a given name and a date of birth by which we determine age, horoscope, and so on. In physical terms there are height and weight, and for humans, color is generally used to describe racial origin. As a few extra properties for the human, we have added country, location, and occupation. By encapsulating certain code and data in a parent class, software applications can inherit the functionality of the parent class and easily expand upon it. For example, a graphics class with functions for drawing primitives such as single pixels and lines can be inherited by a 3-D graphics class that uses the basic methods in a more specified context. The same primitives class could be inherited to an architecture drawing program, a statistics program, or a computer game, if you wish—although that would probably require some tweaking. In OOP, the units are to be reusable and protected, and only do the task they were programmed for to return the expected and projected result.

Summary

In this chapter we have looked at the basics of Perl. As a language, Perl has three data types: the scalar variable, the array of scalar variables, and the associative array of scalar variables. The scalar variable can contain both numerical and character data, and there are both a regular expression engine and many built-in functions and operators that apply to the manipulation of the values of scalar data. Not exactly a data type, the reference is a scalar that points to the memory address of a variable such as a scalar variable or an array. This allows complex data structures such as lists of lists to be constructed. The language supplies control structures to regulate the flow of a program written in Perl. A conditional control statement can be used to execute a block of code only when a specified condition is met, and a loop control statement will execute a block of code a given number of times. Blocks of code may also be labeled in order to make it easier to handle the program flow programmatically. As a language, Perl fully supports a classic model and an object-oriented model of programming. On the most basic foundation of modular programming, Perl provides subroutines that enable encapsulation and reuse of code. A subroutine can consist of passed data, such as a scalar variable, on which operations are to be performed. Such a scalar variable passed to a subroutine is formally called a *parameter*. To complete this circle of passing variables, the subroutine can return the manipulated data to the point of the program that called the subroutine. The one thing to notice about parameters, however, is that when an array is passed, it must be passed to the subroutine by a reference to the array or else the subroutine will not receive every element of the array. A group of commonly used subroutines can be placed in a package and easily reused by future programs by saving the package as a Perl module, which has the file extension .pm. In general, a Perl module either builds upon the functionality of Perl by writing Perl code that is reusable, or extends the functionality of Perl by creating a module in a different language such as C. A standard set of modules known as the standard Perl modules are included with the installation of Perl. Since Perl supports an object-oriented programming model, a module or a program can be written as such, whereas a class is created as a placeholder for a set of variables and subroutines, of which selected variables and selected subroutines are exposed as the functionality of the class. In OOP terminology, variables become known as *properties*, and subroutines become known as *methods*. These properties and methods are accessed through an object, which is a reference to a class and is in fact the only direct way to access the class. If you write a module, it can be tailored to be easily installed with Perl Package Manager (PPM) from ActiveState. Many popular modules are already installable through PPM, and the number is constantly increasing. The reason is simple. It used to be a rather tedious process to install modules, and several pages of documentation would deal with how to install a module. With PPM, however, installing a module became a very convenient and quick process. If you want to install a module that is not yet available through PPM, you can look in the Perl documentation for instructions. The Perl documentation comes with the installation of Perl, and it is a very large set of documents that deal with every aspect of Perl. It contains everything about the language, frequently asked questions, and everything about the standard Perl modules. It is a very good compilation of documents, and if you are having Perl problems early on, you are guaranteed to find some answers in those documents.

From here, we will move on to programming the Active Server Pages objects that work at the ground level of the Web server.

Further Reference

- See "Tom's Object Oriented Tutorial for Perl" by Tom Christiansen. It is in the core Perl documentation, and it covers issues such as constructors, class data, inheritance, and alternate object representations. Read it from the command prompt by entering perldoc perltoot.

- See "Perl Objects" in the core Perl documentation for a more in-depth paper on Perl objects, what they are, how they come into being, and how to write your own destructors. Read it from the command prompt by entering perldoc perlobj.

- See "Bag'o Object Tricks" in the core Perl documentation for hints on how to use Perl's object-oriented features. Read it from the command prompt by entering perldoc perlbot.

- See "How to Hide an Object Class in a Simple Variable" by Tom Christiansen, and the TIEHANDLE by Sven Verdoolaege and Doug MacEachern. Read it from the command prompt by entering perldoc perltie.

## CHAPTER 3

Elevating the Stateless Internet

I t is often said that the Internet HTTP protocol with which servers communicate is a *stateless protocol.* The essence of that statement is that the client, or user, is neither unique nor identified by a standard Web server on the Internet. Regardless of how long, how frequently, or how extensively the client has previously been on the Web server, with each request for a document the server persists in regarding the client as a new caller. It simply lacks memory, and that makes it stateless. In the same breath in which HTTP is mentioned, the phrase *maintaining state* normally ties in.

Maintaining state entails finding a solution to the stateless nature of communicating over the Internet. There are several reasons for such a solution, because the client would then be both unique and identified by the Web server, which itself can be built upon by every Web application. A lasting effect is that the script is enabled to store variables associated with the client and can assign these variables some values determined by the client's action. In an online store, the maintained state produces an effective way of representing a shopping cart. When state is maintained, the server does not forget about the client after each page.

In the same sense that there is an apparent need for client-associated variables, there is global content that must be able to maintain its state. Contrary to the client state, a global variable maintains its state for the lifetime of the Web server, and its function is to provide its contents to every client or gather content that relates to every client. For example, an advanced log system relates to each client and can either keep its statistics to itself or provide the clients with them. In essence, for both purposes that have been presented, Active Server Pages lets two objects work behind the scenes to ensure this functionality: The Session object works for the client-specific content and the Application object for the global content.

Introducing the Not-So-Visible ASP Objects

With Active Server Pages, you are able to provide real solutions for most online services without pulling a lot of excess weight during development. First, however, as with any application-level programming interface, there are key points that must first be learned before this one can be used efficiently. In general, the object interfaces are important, but with the Session and Application objects it is slightly different. The areas of usage are ranked as more important because it is important to know where to apply them. Essentially, in ASP, these objects are not very visible, nor does the program make a lot of noise about them. Yet they create most of the weight—and tons of excess weight if not used properly.

To begin with the Session object, from the perspective of viewing all clients that are online on a service as a group, a single client can be associated with a set of variables such as scalars, arrays, or objects, and these variables will not be available to any other client. For each individual client, there is a unique Session object generated and attached to the client, and this object points to a location on the server. In that particular place, the contents that are stored in the client's Session objects are saved on the server side, and remain until the Session object is destroyed.

On the other hand, the Application object is a set object. It is only one object, and is the same for every client. In fact, it is used either implicitly or explicitly to share its contents between the clients within a given territory. When the Application object is used implicitly, the administrator or programmer stores data in it for later examination. Explicit contents are available directly to the client on the screen. Because the Application object server functions for many users, it is very capable of handling concurrency issues between them yet gives access to a perfect store of data. In the same manner as the session stores its contents, most data types, including external objects such as ADO record sets, can be stored on the server side. But it may not be a good idea to store external objects on the server side because they may consume more memory than anticipated. Unlike the Session object, however, the Application object is destroyed only once—when the service is ended.

What You Need to Know about Applications

In Chapter 1, we tried to define the deceptive word *application*. It is a double-sided word that means a different thing in each context. In order for everything to make sense, we distinguished between the two meanings, and for the sake of security and sanity, let's do a quick repetition of what was learned. The applications that we work with in Internet Information Services and Active Server Pages are closely related, as the following list shows:

- The IIS application is a directory marked as application root by the administrator. From the root, all subdirectories include the application. Chapter 1 describes how to set up an application root.

- The ASP Application object is a built-in object that is designed for sharing data between the clients within a defined IIS application.

In illustration, an IIS application defines its sector within the Web service. IIS is not limited to only one application, so it is easy to tailor specific settings within the Web service by dividing it into IIS applications. In each such application, a dedicated ASP application is present, and it can be programmed to store data. A concrete example is the classic visitor counter—seen literally everywhere—where a scalar variable is stored in the ASP Application object. As a result, regardless of where in the IIS application the client is, the counter is applicable. And it can increment by 1 and keep track of the visitors with ease. But how does it actually do that?

In order to introduce the next object in a friendly manner, we will elaborate on how the counter application keeps track of the number of visitors. It is possible to count the number of users very accurately by incrementing the counter when a new session begins. With few exceptions, a new session occurs every time a new visitor comes to the Web page. For the exact purpose of initializing code or variables, the Session object has a start-up event. By placing a script that performs a small operation on an application-level variable at runtime of this start-up event, a counter can be easily incremented in an accurate manner. The most logical way to interact with these Application and Session objects is by using the events related to them; and in the life cycle of the Session and Application, the events occur at the beginning and the end of the respective objects.

The Events

In Active Server Pages, the Session and Application objects are different from other built-in objects, and a major difference is that they have a life cycle.

In an object's life cycle, there are four events that occur in four certain situations and only in those situations. You can specify code that belongs to these events by declaring it in a file that is global to the IIS application and recognized by the IIS application.

First, an event-level variable that is to use either the Application object or the Session object must be declared in a file that is named Global.asa. Within the file, there are four events that you declare in your favorite scripting language. Then the file must be physically located in the root of the IIS application because the application automatically looks for the file there.

```
<SCRIPT LANGUAGE="PerlScript" RUNAT="Server">
sub Application_OnStart
{
#    ... code ...
}

sub Application_OnEnd
{
#    ... code ...
}

sub Session_OnStart
{
#    ... code ...
}
```

```
sub Session_OnEnd
{
#     ... code ...
}
```

```
</SCRIPT>
```

As seen in Global.asa, these events are regular subroutines that can contain ordinary PerlScript, and as far as the eye can see there is nothing unusual about the file. Events, however, are special because they are automatically called when a certain action or physical event is triggered. Therefore, in the case of ASP, it is quite predictable when this will occur, as we will see.

Sharing Data on the Web

When the IIS application has been configured, the ASP Application object can be deployed. In the Application object, there are two collections for storing the data that will be accessed from the object: the Contents collection and the StaticObjects collection.

First, a static object is an object that was added to the ASP Application and was declared using the <OBJECT> tag. Normally, components are declared as global with this tag, and the object cannot be removed by any other means than restarting the application. These objects end up in the StaticObjects collection. However, there is of course a real advantage and reason to use the tag: It saves memory and therefore increases performance throughout the application simply because the object will only be instantiated first when a method or a property of it is called.

On the contrary, the Contents collection contains only what was either added by script commands during a Web application or declared inside the Application's events. In this collection, an item can be added at any time, and with ASP 3 the Contents collections have been provided with two methods for removing items from the collection and free memory. These methods are Remove(item), which will destroy a single item, and RemoveAll(), which will remove every item in the collection.

Application Events in Global.asa

When the items of either collection in the ASP application are going to be defined, there are two events that can be used for working with the global content when the IIS application starts and stops.

Event: Application_OnStart

The genesis of events, Application_OnStart is run only once, and it is a perfect event for adding variables that will be globally shared throughout the application.

When it executes, there must be no application variables present. Such a situation occurs in one of two ways:

- The Web server is started for the first time.
- The existing application variables are unloaded from Internet Services Manager.

Event: Application_OnEnd

When no more sessions are active and when the application is ended, the Application_OnEnd event is run. Similar to its cousin, Application_OnStart, this application will only run the event one time during the lifetime of the served application. Although the MapPath() method of the Server object is not callable from here, it is a good place to clean up temporary files or objects that have been used throughout the application, thus freeing memory.

Adding Items to the Contents Collection

To add a variable such as a simple counter to the Contents collection, it can be put in the OnStart event. The Application_OnStart event will be run with the very first session that is launched within the IIS application. In Global.asa, the variable only needs to be declared and initialized once. This one line in the preceding event creates a new application variable in the Contents collection of the application.

```
sub Application_OnStart
{
# Add the variable counter and initialize it to 1
#
$Application->Contents->SetProperty('Item', 'Counter', 1);
}
```

It is not necessary to declare application variables within the Global.asa, because they can be declared at any place and time by script command.

In contrast, it is equally easy to remove items from the Contents collection.

```
<%
# Method 1: Remove all items in the Contents-collection
#
$Application->Contents->RemoveAll();

# Method 2: Remove one item in the Contents-collection
#
$Application->Contents->Remove('NumberOfVisits');
%>
```

In cases where an array or an object is set in the event or during script processing, it is very easy to add such items, as will be seen in later examples. On a final note, during the lifetime of the application, Application_OnStart is run only once, so there is no need to worry about a concurrency situation occurring where two clients try to modify the same value.

Issues of Concurrency

When two clients attempt to modify the same value at the same time, a concurrency issue occurs. Fortunately, the ASP Application object was designed for these situations.

Because the collection items may have to be modified, a Lock() and Unlock() method is provided to prevent the data from being corrupted by an accident of concurrency. The methods are absolutely not necessary when reading the data, and using them there by mistake would seriously slow down the Web service. When writing data to the collection, however, the methods will keep several users from trying to write to the same location at the same time. There the script must lock the Application object for each user; thus a side effect is that the ASP Application object becomes unavailable to other requests for its data. Clients waiting to read or write from the application object will be forced to take turns locking the object, doing its work, and then unlocking the object. As a result, the service can become slow, and that is a valid reason for limiting usage of the ASP Application object.

In terms of usage, a classic example of how to use the Application object is to create a counter that shows the number of clients currently logged onto the site. Such a counter, exposed to all users, is an application variable that is shared. This means that with the start and end of each session, the Application object is locked. Everything is programmed in the Global.asa events of the Session object.

```perl
<SCRIPT LANGUAGE=PERLSCRIPT RUNAT=SERVER>
sub Application_OnStart
{
    $Application->Contents->SetProperty('Item', 'NumOfUsers', 0);
}

sub Application_OnEnd
{
}

sub Session_OnStart
{
    # Lock the application to the current client
    #
    $Application->Lock();

    # Update the current value of the NumOfUsers variable
    #
    $Application->Contents->SetProperty('Item', 'NumOfUsers',
                $Application->Contents('NumOfUsers')+1);

    # Release the application for the next client
    #
    $Application->Unlock();
}

sub Session_OnEnd
{
    # Lock the application to the current client
    #
    $Application->Lock();

    # Update the current value of the NumOfUsers variable
    #
    $Application->Contents->SetProperty('Item', 'NumOfUsers',
                $Application->Contents('NumOfUsers')-1);

    # Release the application for the next client
```

```
     #
     $Application->Unlock()
}
```

```
</SCRIPT>
```

In summary, it is completely optional to use the events shown in this example to add application variables. When used from the beginning, Application_OnStart is run when the first session is assigned after the Web server has been started. Application_OnEnd is run after the last session before the Web server is shut down. By design only the server and Application object are available from that event and the MapPath() method of the Server object is disabled at that point.

Cleaning Up the Application

When experimenting with Global.asa and the Application object, following the next few steps can unload the existing application variables:

1. Open Internet Services Manager.
2. Right-click on the IIS application you want to unload and choose Properties.
3. Find the Home Directory tab.
4. Click on Unload.

If Unload button is shaded, it means that no application variables have yet been added to the object.

The Session Object

Not only application scoped objects are present; there can be Session Scoped objects declared within Global.asa. A number of factors must be taken into consideration before doing this, however. To declare objects with application or session scope, use the <OBJECT> tag to create your object when possible. This prevents the object from being explicitly created and in memory before a method or property that belongs to it is utilized. As a result, a good deal of memory that would be consumed by an idle object is saved.

```
<OBJECT RUNAT=Server SCOPE=Session ID=MyInfo
PROGID="MSWC.MyInfo">
```

In this example, the IIS installable component object is declared to run at the server with a session scope. A technical benefit of using this approach is that it saves memory on startup. However, it is equally important to free the memory by ending the session on time. When working with sessions, set the time-out of the session to less than the default value if you are using an object in Global.asa. More importantly, make sure that the service is scalable enough to handle what is put on it. It is absolutely not recommended to store other objects than the Microsoft installable components such as the Microsoft AdRotator with an application scope. Remember to restart the application after changes have been applied to the Global.asa file or else an error will be returned.

Session Events in Global.asa

Before moving on to how the Session object works, let's quickly look over what events belong to this object.

Event: Session_OnStart

With each new visitor that is currently not in a session, the Session_OnStart event is run. It is only run once during the session, and the variables declared and initialized in the Session object are by default not available to any other sessions since each session is unique.

Event: Session_OnEnd

A session can end in one of two ways, and either way the Session_OnEnd event is called. Session_OnEnd is called either when the session times out because it is idle or when it is abandoned by script command that calls the Abandon() method of the Session object.

The Session Object's Process

The Session object has a rather simple process. However, it includes a number of tasks that must be accomplished.

The scenario for getting the session to start is the following:

1. A client requests a Web page within the IIS application.
2. A positive response comes from the server, and included is a cookie with a Session ID.
3. The client accepts the cookie, and the session is instantiated.

In detail, the session can be a bit more elaborate than that. The Web server minimizes the number of cookies it sends out, so even though a session is started, it does not mean that a cookie is sent for each session. Once a cookie has been set, the server will reuse it to generate new sessions for the client. However, a cookie is only issued when the client visits the page for the first time after restarting the browser or when the server on which the application resides is restarted.

With the first cookie, a Session ID is included. When the Session ID is deleted, it is because the session either timed out or was abandoned by script command. The next time the user visits the Web page, the cookie is read from the client, and a new Session ID is associated with the cookie.

The Session ID is used to associate the current session with the data of the session, such as variables created either in the events or by script. On the server, the session data associated with the client is stored in collections that can be read from and written to by script command. For example:

```
<HTML>
<BODY>
```

```
<TITLE> Example: The Session Object </TITLE>

Welcome Session <%=$Server->{SessionID}%>
<BR>

<%
# The current value of the Session-variable Counter
#
$currValue = $Session->Contents('Counter');

# Increment the value by one
#
$Session->Contents->SetProperty('Item', 'Counter',
$currValue+1);
%>

<BR>

<%=$Session->{Counter}%>

<BR>Please Hit Reload/Refresh To Increment The Counter

</BODY>
</HTML>
```

When you click Refresh or Reload in your browser while running this example, the counter variable in the Contents collection will increment by 1. The item does not have to be in the session earlier, because the call to set its property simply adds on the value of the current value. To add items to the Session object by script command, you must add them to the Contents collection. As previously mentioned, this can be done in either your .asp pages or in Global.asa, which runs the Session events each time a new session is generated.

When removing Items from the Contents collection, the Remove() and RemoveAll() methods have been provided with ASP 3. Either you specify an item in the Remove() method or call RemoveAll(), or all items in the collection will automatically be deleted.

```
# SessionOne.asp
#
<%=$Session->{SessionID}%>
<A HREF="SessionTwo.asp">Check Session ID Again</A>

# SessionTwo.asp
#
<%=$Session->{SessionID}%>
<A HREF="sessionOne.asp">Go Back To Check Session ID Again</A>
```

Not everyone will use the Session object. If your application has no need for the Session object, you should disable the session state immediately because it consumes memory and decreases performance. There is a page command for turning off the session state for individual pages:

```
<%@ENABLESESSIONSTATE=FALSE%>
```

In order to disable the sessions from Internet Services Manager in Microsoft Management Console, do the following:

1. Find the IIS application in which you want to disable sessions.
2. Right-click on it and choose Properties.
3. Find the Home Directory tab.
4. Click on the Configuration button.
5. Find the App Options tab.
6. Uncheck Enable Session State.

Overview: The Application

Table 3.1 displays the properties, methods, and collections of the Application object.

Overview: The Session

Table 3.2 displays the properties, methods, and collections of the Session object.

Table 3.1 The Application Object

	DESCRIPTION
Collection	
Contents	Items added by script command.
StaticObjects	Items added by OBJECT.
Method	
Lock	Locks the application so that only the current user can modify it.
Unlock	Unlocks the application so a new user can modify it.
Contents->Remove(item)	Removes item from the Contents collection.
Contents->RemoveAll()	Removes all items in the Contents collection.
Event	
Application_OnStart	Runs the first session after the application is started.
Application_OnEnd	Runs after the last session.

Table 3.2 The Session Object

	DESCRIPTION
Collection	
Contents	Items added by script command.
StaticObjects	Items added by OBJECT.
Method	
Abandon()	Abandons the current session, destroys all objects in it, and restores resources.
Contents->Remove(item)	Removes item from the Contents collection.
Contents->RemoveAll()	Removes all items in the Contents collection.
Property	
CodePage	CodePage or character set that is used to display the current page.
LCID	Location identifier, or locale identifier.
Session ID	Unique number associating the client with a data store on the server.
Time-out	Session time-out in minutes. Default is 10.
Event	
Session_OnStart	Runs at the beginning of the session.
Session_OnEnd	Runs at the end of the session.

Summary

In this chapter we have learned the ASP objects that store data, such as scalar variables, arrays, and objects on the server side. We have also revisited the word application, which was first mentioned in Chapter 1. It is important to distinguish between the ASP Application object and the IIS application because an IIS application is a directory that has been defined as an IIS application by the administrator of the server. The ASP Application object, on the other hand, is initialized when the Web server is started for the first time, and it resides within an IIS application. Every client that is physically inside the territory of an IIS application on the Web server shares a single ASP Application object. Variables that belong to the ASP Application can be read and written. However, these variables are shared between all users within the IIS application, so only data that concerns every client should be placed within the ASP Application object. The data is erased removed by script command, when the Web server is restarted, or when the variables of the ASP Application are manually unloaded. In contrast to globally shared variables, ASP provides the Session object, which works with storing data that is associated with each unique client. Like the ASP Application object, the session stores its data on the server side, but each client has a private Session object, and that object is not available to anyone else but the scripting engine. The data in this object can be removed by script command, but it can also be removed because the session times out or is deliberately abandoned. Both the Application object and the Session object have events related to code that should be executed when they are first created and when they are destroyed. These events are contained in a file named Global.asa, and this file can be used to execute your own code and create your own variables when these events occur.

In the next chapter, we will learn how to retrieve data from the client, such as the contents of a form that was filled out and sent back to the server, and we will see how we can send responses to a client in the form of raw data.

## CHAPTER 4

Practical Active Server Pages

As a scripting host, Active Server Pages deepens the relationship between the client and the server. First, a chief factor is the ability to use a scripting language without special configuration or external process launch. The scripting language can be embedded and processed inline within HTML, and that makes Active Server Pages attractive. Second, Web services are extended by learning, knowing, and extending the language of choice, so how far a Web service can be driven is equal to the potential of the language chosen for the project. In this instance, PerlScript is a wise decision because it is a far more powerful ActiveX Scripting Engine than many of its competitors. Finally, the server side where the scripting host resides is in itself a piece of machinery. For example, should the client pass extra content, such as form data, an uploaded file, or a digital certificate for security and identification purposes, the scripting host gathers all the information and exposes it to the scripting engine. The Response and Request objects in ASP enable dynamic exchange and communication between client and server.

Levels of Communication

In general, the flow of data on the Internet is embodied in the HTTP protocol, and this is what enables communication. When a browser sends an HTTP request to a Web server, for example, it normally says that it wants to view a page that is located within the server's URL. The server then processes the request and returns a header to the browser indicating the status of the request. If the status indicates success, a header that describes the content is sent with the document.

As trivial as it seems, HTTP requests can become far more advanced by letting the client send some additional information in the request. An online document could provide an online form with a number of elements to fill out and send to the server for processing. Moreover, the user might need to upload a file, verify the client's identity in a secure environment, or pass a cookie with customization information about preferred viewing of the Web pages. For such requests, the backbones of most scripts turn to the Request object for processing the information. The Request object is concerned solely with gathering data that is important to and requested by the Web application. It neither outputs nor passes to the client any kind of content or headers. In essence, the Request object only works with information sent from the client to the server.

The ASP Response object is in charge of data flowing from server to client, and can control headers plus content. It can redirect the browser to a new location, send a status code, or simply output variables in HTML, to name but a few functions. In most cases, the Response object works in conjunction with the Request object to make the script as active as possible.

In short, the HTTP protocol has been introduced in a way that does not classify as more than briefly. Most parts and purposes of the protocol can be controlled by the Response object. When the script gathers data sent by the client to the server, however, the Request object collects and exposes the bytes and variables. These two objects work in conjunction when a script delivers truly dynamic Web pages.

Taking Charge over the HTTP Stream

Although working as separate entities, the Response and Request objects essentially live in virtual symbiosis. Each has its own collections, methods, and properties. The Request object has five collections in which the data from an HTTP request are stored, as follows:

- ClientCertificate
- Cookies
- Form
- QueryString
- ServerVariables

The Response object has only one collection, and although the name of this collection is shared by both objects, each object is concerned with its own task rather than what the other one is doing.

- Cookies

The Response object writes the cookie to the client, and when the cookie has been written, the Request object is used to read the cookie.

An Old Recipe: Cookies

A standard since HTML 2.0, the cookie quickly became a popular and practical way of storing data. There are, however, a number of guidelines for cookies.

First, the client's browser can be set to deny all cookies. This is not at all unusual, and there are many reasons why this setting might be used. Next, when using cookies, let the client know that they are being used and for what purpose they are being used, because if the client does not accept cookies by default, some explanation might change the habit.

With these guidelines in mind, the cookie is an entity that is both read and written by sending its keys and values in the HTTP header. After it has been sent and accepted by the client, the cookie has to be stored somewhere. The location is the client's hard disk, and this is where the myths about cookies arise. One of the biggest myths is that a cookie when sent can be run as a script that damages the client's machine or inserts a virus. This is a complete and utter fallacy. There are some facts to note about cookies, however:

- The user can tamper with cookies. Therefore, never store information that is sensitive to your business or the client in the cookie.

- Cookies are not unique in any way, shape, or form and they can be copied from one machine to another, so do not rely on them being unique in any situation.

Common sense will tell you that storing information such as passwords, addresses, and credit card numbers is generally a bad idea when working with cookies. There are, however, many good examples of when cookies can be applied.

When to Serve Cookies

The question of when cookies should be served is probably best answered by examining when they should be avoided. It is not recommended to make cookies the backbone of a serious application, although for site improvisation you can use them to personalize visits for each client or transparently gather feedback for your Web site. For example, a client might want to customize the look and feel of the page, and cookies give that possibility by storing preferred font size, colors, navigation parameters, and so forth. Next, a cookie can be used to determine what banners in an advertisement system the client has viewed or when the client last visited the Web page.

Setting a cookie is different with IIS 5 than with older versions of IIS because the Response object's Buffer property, which controls how data is sent back to the browser, is set to have buffering on. The effect is the following:

- Buffering on allows content such as HTML to be sent before the cookie is written.

- Buffering off requires that no content at all be sent before the cookie is written.

Turning the Buffer property of the Response object on or off is easy, and the only thing to remember is that the property needs to be set before any content is output.

Example 1: Setting the buffer property to true then sending output

```
<%@Language=PerlScript%>
<%
$Response->{Buffer} = 1; # Buffering on
%>
<HTML>
<BODY BGCOLOR="White">
```

Example 2: Setting the buffer property to false

```
$Response->{Buffer} = 0; # Buffering off
```

A New Cookie

Active Server Pages bakes cookies as items of a collection. You set the keys and values of a cookie; thus the SetProperty() method has to be used to set the item. Creating a cookie is simple.

```
<%
# Create the cookie named Client
#
$Response->Cookies->SetProperty('Item',
                                'Client',
                                'Preferences' );
%>
```

There are a number of attributes that can be set to define a cookie (Table 4.1). The Domain attribute determines the domain where the cookies are exchanged—normally your own domain. The Expires attribute is the date the cookie expires, and it can be safely ignored if the cookie should not be saved for longer than the end of the current session.

Table 4.1 Attributes for Setting a Cookie

ATTRIBUTE	DESCRIPTION
Domain	When the client issues an HTTP request, the cookie is only sent if the requested URL is within the domain. This attribute is used to let one domain own the cookie.
Expires	The date in format MM DD, YY. For example, December 1, 2005.
Path	Similar to Domain, but the cookie will only be sent when a request is made for the specified path and its subdirectories. For example, "/main//members/".
Secure	True or false for whether the connection between the client and the server is secure before the cookie is written.

A Cookie with Subkeys

A cookie can contain subkeys, and they are key and value pairs that can be read from the cookie. The following is an example of how to set subkeys in a cookie:

```
<%
# Create the cookie named Client
#
$Response->Cookies->SetProperty('Item', 'Client',
'Preferences');

# Set the Expires-attribute
#
$Response->Cookies('Client')->{Expires} = "December 1, 2005";

# Subkey 1: Textcolor
#
$Response->Cookies('Client')->SetProperty('Item',
                                          'Textcolor',
                                          'White');
# Subkey 2: Background
#
$Response->Cookies('Client')->SetProperty('Item',
                                           'Background',
                                           'Black');
%>
```

The HasKeys property of the Cookies collection can detect whether a cookie has subkeys and return the answer.

```
<%
# If there are subkeys in the cookie, notify the browser
#
if( $Request->Cookies($name)->{HasKeys} ) {
    $Response->Write("Has subkeys … ");
    }
%>
```

Reading Cookies

It is not a good idea to avoid writing subroutines for reading cookies, so let's write two of them to check the cookie and any subitems in the cookie. The first subroutine iterates the top-level Cookies collection. It reads the HasKeys property to see whether or not there are subkeys present. (See Table 4.2 for a description of cookie properties.) If present, the second subroutine is called to iterate all of the subkeys.

```
<%
use Win32::OLE qw('in');

getCookieKeys();
%>
```

Table 4.2 The Properties of a Cookie

PROPERTY	DESCRIPTION
HasKeys	Returns true or false whether or not the cookie has subkeys
Count	Counts the number of subitems

```
<%
sub getCookieKeys
{
    foreach my $key (in($Request->Cookies)) {
        $Response->Write("Name: $key<BR>");
        if( $Request->Cookies($key)->{HasKeys} ) {
            getCookieSubKeys($key);
            }
            else {
                my $value = $Request->Cookies($key)->Item();
                $Response->Write("Value: $value<BR>")
                }
        }
}
%>

<%
sub getCookieSubKeys
{
    my $key = shift;

    foreach my $subkey (in($Request->Cookies($key))) {
        $Response->Write("$key: ");
        $Response->Write($Request->Cookies($key)-
>Item($subkey));
        $Response->Write("<BR>");
        }
}
%>
```

Alternatively, since the cookie has a Count property—as do all collections—the sub-keys can be iterated by index instead of key.

```
<%
sub getCountCookieSubKeys
{
    my $key = shift;
    my $numKeys = $Request->Cookies($key)->{Count};

    for($i=0; $i<=$numKeys; $i++) {
        my ($subVal) = $Request->Cookies($key)->Item($i);
        $Response->Write("$i: $subVal<BR>");
        }
}
%>
```

Communicating with the Client

When the browser sends data to a server, a red thread runs through the theme. It is the fact that the data is in memory, thus temporary, so essentially it is passed from the one page to another page where it is later extracted and operated on by the script. This in-memory data is only present on the current page where it has been extracted. However, several ways exist of passing the variables from one page to the other and thus maintaining a temporary state of the client. Either way of sending the data from an online form has its advantages and disadvantages, both of which will be balanced while looking at how to extract data that is sent from the client's browser.

Collecting Items in the Query String

To begin, the HTTP query string embeds its variables as a part of the URL. When a page is requested and the query string is present in the URL, the ASP Request object's collection is used to access the values.

The Features of a Query String

The query string approach has certain characteristics that can be summarized as follows:

- The HTML form tag must define that the method GET is used for submitting the form, or else the query string will not be used.

- The maximum size of the sent data is restricted to approximately 2000 characters since the physical limitation is the length of a URL.

- The variables are appended to the URL, and thus visible in the URL.

While there are a number of different elements that make up a form, such as input boxes, check boxes, and drop-down select menus, these only play a part when accessing the variables from the collection. In order to prepare the form, two primary values must be specified in its form element: the URL to which the action will steer the browser, and how the data is sent. The following is an example of a simple form that sends the values of the form elements with the query string to the script validateform .asp.

```
<FORM ACTION="/validateform.asp" METHOD="GET">
Please type your name here then submit query:
<INPUT TYPE="Textfield" NAME="Fullname">
<INPUT TYPE="Submit">
</FORM>
```

This HTML code can be broken down into four parts. Two are the important attributes of the FORM tag, and the other two are the elements of the complete form:

- ACTION points to the URL to which the data will be sent and processed.

- METHOD specifies that the GET method should be used, which results in the data being embedded in the query string.

- INPUT TYPE is the type of element that is to be used, and Fullname is a text field into which the client can enter data.

- Submit is a reserved input type that produces a button on the screen that allows the data to be sent when the client clicks on the button.

In essence, the data passed by the form illustrated in this example will be appended to the URL and sent in what is known as the QueryString environment variable. In the QueryString collection, the variables can be accessed either by index or key. In the previous example, the only data filled out was that contained in the Fullname field. To access that data, the following syntax is all it takes:

```
<%
$Request->QueryString('Fullname')->Item();
%>
```

When a form is submitted, the URL likely looks similar to http://www.domain.com?message=hello in cases where the data is passed by the QueryString. There are positive and less positive sides to this. The positive note is that variables can be passed with normal HREF links by using the syntax <A HREF="/thatpage.asp?variable=green"> Click me!</A>. The flip side with using GET is that the data is visible in the URL, so this method is not suitable for sending sensitive data such as passwords.

In-Memory Storage of Data

When necessary, there are several ways to keep an in-memory store of the information sent from the client.

Storing the Items in a Hash

To store the name and value pair in a hash, the name by which to reference the hash is the name the form element held, and likewise the value is the value of the element.

```
foreach my $item (Win32::OLE::in ($Request->QueryString)) {
    $FORMDATA{$item} = $Request->QueryString($item)->Item();
    }
```

To do the same thing with regular arrays, which index by integer, we use the built-in push function to add the values of the submitted form to the array's "stack." The difference between this approach and the previous approach is that you now will have access to the elements by index instead of key name.

```
foreach my $item (Win32::OLE::in ($Request->QueryString)) {
    push @FORMDATA, $Request->QueryString($item)->Item();
    }
```

Storing the Variables in a Cookie

Many times the information gathered by the Request object can be used in cookies. When customizing a Web page, it is useful to pick up information from the Query-String, set it in a cookie, and read the values of the cookie. Here is a simple example:

```
<%
# Get the desired backgroundcolor
#
my $colorBackground = $Request->QueryString('BACKGROUND')-
>Item();

# Get the desired textcolor
#
my $colorText = $Request->QueryString('TEXTCOLOR')->Item();

# Create the cookie
#
$Response->Cookies->SetProperty('Item', 'User', 'Preferences');

# Set the expires-attribute
#
$Response->Cookies('User')->{Expires} = "July 16, 2010";
# Set the domain-attribute
#
$Response->Cookies('User')->{Domain}  = "127.0.0.1";

# Set the Background-subkey
#
$Response->Cookies('User')->SetProperty('Item',
                                        'Background',
                                         $colorBackground);

# Set the textcolor-subkey
#
$Response->Cookies('User')->SetProperty('Item',
                                        'Textcolor',
                                         $colorText);

# If the querystring passed a value then use the cookie-values for
# background and text - twisted logic.
#
if ($Request->QueryString->Item() )
{
%>
<BODY BGCOLOR = "<%=$Request->Cookies('User')-
>Item('Background')%>"
     TEXT    = "<%=$Request->Cookies('User')-
>Item('Textcolor')%>">
<%
}

# Otherwise, use the default settings
#
else {
%>
     <BODY BGCOLOR="WHITE" TEXT="BLACK">
<%
     }
```

```
%>

<H1>Cookies And QueryString</H1>
<FORM ACTION="cookies.asp" METHOD="GET">

<TABLE BORDER=0>
<TR>
<TD>Red</TD>
<TD><INPUT TYPE="RADIO" NAME="BACKGROUND" VALUE="#FF0000"></TD>
</TR>

<TR>
<TD>Green</TD>
<TD><INPUT TYPE="RADIO" NAME="BACKGROUND" VALUE="#00FF00"></TD>
</TR>
<TR>
<TD>Blue</TD>
<TD><INPUT TYPE="RADIO" NAME="BACKGROUND"
VALUE="#0000FF"></TD></TR>
<TR>
<TD>Black<INPUT TYPE="RADIO" NAME="TEXTCOLOR"
VALUE="#000000"></TD>
<TD>White <INPUT TYPE="RADIO" NAME="TEXTCOLOR"
VALUE="#FFFFFF"></TD>
</TR>
<TR>
<TD COLSPAN="2"><INPUT TYPE="SUBMIT"></TD>
</TR>
</TABLE>
```

Example: Combining the Query String and the Session

As a summary of everything we just discussed, with one additional bit of knowledge about the QueryString collection, we will build a script that iterates the values of a form and stores its values in the session object. What makes this application different from the previous examples is the use of two multiselect elements. These elements will return an array, so a reference to the array will be stored in the Session object's Contents collection, and when all data is processed, it will be output to the screen. To detect an index of a variable in the QueryString, the Count property must be used. In essence, if the item contains more than one variable, the Count property will return the number of variables in the item. If there are several items, in plain text they will be comma-separated.

```
<TITLE> Demo: Formdata and Session </TITLE>
<HTML>
<BODY>
<!--
Warning: A lot of comments in this script

This example demonstrates the use of the Request object
and the session object.
```

The variables passed with the multiselect are parsed and
displayed to the screen. Alternatively, if "Store in
Session" was the pressed button, the variables will be
stored as array references in the session object, and
then displayed to the screen with the other values.
-->

```
<TABLE WIDTH="310" ALIGN="CENTER">
<TR>
<TD><FONT FACE="VERDANA" SIZE="-1">

<%
# Use the "in"-function of the OLE-module to iterate a collection
#
use Win32::OLE qw(in);

# Call the controlling subroutine
#
Main();
%>

<%
#######################################################################
#
# Subroutine:   Main
# Parameters:   None
# Description:  The controlling subroutine. All other subroutines
#                   are called from Main.
#######################################################################

sub Main
{
# Set StoreSession equal to one if the SUBMIT-button
# named COMMAND was of the value 'Store in Session'.
# This is how we determine whether to store or not
# to store the Querystring-variables in the session
# object. SUBMIT-elements of the form can share the
# same name because it is only the value which is
# passed and stored in the Request object.
#
    my $StoreSession = 1
        if ($Request->QueryString('COMMAND')->Item
        eq 'Store In Session');

# Iterate the QueryString-collection of the Request object
# with the already imported "in"-method. Each item in the
# collection will be stored in the scalar "$Item". Each item
# also return the number of elements in itself - only needed
# when multiple options are available - and unless we are
# dealing with the COMMAND element of the Form, the PrintItems-
# subroutine is called.
#
```

```perl
    foreach my $Item (in ($Request->QueryString)) {
        my $numItems = $Request->QueryString($Item)->{Count};

        PrintItems($StoreSession, $Item, $numItems)

        unless ($Item eq 'COMMAND');

        }

# In case it was issued that each item is stored in the session
# object, then call the subroutine which prints the stored values.
#
    PrintSession() if $StoreSession;
}
%>

<%
#######################################################################
# Subroutine:    PrintSession
# Parameters:    None
# Description:   Prints the value of any array references in
#           the session object.
#######################################################################
sub PrintSession
{
# Again, the "in"-method iterates all items in a collection.
# The Contents collection contain those values which were
# added by script command during the application.
# First, output the name of the array that is stored.
# Then, loop each element of the array reference.
#
# Note:
# 1) " " is HTML which functions the same as hitting
#    the space-key does.
# 2) $_ is a special variable where values from a for loop
#    such as the one used can be accessed.
# 3) The loop basically will call Response Write with two
#    spaces, the special variable $_, and a <BR>-tag for
#    as long as there is an element in the array reference
#    in Session->Contents.
#
    foreach $i (in ($Session->Contents)) {
        $Response->Write("<B>Session stored array $i
...</b><BR>");

        # Print each item in the array stored in the Session
        #
        $Response->Write("  $_<BR>")
            for ( @{$Session->Contents($i)} );
        }
}
%>

<%
```

```
#####################################################################
# Subroutine:   PrintItems
# Parameters:
# 1) Flag     - Whether to store the values in the session
#           object or not.
# 2) Item     - The key(name) of the Item in the QueryString
#             that is the current.
# 3) numItems - The index-length of the Item in the Querystring.#
#
# Description: When there is more than one option selected in
#           a form element, the Item in the querystring will
#           have an index-value. That value is used to loop
#           the values by the index and push then to a
#               temporary variable if Flag(StoreSession( is equal
#               to one. Then if Flag is equal to one, pass the
#               array by reference to the Session object then
#               undefine the array so that we can reuse it.
#####################################################################
sub PrintItems
{
    # Read in the parameters
    #
    my ($Flag, $Item, $numItems) = @_;

    # The number of items in the item
    #
    $Response->Write("<B>There are $numItems items in
                    $Item...</B><BR>");

    # Loop and push the values to an array
    #
    for($i=1; $i<=$numItems; $i++) {
        my $valOfItem = $Request->QueryString($Item)->Item($i);

        $Response->Write("  Item $i:
$valOfItem<BR>");

        push (@temp, $valOfItem) if ($Flag==1);
        }

    # Store the array-reference in the Session-object if lagged
    #
    $Session->Contents->SetProperty('Item', $Item, \@temp)
    if ($Flag==1);

    # Undefine the array
    #
    undef @temp;
}
%>
</TR>
</TD>
</TABLE>
```

```
<CENTER>
<FORM ACTION="MultiSelect.asp" METHOD="GET">

<TABLE WIDH=300>
<TR><TD WIDTH="150" BGCOLOR="#EEEEEE">
<SELECT NAME="MultiSelect1" SIZE=4 MULTIPLE WIDTH=150>
<OPTION SELECTED> Red
<OPTION> Green
<OPTION SELECTED> Blue
<OPTION> Orange
</SELECT></TD>

<TD WIDTH="150" BGCOLOR="#EEEEEE">
<SELECT NAME="MultiSelect2" SIZE=4 MULTIPLE WIDTH=150>
<OPTION SELECTED> Winter
<OPTION> Summer
<OPTION SELECTED> Spring
<OPTION> Autumn
</SELECT>
</TD></TR>

<TR>
<TD WIDTH="150" ALIGN="LEFT">
<INPUT NAME="COMMAND" TYPE="SUBMIT" VALUE="View On Screen">
</TD>
<TD WIDTH="150" ALIGN="RIGHT">
<INPUT NAME="COMMAND" TYPE="SUBMIT" VALUE="Store In Session">
</TD>
</TR>
</FORM>

<TR>
<TD COLSPAN="2">
<FONT FACE="ARIAL" SIZE="-2">
<BR>* Use "Store in Session" to display the values in the session
     object
<BR>* Use "View on Screen" to see the parsed formdata
</FONT>
</TD>
</TR>
</TABLE>
```

Validate Submitted Data as Clean and Legal Entries

In any case, when data—sensitive or not—is sent with the QueryString or another way, some emphasis is put on validating the data.

Checking the Form Fields

First, verify that some type of data was sent. Let's illustrate an example of a log-in and password form that requires both fields to be filled out before it takes further action. The following is the file login.asp:

```
<TITLE> Please Use Your Membername And Password To Login
</TITLE>
<HTML>
<BODY>
<%
# In case a value is detected in the QueryString
#
if( $Request->QueryString->Item() )
{
    # Get the login
    #
    my $login = $Request->QueryString('LOGIN')->Item();

    # Get the password
    #
    my $pwd = $Request->QueryString('PWD')->Item();

    # If the value of $login is a null value, remind
    # the client of entering the field
    #
    if(! $login) {
        $Response->Write("Please Enter A Login Name <BR>");
        }

        # In case the login was filled out, then check
        # if the value of $pwd is a null value.
        #
        elsif(! $pwd) {
            $Response->Write("Please Enter A Password <BR>");
            }

            # In case both tests passed, try and verify the
            # login/password pair in a database or something
            #
            else {
            verifyIdentity($login, $pwd);
            }
}
%>

<FORM ACTION="login.asp" METHOD="GET">
<BR>Login <INPUT TYPE="TEXTFIELD" NAME="LOGIN">
<BR>Password <INPUT TYPE="TEXTFIELD" NAME="PWD">
<BR><INPUT TYPE="SUBMIT">
</FORM>
</HTML>
</BODY>
```

On the ASP side, because these variables are items in a collection, the Item() method is used to return their value, while omitting the call to Item() would return the reference to the value. The Item() method can take an optional parameter that specifies the index of the variable. But this is only necessary if the variable has multiple options, such as a multiselect element would have.

Inside the if clause there are two more checks. Contrary to ignoring code in case of null values, we set the script to react and to provide notification if there is a null value. For example, a client could manually add a QueryString and send it to our script, which then would enter the first loop and try to retrieve the variables LOGIN and PWD. If either one of the variables is not equal to or greater than nothing, we assume that the user forgot to enter something into the text field, and flag that it needs attention. Otherwise, if it matches none of the criteria, then it has passed successfully, and the subroutine validateData is called with the parameters to verify the identity in our fictitious database.

The previous example is recursive because it calls itself to check the data. Furthermore, the least exhaustive data validity check possible is performed—especially considering the powerful regular expressions of Perl! The script only makes sure that no null values were passed and does not care what was sent. In bits and pieces, whether or not the block of code belonging to the first if statement is entered depends on whether the QueryString is greater than null. If not, no further script commands are executed since everything within the curly brackets will be ignored. However, if the QueryString has a value greater than nothing, then each variable is requested by key. The key is always the same name the elements were given in the Web form.

Checking for a Two-Letter State

```
CheckState("f1"); # returns 0 for success
CheckState("34"); # returns 1 for failure due to the digits

sub CheckState
{
    my ($param) = uc shift;
    $param=~/^([A-Z]{2})$/ ? 0 : 1;
}
```

Formatting Names

```
FormatName("jOhN"); #returns "John"

sub FormatName
{
    my $temp = lc shift;
    return ucfirst($temp);
}
```

Checking a Five-Digit Zip Code

```
CheckZip("fsd12"); # returns 1 for failure due to the characters
CheckZip("12343"); # returns 0 for success

sub CheckZip
{
```

```
    my ($param) = shift;
    $param=~/^(\d{5})$/ ? 0 : 1;
}
```

Checking a Phone Number in Format 888-888-8888

```
CheckPhone("112-3233-232"); # returns 1 for failure to follow format
CheckPhone("112-323-3232"); # returns 0 for success

sub CheckPhone
{
    my ($param) = shift;
    $param=~/^(\d{3})-(\d{3})-(\d{4})$/ ? 0 : 1;
}
```

How to Respond to the Client

There are several ways to treat a successful or failed log-in attempt: for example, redirection of the browser, altering the status headers or appending a message to the Web server log, or storing the data for later use.

Sending a Status Header

The Response object can be used to send a status header if either of the validation tests fails. Consider the following:

```
if(LogInFailed()) {
    $Response->{Status} = "401 Unauthorized";
    }
```

Redirecting the Browser

Regardless of how the validation failed, the browser can be redirected to a new page where the user is given the option of reporting an error, is informed that the log-in failed, or is sent to a registration page. In the following example, LogInFailed() is a made-up subroutine that returns 1, which will make the if statement execute its code if the login fails:

```
if(LogInFailed()) {
    $Response->Redirect($url);
    }
```

In some cases, Redirect() can be used to send the user to a new page after a successful log-in, requiring that some variables of the old data be available on the new page.

```
if(LoggedIn()) {

$url="http://www.mysite.com/members/welcome.asp?login=$login";
    $Response->Redirect($url);
}
```

The Form Collection

In contrast to the QueryString, the Form collection has a number of opposing definitions of what is allowed.

- The Form method used has to be POST.
- There is no limitation on the number of characters.
- The data is not sent in the URL (invisible data).

When the POST method is used, the data will be parsed and ready in the Form collection—a collection that is identical to the QueryString.

Example: Fetching a Remote Web Page

Let's illustrate the Form called with an example.

```
<TITLE> Example: Request a Webpage </TITLE>
<HTML>
<BODY>
<!--
The following example will demonstrate how to retrieve
a value passed with the POST method of the Form-element.

What is passed by POST will be stored in the Form-collection
of the Request-object. When we have returned the value of
the "URL"-item, it is stored in the scalar "$getURL" and
below the contents of this webpage, the contents of the
requested URL is displayed.
-->

<%
# Use the LWP::Simple module, which makes it easy to fetch a webpage
#
use LWP::Simple;

# The get-method of LWP::Simple will get a webpage
#
my $urlContents = get( $Request->Form("URL")->Item() );
%>

<FORM ACTION="RequestURL.asp" METHOD="POST">
<TABLE WIDTH="140" BORDER="0" CELLSPACING="0" CELLPADDING="3">
<TR>
<TD HEIGHT="20" BGCOLOR="#EE0000" ALIGN="LEFT">
<FONT FACE="ARIAL" COLOR="#FFFFFF">
<B>Download URL:</B></FONT>
</TD>
</TR>
<TR>
<TD BGCOLOR="#EEEEEE" ALIGN="CENTER">
<INPUT TYPE="TEXTFIELD" NAME="URL" SIZE="20">
```

```
</TD>
</TR>
<TR>
<TD BGCOLOR="#F6F6F6" ALIGN="RIGHT">
<INPUT TYPE="SUBMIT" VALUE="Go Get It!">
</TD>
</TR>
</TABLE>
</FORM>

<!--
Display the return-value of the webpage that was
sent to be fetched.
-->
<BR>
You Requested "<%=$urlContents=~/<TITLE>(.*?)<\/TITLE>/si%>":
<BR>
<%=$urlContents%>
</BODY>
</HTML>
```

When you enter the URL of a Web page, the LWP::Simple module will connect to it and return the contents to a string that is later displayed to the screen. Before the string is displayed, the title of the Web page is extracted by regular expression and printed to the screen.

Client Certificates for Security

On the Internet, sensitive data is passed every hour of the day. Security measures are taken to prevent data from being intercepted, misused, or falsified. Development within this field is always on the move forward and improvements in Web service security are always in progress to ensure the highest possible security.

In the field of improvement, one such technology is public-key cryptography in the form of digital certificates. An example of an environment in which certificates can be used is Secure Socket Layers (SSL), which is an encrypted type of HTTP protocol whose web begins its URL with https://.

Digital certificates are used to identify both the server and the client. An authority that approves and registers the Web service's legibility signs the server certificate. This signed certificate is presented to the client as evidence of the quality of service. On the other end, client identification occurs when the server requests the certification fields that the browser issues with a request to the server. The fields in the client certificate are specified as an X.509 standard, and they are described in Table 4.3.

The flags that are used to provide additional client information will be available in a special file when a certificate has been obtained from an authority. The subfields mentioned in Table 4.3 relate to the identification of the client certificate. Each subfield has its name value separated by an equal sign in the format C=US and its term in each pair separated by a comma. However, to request a certain subfield instead of the

Table 4.3 The Fields of the Client Certificate

FIELD	DESCRIPTION
Certificate	The certificate in a string of binary data in ASN.1 format.
Flags	Flags that may contain additional client information. The flags are ceCertPresent, which indicates that a client certificate is already present with the client, and ceUnrecognizedUser, which indicates that the last certification was for an unknown user.
Issuer	A set of subfields that provide information about the client. For convenience, these subfields are specified in Table 4.4.
SerialNumber	A serial number in ASCII form that represents hexadecimal bytes organized as in the following example: FA-04-EE-2E.
Subject	A set of subfields dealing with the subject of the certificate.
ValidFrom	A date indicating at what time the certificate becomes valid.
ValidUntil	The opposite of ValidFrom, specifying the expiration date of the certificate.

whole set of subfields, the key of the subfield can be appended to the field (for example, IssuerC). Table 4.4 describes these keys more fully.

In order to work with client certificates, the Web server must be configured for the task. It must be configured to use and request certificates, and that includes requesting an authority to validate the legibility of the certificate. This process of creating a certified server can be initiated under the Document Security tab of Internet Information Manager. The signature on the certificate, however, is not free.

When the certificate has been obtained, IIS can be set to accept, ignore, or require client certificates. To ignore a client certificate means to disregard its value. Whether or not the client sends a certificate, it is not the choice of authentication for the server and thus it has no value to either party. Instead the server could choose authentication

Table 4.4 Subfields that Physically Identify the Client

SUBFIELD	DESCRIPTION
C	Country of origin
O	Company or organization
OU	Organization unit
CN	Subject key only: common name of the user
L	Locality
S	State or province
T	Title of person or organization
GN	Given name
I	Initials

by asking for a user name or password to identify the user. One step up on the security scale is to accept client certificates. This means that if a certificate is sent, then it is used as the preferred method of authentication. However, if a certificate is not issued, another form of authentication will be chosen. The only setting that mandates a client certificate is Require.

Server Variables

Retrieval of useful information about the current user session is greatly assisted by the server variables that ASP creates each time an application is executed. Previously, it was mentioned that the QueryString is a parsed version of the environment variable with the same name, and that is one part of what the server variables do. They hold information passed by the browser about the browser, the user's location, and the server. This information can become very useful. For example, you may want to build a form-handling routine that works without knowing how the data is sent. From the REQUEST_METHOD variable, you would read how the data was sent; it will say either POST or GET.

```
<%
# Get the request-method that was used for the page
#
my $reqMethod = $Request->ServerVariables('REQUEST_METHOD')-
>Item();

    # Do the following if the POST-method was used
    #
    if( $reqMethod eq 'POST') {
        # ... get the Form-collection ...
        }

        # Do the following if the GET-method was used
        #
        else {
            # ... get the QueryString-collection ...
            }
%>
```

Which variables are useful really depends on your needs. The next example will dump all server variables to the screen.

Example: Dumping All Server Variables

```
<%@Language=PerlScript%>
<HTML>
<TITLE> Example: Server Variables </TITLE>
<BODY>
<TABLE WIDTH="600" ALIGN="CENTER" BORDER="1" CELLSPACING="0">
<TR>
<TD WIDTH="150" BGCOLOR="BLACK'>
<FONT FACE="ARIAL" COLOR="WHITE"><B>Name</B></FONT>
</TD>
```

```
<TD WIDTH="450" BGCOLOR="BLACK">
<FONT FACE="ARIAL" COLOR="WHITE"><B>Value</B></FONT>
</TD>

</TR>
<%
# Get every server-variable in the collection
#
foreach $i (Win32::OLE::in($Request->ServerVariables)) {

    # Set the name and value of each variable in a neatly
    # laid out HTML-table
    #
    $htmlOutput .= '<TR><TD ALIGN="LEFT" VALIGN="TOP">';
    $htmlOutput .= '<FONT FACE="VERDANA" SIZE="-1">';
    $htmlOutput .= "<B>$i</B>";
    $htmlOutput .= '</FONT>';
    $htmlOutput .= '</TD><TD ALIGN="LEFT" VALIGN="TOP">';
    $htmlOutput .= '<FONT FACE="VERDANA" SIZE="-1"
                        COLOR="#121212">';

    $htmlOutput .= $Request->ServerVariables($i)->Item();
    $htmlOutput .= '</TD></TR>';
     }

    $Response->Write($htmlOutput);
%>
</TABLE>
</BODY>
</HTML>
```

In this example, the server variables were stored in a scalar variable before being out-putted to the screen. This is the fastest way of outputting data generated by the script, because you prevent a series of unnecessary calls to the Response object. So, instead of the table cells and values for each server variable being outputted, they are stored in a scalar variable and are outputted only after the loop has finished iterating the collection. Many scripts become unnecessarily slow because they make repeated calls to the Response object. The scripting engine is best used when performing its operations and not outputting content bit by bit to the screen.

A Note for the COM Developer

If you are not a COM developer, you may safely skip this section without loss of continuity as we move on with ASP and ADO. When writing COM components in Perl, you can cause them to interact with the built-in ASP objects, and we will look at how this is done.

In IIS version 3.0 and later, you can use the IScriptingContext interface to access built-in ASP objects—but although that method is still functional, it is not recommended. It is instead recommended that you use an ObjectContext object. However, do not confuse that object with the ASP ObjectContext object, because the instance we will look at is richer in terms of the data it exposes. The ObjectContext object will maintain information about the context of an instance of a COM component. This is interesting because it enables you to easily create reference to an ASP built-in object and make your components interact with the abilities of the ASP objects. Let's look at some PerlScript code that grabs the ASP Response object and calls a method by way of this object:

```
<Script Language="PerlScript" Runat="Server">
use Win32::OLE;


$obj = Win32::OLE->new("MTxAS.Appserver.1");
$objContext = $obj->GetObjectContext();


$responseRef = $objContext->Item("Response");
$responseRef->Write("Hello World");
</Script>
```

You can use this code in an .asp page just to test it, and you can access any single ASP object or multiple ASP objects by specifying your object in the call $objContext->Item("object"). However, the version number of MttxAS.Appserver on your server may be different than the one that appears in the previous example. In addition, a component that uses the ASP objects must be running in IIS context where the AS objects can be accessed. When all this is taken account of, you can use all your knowledge of ASP when building COM components for IIS.

Overview: The Response Object

Table 4.5 displays the properties, methods, and collections of the Response object.

Overview: The Request Object

Table 4.6 displays the properties, methods, and collections of the Request object.

Table 4.5 The Response Object

	DESCRIPTION
Collection	
Cookies	Creates a cookie or sets the value of an existing cookie.
Method	
AddHeader(name, value)	Adds the new HTML header *ncme* with *value*. With buffering on, a header can be added at any time. However, buffering off requires that no content be sent to the client before AddHeader is called.
	Continues

Table 4.5 The Response Object *(Continued)*

COLLECTION	DESCRIPTION
AppendToLog(scalar)	Appends a message to the Web server's log. Notice that due to the format of the log, the message can contain no commas.
BinaryWrite(data)	Writes *data* of unsigned 1-byte characters(VT_ARRAY|VT_UI1) to the standard output: for example, a binary file such as an image.
Clear( )	Clears the body of any buffered HTML output.
End( )	Ends processing of the current ASP document and returns the result.
Flush( )	When output is buffered, calling flush will send it to the output.
Redirect(URL)	Sends a message to the browser that it should redirect to *URL*.
Write(scalar)	Writes *scalar* to the output.
Property	
Buffer = TRUE|FALSE	Turns page buffering on/off. When set to TRUE (1), no output will be sent to the client until all scripts and other content are done processing; this is the default setting for IIS5. When the buffering is FALSE, or turned off, the content is outputted while being processed.
CacheControl = scalar	Can be set to either Private or Public. The default value is Private. However, the majority of proxy services will not be able to cache those pages. Instead, when cache is set to Public, proxy servers will cache.
Charset = scalar	Places the name of the character set to use for the page in the content type header.
ContentType = scalar	Describes the content type being sent in the response.
Expires = minutes	The length in minutes before a cached page expires in the client browser. For immediate expiration, the number of minutes can be set to −1 or another negative number.
ExpiresAbsolute	The date and time when the page expires in the format Month DD, YYYY HH:MM:SS where HH is set according to 24 hour time. For example: December 21, 2002 17:07:30
IsClientConnected	Returns whether or not a client is connected to the server.
PICS = scalar	Scalar that is a PICSLabel.
Status = Value	A three-digit status code and a string of text that describes the status.

Table 4.6 The Request Object

	DESCRIPTION
Collection	
ClientCertificate	Client certification fields in a digital certificate.
Cookies	Cookies sent in the HTTP header.
Form	Form elements posted to the HTTP body.
QueryString	Variables passed in the HTTP query string.
ServerVariables	Environment variables.
Method	
BinaryRead(bytes)	Number of bytes to read from the HTTP body. This method returns VT_ARRAY|VT_UI1 unsigned 1-byte character stream of the number of bytes read from the HTTP body.
Property	
TotalBytes	Returns the number of bytes in the HTTP body.

Summary

In this chapter we have learned how ASP is used to collect information from the client, and we have learned how we can send data to the client's browser using ASP. The Request object is responsible for collecting information that the client sends with each request to the server. There are many types of information that the Request object can provide the script engine; for example, the contents of a submitted Web form, server environment variables, the values of cookies, and the certification fields of a digital client certificate. When the client fills out a Web form and submits the values, it is always a good idea to ensure that each element of the submitted form contains a valid value. Perl's regular expression engine is perfect for that task. Digital certificates can only be used on a certified server, and such a server cannot be run out of the box. A certification process is necessary, and certain costs are involved before the process is completed. Instead of collecting various data, the Response object feeds data to the client's browser. When the scripting engine produces content such as text for the client to view, the Response object is used to output the content. The object's Write method is used to pass textual data, and the BinaryWrite method is used to pass binary data to the client. Not only can you write to the client, but it is also possible to append strings to the Web server log, redirect the client's browser to a different URL, or simply stop the processing of the current page. In correlation with the Request object, which can read the values of cookies, the Response object is used to set the values that are contained within cookies. In many applications, these two objects work very closely together.

In the next chapter, we will look at a mix of ASP objects and the purposes for which these objects can be used.

## CHAPTER 5

The Special Utility Objects

For special tasks, Active Server Pages provides standard utility methods and properties through a number of objects. The Server object is a set of utility methods and properties, and the theme that runs through the toolkit is that everything it provides is located on the server side. However, its range of uses is rather wide, encompassing everything from creating a class instance of an external COM component object to executing separate Active Server Pages documents as if they were subroutines. In a transactional environment, the ObjectContext object is used to either commit or abort the current transaction. It is a smaller version of the COM ObjectContext object, and implements only two standard methods and has two events related to itself. When an error occurs in an ASP page, the ASPError object will contain information about the incident. It returns a number of error messages on a number of different levels.

The Swiss Army Knife of ASP

Contrary to the other built-in ASP objects, the Server object provides functionality that resides on the server side. This object is the Swiss army knife of ASP; it has a wide variety of methods and properties that define some type of utility.

The Server's Property

Being the Server object of ASP, the only property that really applies is setting the number of seconds for which a script can run before returning an error.

ScriptTimeout

The ScriptTimeout property can be set in Internet Services Manager. It defines, for the scope of the page, how long a script is allowed to be processed before it should return an error. This value is defined in seconds.

```
<%
$Server->{ScriptTimeout} = 60
%>
```

In this example the time-out would occur after one minute, but there is one catch. The time-out cannot be fewer seconds than currently specified in the AspScriptTimeout in the Metabase properties, so in many cases you will be better off defining the Script-Timeout in Internet Services Manager.

The Utility Methods

The Server object exposes simple methods for encoding and decoding strings, up to the possibility of including external COM component objects in Active Server Pages documents.

The CreateObject() Method

Whether you have written a proprietary component or are using a product created by someone else, the CreateObject() method can create an instance of that component.

```
<%
$adoConn = $Server->CreateObject("ADODB.Connection");
%>
```

For this ADO Connection object, as for any other object created by CreateObject, neither application nor session scope can be modified; the values given when the object was created must be used. An object created inside a page with CreateObject will have page scope and will be freed from memory when the page is done processing. There is, however, nothing to prevent the object from being placed inside the Session object.

Since the Connection object of ActiveX Data Objects has been created and introduced, you can access its methods and properties through the local instance.

```
<%
$adoConn->{Timeout} = 100;
$adoConn->Open("someServer");
%>
```

The Execute() Method

As an option for including files that are greatly disadvantaged in interactive environments and code libraries, the Execute() method can execute external .asp pages.

You can use either the physical or virtual path to the file you wish to execute. Furthermore, a QueryString can be included in the call.

The GetLastError() Method

With ASP 3, a 500;100 error message was designed to be customized and presented by the Web application when an error occurs. The Transfer() method of the server automatically takes the client to the custom page, and the GetLastError() method can be used to examine or present the ASPError object. The default Web site is generally customized for the file 500-100.asp.

The HTMLEncode() Method

On the Internet, certain strings can produce unwanted results. For example, the < and > characters cannot be outputted as expected in the documents. Instead, they have to be encoded. To solve this issue, the HTMLEncode() method will encode any such characters to an understandable form for the browser, and in turn this will prevent clients from sending data such as HTML or JavaScript, for example, to your Web application.

```
$valForm = $Server->HMTLEncode( $Request->Form("comment")-
>Item() );
```

The MapPath() Method

An extremely useful method, MapPath() will map the path to a given file. By giving the virtual path to a file on the server, the MapPath() method will locate it by the physical path on the machine. For example, MapPath() could turn /cgi-bin/helloworld.pl into c:\inetpub\cgi-bin\helloworld.pl.

A common scenario where this can be used is when opening databases, or when opening a file such as the following:

```
open(F, $Server->MapPath("/CGI-BIN/File.dat") );
```

An example follows:

```
<TITLE>Sign GuestBook - PerlScript Example</TITLE>
<BODY BGCOLOR="WHITE" TEXT="WHITE">

<%@Language=PerlScript%>
<%
open(F, $Server->MapPath("/guestbook.dat"));

while(<F>) {
    chop;
    split(/\t/);
    $output .= '<A HREF="mailto:';
    $output .= $_[1];
    $output .= '">';
    $output .= $_[0];
    $output .= "</A> says: <BR> $_[2] <BR><BR>";
}

close(F);
%>
```

```
<FONT FACE="ARIAL" SIZE=-1 COLOR="BLACK">
    <%=$output%>
</FONT>

<TABLE width=300 bgcolor=orange cellspacing=1 border=1 align=center>
<FORM ACTION="Guestbookwrite.asp" METHOD="GET">
<TR>

<TD width=100>
    <FONT FACE="ARIAL" SIZE=-1 COLOR="WHITE">Name:
</TD>

<TD width=200 ALIGN="RIGHT">
    <INPUT TYPE=TEXTFIELD NAME="Name">
</TD>

</TR>
<TR>

<TD width=100>
    <FONT FACE="ARIAL" SIZE=-1 COLOR="WHITE">Email:
</TD>
<TD width=200 ALIGN="RIGHT">
    <INPUT TYPE=TEXTFIELD NAME="Email">
</TD>

</TR>
<TR>

<TD width=100>
    <FONT FACE="ARIAL" SIZE=-1 COLOR="WHITE">Comment:
</TD>

<TD width=200 ALIGN="RIGHT">
    <INPUT TYPE=TEXTFIELD NAME="Comment">
</TD>

</TR>
<TR>

<TD colspan=2 align="right">
<INPUT TYPE=SUBMIT VALUE="Sign Guestbook">
</TD>

</TR>

</FORM>
</TABLE>
```

The next bit of code is the part that gets the information passed from the client and writes it to the guestbook.

```
<%@language=perlscript%>
<%
my($file) = $Server->MapPath("/Guestbook.dat");
my($entry) = join "\t", ($Request->QueryString("Name")->Item,
```

```
                          $Request->QueryString("Email")->Item,
                          $Request->QueryString("Comment")->Item),
                "\n";

     open(F, ">>$file") || $Response->Redirect("/Error.asp");
     flock F, 2;
     print F $entry;
     close(F);
     $Response->Redirect("/Guestbook.asp");
%>
```

Thank you for signing the guestbook!

The Transfer() Method

The Transfer() method is a new way of maintaining state. Instead of telling the browser to redirect to a new page, the server will automatically transfer the user to the new page. In addition, each built-in object will maintain state. For example, the requested and received values of a form in the Request object. The client and the data can be transferred to a new page, thus eliminating the use of ugly methods such as:

```
$Response->Redirect("http://www.mysite.com?variable=$a");
```

URLEncode() Method

URLEncode() will encode a string so that it is valid to be passed in the URL.

Overview: The Server Object

Table 5.1 discusses aspects of the Server object.

A Transactional Utility

ObjectContext is used to either commit or abort a transaction. It is a subset of COM ObjectContext and as such it implements only two methods and two events.

Controlling Transactions

The two methods of ObjectContext are used to set the destiny of a transaction that has been invoked in an ASP page. In order for a page to run in a transaction, the @TRANS-ACTION page command must be on the first line of the document.

```
<%@TRANSACTION=value%>
```

Table 5.2 shows the four values that can be used when setting the transactional state.

If there is more than one page involved in a transaction, each page must invoke a transaction directive.

Table 5.1 The Server Object

	DESCRIPTION
Property	
ScriptTimeout	The number of seconds a script can run before returning an error
Method	
CreateObject(progID)	Creates a class instance of a COM component that is located by the string *progID*
Execute(path)	Executes the .asp file in the absolute or relative location *path*
GetLastError()	Returns an ASPError object with information about the error
HTMLEncode(string)	Encodes *string* into a valid format for displaying certain characters as text instead of HTML to an HTML browser
MapPath(path)	Returns the physical path of the virtual path in *path*
Transfer(path)	Transfers a client to *path* and maintains the state of the built-in objects such as the Request object
URLEncode(string)	Encodes *string* so that it qualifies as a URL with its character conventions

The ObjectContext Object

Table 5.3 discusses the ObjectContext object.

Everything about Errors

When an error occurs during an ASP page, an ASPError object will be created by IIS. Later, you can examine the error object's properties for information about the error.

Table 5.2 The Type of Transaction for the Document

VALUE	MEANING
Required	The script initiates a transaction.
Requires_New	The script initiates a transaction.
Supported	The script does not initiate a transaction.
Not_Supported	The script does not initiate a transaction.

Table 5.3 The ObjectContext Object

DESCRIPTION	
Method	
SetAbort( )	Used to abort a script-initiated transaction because something in the transaction did not complete and the updates should be prevented.
SetComplete( )	Makes a change final and completes the transaction. It has a higher priority than SetAbort( ) and thus will override any previous calls to SetAbort( ). If all COM components used in the transaction also call SetComplete( ), the transaction is fully completed.
Events	
OnTransactionAbort	If defined in the script, this event is run if the SetAbort( ) method is called.
OnTransactionCommit	If defined in the script, this event is run if the transaction commits.

The ASPError Object

A number of sources for detailed information about the occurred error are available in the ASPError object's properties (Table 5.4).

Summary

In this chapter we have looked at objects that serve various purposes. Dealing strictly with what happens on the server side, the Server object exposes a number of methods

Table 5.4 The ASPError Object Properties

PROPERTY	DESCRIPTION
ASPCode	A string with an IIS error code
Number	A long integer that contains the error code returned by a COM component
Source	A string that details whether the error occurred because of IIS, ActiveX Scripting Engine, or a COM component
FileName	A string with the name of the .asp file where the error was generated
LineNumber	A long integer with the line number where the error was generated
Description	A string with short description of the error
ASPDescription	A string that returns a more detailed description of the error (if applicable) than the description given by the Description property

and properties ranging from creating instances of external COM objects within the ASP page to setting the time-out of the scripting engine that is being used in the ASP document. For transactional environments, the ObjectContext object can be used either to commit or abort a transaction. This object can only be used with transactions launched by a script within an ASP document. In case of an error, an ASPError object is generated. The ASPError object can be closely examined to find the causes of the error, so that a remedy can be found that ensures that the error will not occur again.

Up next are the basics needed for understanding Universal Data Access and for beginning programming of the ActiveX Data Objects for data access.

## CHAPTER 6

Universal Data Access

U niversal Data Access (UDA) is a strategy for data access from Microsoft. In contrast to other industry standards that provide similar access, UDA is not limited to only one type of data. Through UDA, database records, files and folders, and e-mail systems can be accessed by one single interface—thus the data access becomes universal.

Microsoft Data Access Components

Universal Data Access is a strategy implemented by Microsoft Data Access Components (MDAC). Since the components are accessed through the Component Object Model (COM), virtually any programming or scripting language can use MDAC to retrieve data for its application.

The Medicine for Data Access

From one single interface and syntax, MDAC can access data regardless of whether it is relational or nonrelational. This new standard is revolutionary because relational data, such as that in databases, has previously required an application-level programming interface separate from that used for nonrelational data, such as the contents of files. With UDA, each type of data is unified into one standard instead of divided into separate standards.

The two main technologies in MDAC are OLE DB and ADO. First OLE DB enables access to the data store that the application will program, and then ADO provides the simple application-level programming interface for working with the contents of the data store—that is, doing the actual programming. The third technology, which is a part of MDAC, is the older and already established Open Database Connectivity (ODBC) standard. In summary, the most important components of MDAC are the following:

- Object Linking and Embedding Database (OLE DB)
- ActiveX Data Objects (ADO)
- Open Database Connectivity (ODBC)

In Microsoft Data Access Components, the most limited interface of the three is the Open Database Connectivity API. The limitation is in the program's core, where it is designed to work with relational databases only and no other types of data stores. Prior to the development of the ODBC interface, however, database programming could be both a complex and tedious task. The variety of database systems did not support one single simple form of programming to write database applications. On the contrary, a multitude of skills had to be mastered, and this was a major problem in the industry that cried out for a solution.

As a solution to the complexity of database applications development, ODBC addressed the problem of database programming in a new way. Because there was now a standard for programming the relational databases and each vendor could voluntarily write a software device to support the proposed standard, multiple skills were no longer needed. It was only necessary to learn one single interface—the ODBC API. From the moment ODBC hit the market as an open standard, all the database vendor had to do was to provide a support for ODBC before it was employed in applications. For this a database driver was required.

Since ODBC provides its own functions for calling the underlying database to which it is connected, the primary task of the driver is to ensure that the calls from ODBC are translated into the native language of the database and vice versa. For a software device to qualify as a driver, it needs to follow the open ODBC standards for implementation. This is not difficult, however. The result of the clear and open definition suggested that each driver must implement the proposed standard, and therefore it is not necessary to learn anything more than the commands of ODBC alone. What does a driver have to do in order to qualify as a driver? For the driver to work with ODBC, it must support a number of services defined by ODBC. The services, in summary, are the following:

- It must connect to the database.
- It must execute statements in standard SQL syntax.
- It must be capable of returning standard error codes.
- It must provide access and return results from the database.

When the suggested services of an ODBC driver have been implemented and the software device is fully functional, the driver can be applied almost anywhere. For example, on the Internet, a Web-based application can connect to a database by way of ODBC and the ODBC driver. The typical scenario would require three simple stages:

- An application, which on the Internet is a server-side script, must call ODBC.

- A database must receive the call from ODBC.

- A driver must be present to translate calls from the application to the database, and to translate results from the database to the application.

In the real world, most database systems already support ODBC, so it is already widely implemented and established as a way of data access for applications. But while it is true that ODBC is a solution for working with relational databases, the need to perform the same operations on nonrelational data is left unanswered by ODBC. Therefore, Universal Data Access responds not only to the absent services of ODBC in the form of MDAC, but also to the existing functionality of ODBC—providing one single interface for all types of data stores.

As a technology that supports a wide range of data such as file systems, e-mail systems, and binary and textual data, Microsoft Data Access Components—much like ODBC—needs an implementation to connect to a database. The component that is closest to the data store, and is easily compared to having the same function as the driver has for ODBC, is the OLE DB technology. The difference between how ODBC and OLE DB are deployed by an application is very distinctive in one point:

- ODBC was designed to run in a multiplatform environment.

- OLE DB was designed to run in a COM environment.

As a standard, OLE DB is meant to provide universal data access. However, it is a rather complex, low-level interface that enables any type of data store to be exposed. The first type of data access that OLE DB provided was to ODBC-compliant databases. What it essentially did was to make the old approach of connecting to databases through an ODBC layer callable by way of the new interface. As an implementation, the new interface was called the OLE DB provider for ODBC, and with a completely new programming interface, the services of ODBC were provided by MDAC. In terms of implementation, OLE DB essentially had to make sure all calls were accurately funneled into ODBC from the calling application. From there on ODBC would perform its core services and connect itself to the database via its original driver. In itself, ODBC was never rewritten, but OLE DB was written to interface it and provide its many services.

In the situations where OLE DB is used, regardless of what functionality it exposes, it will generally tie an application to the database that it exposes. OLE DB is an open standard that can be used by practically anyone who wants to write a software device that introduces a new or not-yet-implemented data store into UDA or to access an already-implemented data store for programming. Although it gives fast and powerful access, it is not available to every language. A scripting language, for example, is not low-level or close enough to the metal to use OLE DB as its solution for data access. C++, on the other hand, is a language that can utilize OLE DB, and in two common scenarios it would be rewarding to use OLE DB alone:

- When application development requires fast, but not necessarily simple, access to a data store

- When a data provider is developed to allow a previously unimplemented data store to expose its functionality to an application

For the Internet developer, OLE DB will not be directly accessed through Web pages such as Active Server Pages documents. A scripting language is not compatible with the programming language required to program OLE DB. However, the solution offered by MDAC is an application-level programming interface for every type of programming and scripting language that supports OLE and COM—ActiveX Data Objects.

ActiveX Data Objects (ADO) is a high-level interface. It essentially provides access as an application-level programming interface to OLE DB, which in turn speaks with the underlying source, as usual. Data access through ADO is slower than it would be using OLE DB directly, but there are a number of valid reasons that remain in favor of ADO despite the lessened performance.

- ADO is necessary for Internet development with scripting languages.
- ADO is applicable in more languages than OLE DB.
- ADO is easier to learn than OLE DB.

In essence, up until the strategy of Universal Data Access, database programming was commonly done through the open-standard ODBC. While ODBC was limited to relational databases, MDAC would come to provide access to what was considered not ODBC territory—nonrelational data such as file systems and e-mail systems. However, MDAC had gone one step further and provided its interface for relational databases as well. MDAC provides its data access through the OLE DB layer, which is not accessible through a scripting language. OLE DB is an open standard, like ODBC, and it provides a standard for implementing universal data access to all types of data. OLE DB is already giving access to ODBC, and, as a result, the databases that use an ODBC driver for their tasks are compatible with MDAC. There is a performance loss involved when using the OLE DB provider for ODBC because data goes through so many instances before it reaches the data store. Consequently, most database systems now have native OLE DB providers and it is not necessary to use the OLE DB provider for ODBC. The limitation of OLE DB is its small support for programming and scripting languages. This limitation, however, is overcome by ActiveX Data Objects. ADO is called a high-level interface to the services provided by OLE DB, and this means that it provides a simplified interface that allows you to work with OLE DB without noticing its complexity. ADO is applicable from any language—scripting or programming—that supports Object Linking and Embedding (OLE) and the Component Object Model (COM). ADO is the technology used within MDAC when developing Internet and desktop applications. A very easy interface to learn, it provides access to relational and nonrelational data stores.

A and Ω of Relational Databases

The most common type—and probably the oldest type—of database is a relational database. There are two segments of the relational database that make up the foundation—the *data* and the *metadata*.

The metadata describes the structure and creates the layout of the relational database. Stored in the *data dictionary*, the metadata holds information about the tables, columns, indexes, and the other objects that make up the database. The metadata is not the original content that is entered into the database or read from it. Instead it is what defines which manually entered data is populating the database, and how and where this occurs.

When data is inserted into the database, it is inserted into a table (Figure 6.1). A table is a two-dimensional array of rows and columns, with the number of rows and columns depending on how the database is designed. Each column will have its own unique name, size, and type of data stored. For example, a column can store text, currency, date, and numeric values, to name only a few. When a value is going to be accessed in the two-dimensional array, it normally relates to the name of the columns and the value of the columns. The columns physically stretch themselves from the left to the right, and when each column in a row has been set to a value, a record is created. The next time the values are set the position in the table must be moved; hence a new row in the two-dimensional array.

The following example illustrates tables, columns, and records. The database table is named Students and it has three columns: StudentID, Firstname, and Lastname. There are four records in the table, as illustrated in the following text.

Translated into a real-world situation, each student in a school is unique as a person, but is identified by a student identification card or number. For example, the identification card might have a scan code with a special number that is read in order to verify the identity of the student who is, for example, borrowing a book from the library. Figure 6.1 displays a less modern method where the students for some reason are identified by the ID numbers that they have been given as students—it serves as a unique identifier.

Students

StudentID	Firstname	Lastname	
12341	John	Doe	
53462	Mary	Clarke	
75634	Joe	Johnson	
66235	Andy	Haglund	

Figure 6.1 A table in a relational database.

The unique identifier can be used to relate records between several tables in the database. The StudentID column can be present in more than only the table of personal information. Each grade the student has ever held could be stored in a table of grades where the student is identified by the ID number given by the school. The unique identifier introduces what in database terms is called the primary key. A primary key is used to identify who the record belongs to. It is not only useful in one table, but can also be used to identify records belonging to a certain student that are entered into another table. If the main table for information is the personal information about a student, then that student's Student ID would be the primary key, as just described.

In this scenario, the primary key can be used to relate the student to other records in other tables where the same number is present, and the column is used to relate to the student by identification number. However, in a table other than the working table, this is not known as primary key. Instead, it is labeled as the foreign key.

With this information in mind, it is time to look at the language used to access the database—Structured Query Language.

The Structured Query Language

Structured Query Language (SQL) was developed during the 1970s and became an ANSI standard language for adding, manipulating, and accessing data in relational databases in the 1980s. Since its creation, SQL has become widely accepted and is used within database management systems (DBMSs) such as Oracle, Informix, and Microsoft SQL Server, to name a few.

Every language has its parts of speech, and SQL is no exception. Three major parts make up the language and provide its functionality; thus each part of the language has its special purpose for the database system.

- Data Manipulation Language (DML)
- Data Definition Language (DDL)
- Data Control Language (DCL)

These three languages are the most crucial parts of knowledge when it comes to building effective database applications. Data Definition Language enables structure-altering actions of the database, and Data Manipulation Language handles the records in the tables. For secure database actions, Data Control Language will control the events of transactions to ensure that the database work is successful.

Data Manipulation Language

The most frequently used part of SQL and the most important, Data Manipulation Language (DML) was built for managing the records in the database. In terms of functionality, it allows records to be accessed, added, deleted, and updated within a database table (see Tables 6.1 and 6.2). However, in most cases the queries become more complex than that.

Table 6.1 Data Manipulation Language (DML)

CLAUSE	DESCRIPTION
Select	Accesses data to be retrieved from the database
Insert	Inserts a row of new data into the database
Update	Updates existing data in the database
Delete	Deletes a row of existing data in the database

The Select Clause

Select is the clause provided by DML for retrieving a number of records from a database table. A Select clause can be kept very simplistic, but there are some regulations that apply. The clause must specify a table from which the records are to be retrieved, as well as which columns of the database table to return.

```
# Select all columns in the Students table
#
  SELECT *
  FROM   Students;

# Select only the columns Firstname and Lastname ...
#
  SELECT Firstname, Lastname
  FROM   Students;
```

As mentioned, the table and the columns must be present in the Select clause. However, when you either do not know the names of the columns or want to return every single one of them, the asterisk (*) tells the database to return all columns. In contrast, being explicit and specifying the names of the columns as a comma-separated list makes the work a little easier for the database.

Very often a table name, for example, may contain spaces, such as *My Table*. In these cases, explicitly typing it as My Table will return an error from the database. The prob-

Table 6.2 The Syntax

CLAUSE	DESCRIPTION
Select	Defines a list of columns to retrieve from the database
From	Defines which relational table the list of columns should be retrieved from
Where	Defines a criterion that the data must match to be retrieved
Group By	Summarizes the results from the query by column as a group
Having	Defines a criterion for data returned as a group
Order By	Defines by what columns and in what order the retrieved data should be organized

lem is solved by enclosing the table name within square brackets, so that the white space is treated as a part of the clause instead of a command.

```
SELECT FirstName, Lastname FROM table of students;   # Error!
SELECT FirstName, Lastname FROM [table of students]; # Correct
```

So far, so good. No restrictions have yet been put on the records that have been retrieved. However, there are many ways to make the criteria of the Where clause much more effective. For example, there is no limitation saying that only one criterion may be matched. A number of logical operators (Table 6.3) can be used to extend the criteria to require two or more statements to be true, to require one statement to be true, or to falsify a Where clause by disregarding the criteria specified in the clause.

The next example extends the criteria by requiring two Select clauses to match the criteria in order for the records to be returned. It is very easy. The following statement matches everyone who is named Andy Anderson.

```
SELECT * FROM tblStudente
        WHERE Lastname='Anderson'
        AND   Firstname='Andy';
```

In addition to the operators given so far, the queries can be further enhanced by using a number of comparison operators (Table 6.4) to compare values. The next example selects all cars that sell for less than $20,000.

```
# List all cars for less than 20,000
#
  SELECT Car WHERE Price < 20000;
```

The comparison operators are easy and effective to use, and also have a convenient resemblance to the mathematical operators used in various programming and scripting languages.

A more detailed method of describing the matching criteria is by writing comparison predicates. There are several predicates in the SQL standard.

- BETWEEN
- IN
- LIKE
- NULL

Table 6.3 Logical Operators

OPERATOR	DESCRIPTION
AND	Left value must be matched and right value must be matched.
OR	Left value must be matched; if left value is matched, right value is ignored. If left value does not match, right value will be tested, and it returns a match if true.
NOT	Predeclares a criterion as false to be true.

Table 6.4 Comparison Operators

QUERY PREDICATE	DESCRIPTION
=	Left value is equal to right value.
<	Left value is smaller than right value.
>	Left value is greater than right value.
>=	Left value is greater than or equal to right value.
<=	Left value is less than or equal to right value.
<>	Left value is not equal to right value.
!=	Left value is not equal to right value.

- ALL
- DISTINCT
- EXISTS

BETWEEN

The BETWEEN predicate is used to select a number of records that all fit within a certain range. The same thing can be accomplished by comparison of the values. However, BETWEEN offers a more intuitive approach to building the statement.

```
# Get the cars where the price is between 10,000 and 20,000
#
  SELECT Car WHERE Price BETWEEN 10000 AND 20000;
```

BETWEEN could be used to retrieve a set of records for people within a certain age group in a very readable statement.

```
# Get everything about customers who are between 10 and 70 years old
#
  SELECT * FROM Customers WHERE AGE BETWEEN 10 AND 70;
```

In addition, BETWEEN can be used with the most common types of data, such as date and time, characters, and numeric types as seen in the preceding examples. For instance, the following is also valid:

```
# Get the students whose midname-initial is between A and H
#
  SELECT Students WHERE Name_Midname_initial BETWEEN 'A' AND 'H';
```

LIKE

The query predicate *like* is generally used for wild-card matching of strings that make up the Where clause. For example, in Microsoft Access the percent sign (%) is used as a wild card, so the following query would select from the students table everyone whose last name begins with the letter B.

```
# Lastname begins with B
#
```

```
   SELECT * FROM Students WHERE Lastname like 'B%';

# Lastname ends with b
#
   SELECT * FROM Students WHERE Lastname like '%b';
```

As mentioned, logical operators can be combined together. Furthermore, these operators can also be combined with query predicates.

```
# Lastname begins with B and the average is above 60
#
   SELECT * FROM Students WHERE Lastname like 'B%' AND Average > 60;
```

IN

When a column in a relational table has been defined to use character-type data for its field, an operation that concerns the value of that field must enclose the character value within single quotes or else the character will be treated as if it were of numeric value. IN can be used to demonstrate this. The following will retrieve everyone who lives within the countries defined in the criteria.

```
# Get every customer in Ireland and France
#
   SELECT * FROM Customers WHERE Country IN ('Ireland', 'France');
```

The next section will look at how to order the returned data and group the records.

NOT

NOT can be used to make sure the statement does not match. For example, the following would select everyone who is not in Ireland or France:

```
# Get every customer who is not in Ireland and France
#
   SELECT * FROM Customers WHERE Country NOT IN ('Ireland', 'France');
```

This can also be used with the LIKE predicate.

```
# Get all students whose lastname does not begin with a B
#
   SELECT * FROM Students WHERE Lastname NOT LIKE 'B%';
```

NULL

NULL will return records where the specified column has a value of null. For example, to select all students with null averages:

```
# Get all students with a NULL average
#
   SELECT * FROM Student WHERE Average IS NULL;
```

Or, to do the opposite operation:

```
# Get all students without a NULL average
#
   SELECT * FROM Student WHERE Average IS NOT NULL;
```

ALL, DISTINCT

A number of predicates specify the records selected from a query. For example, if nothing else is specified when running a query, most database engines normally assume that the predicate should select all records that match the query. Thus the following two examples are equivalent:

```
# Get all records in Products
#
  SELECT * FROM Products;

# Get all records in Products
#
  SELECT ALL * FROM Products;
```

On the other hand, should there be a need to put some restriction on the records returned, such as in a case where each customer who has ordered a product must not appear more than once in the result, DISTINCT can be used.

```
SELECT DISTINCT CustomerID FROM Orders;
```

In this example, the customer ID will only be returned once, and as a result each unique customer will be listed in the result. In the same manner, if more than one column is specified to be returned, then the program will seek to match all columns only once.

Joining Tables

Although selecting data from one table is fine, in most cases the database tables contain relational data items that are contained in separate tables but related to each other by a unique identifier. The unique identifier is known as a *primary key* and has one or more columns it claims as its own. The table it relates to contains the foreign key, which is identical to the primary key because its value is the primary key.

Tying all this together, to display any current orders in the Orders tables and the information about the customer in the Customers table related to the order, the two tables could be queried separately. However, it would be more convenient to perform a joined operation and retrieve everything in one single round trip.

```
SELECT Customers.*, Orders.*
FROM   Customers, Orders
WHERE  Customers.CustomerID = Orders.CustomerID;
```

The previous join uses the Northwind database, which comes with Microsoft Access, Microsoft SQL Server, and Microsoft Visual Studio. The two tables it works with are Customers and Orders. All columns in both tables are targeted. To the left of the From clause, the columns and tables to fetch are set, and there the dot notation is used to define which table which columns are fetched from. The tables are specified to the right of the From clause. The following Where clause, which can be extended by logical operators, relates the Customer ID in the Customers table to the Customer ID in the Orders table.

Regular joins, as seen in the preceding example, retrieve data from separate tables and relate the columns in those tables by use of an identifier—in most cases a primary key number. The data is then fetched and returned in one single row set or concatenated into one table.

Data Definition Language

Data Definition Language is the standard for defining database objects and creating the structure of the database. Table 6.5 shows the commands that are supported.

CREATE

To create a new table in the database is fairly simple. All that is necessary is to give the table name, the column names, and the data types. The following will create a new table:

```
# Create a table with two columns
#
  CREATE TABLE
            mynewtable (
                      city char(40)
                      year int
                      );
```

DROP

Now let's drop the database table just created.

```
# Drop the table mynewtable
#
  DROP TABLE mynewtable;
```

ALTER

If you want to modify the existing table, the Alter clause is used.

```
# Drop the column year in mynewtable
#
  ALTER TABLE mynewtable
  DROP COLUMN year;
```

Database tables can be added as well.

```
# Add the column Name to mynewtable
#
  ALTER TABLE mynewtable
  ADD COLUMN Name char(50);
```

Table 6.5 Data Definition Language (DDL)

CLAUSE	DESCRIPTION
Create	Creates a new database object or table
Drop	Deletes an existing database object or table
Alter	Alters an existing database object or table

Data Control Language

As a part of Structured Query Language that concerns protecting the database, Data Control Language (Table 6.6) offers support for transactional events.

Actions taken within the scope of a transaction will be pending until COMMIT is called to apply the changes to the underlying database.

ActiveX Data Objects for Data Access

ActiveX Data Objects (ADO) is designed to be easy to learn and easy to use. A front end intended for programming any type of data store, ADO is popular for both desktop and Web applications because of its powerful yet simple application-level programming interface (API).

Behind ADO

In order for ADO to work, there are a number of services that need to work together in the Windows architecture besides ADO. It is important to recognize that although ADO is the interface that enables programming at a given source of data, there are components hidden to the programmer but required for ADO to work. These are the five key components that must work together for a connection between a data store and ADO to be in action:

- A data store
- A data provider
- A data source
- A data consumer
- A client application

The first and last terms are familiar. A data store can be one of several types of data, but it is essentially a label for where data are stored. ADO enables the manipulation and access of many data stores, including the following:

- **Databases.** Oracle, Microsoft SQL Server, and Microsoft Access
- **Spreadsheets.** Microsoft Excel

Table 6.6 Data Control Language (DCT)

COMMAND	DESCRIPTION
COMMIT	Performs the pending changes to the database
ROLLBACK	Cancels all pending changes
GRANT	Permits a certain functionality
REVOKE	Revokes a granted functionality

- **E-mail directories.** Microsoft Exchange
- **Files.** Text files

In the architecture of MDAC, the client application is directly used by the client, and therefore closest to the user or highest up in the pyramid. Below the client application is ADO, which uses OLE DB and the other services implemented by OLE DB, all of which are one step further down the pyramid. At the very bottom, and furthest away from the user, is the data store.

The OLE DB Data Provider

The data provider is located lower in the architectural structure, between the data store and ADO, and as such it can be located, for example, between a relational database and the server-side script that calls the database through ADO. The data provider is often referred to as an *OLE DB provider*, and it basically provides a way to access the data in a store. For example, the native data provider for Microsoft SQL Server provides access to an SQL Server database. In a real-world example, when using ADO, both the data from the relational database and the commands issued by the script have to go through its midpoint in order to communicate completely—both must pass by way of the OLE DB provider.

The OLE DB data provider is the software that makes a data store available to ADO, which in turn is made available to the calling script. When a data provider has been written, the component object model makes it available to the language that wants to use its services. The functions of the OLE DB provider are, in summary:

- Expose the data store to ADO
- Issue native commands at the data store (for example, a native language directly at the data store) or tunnel the calls to an API such as ODBC

Before moving on, let's be clear and say once and for all that ADO does not possess the capacity to connect itself into any data store. On the contrary, it can do very little without a data provider. The provider is required and gives the ability to enable communication between ADO and the data store, and without it the application would not work. Furthermore, as previously mentioned, the OLE DB provider might use ODBC to "talk" to the data store. That doesn't mean that you need to care about ODBC. The only knowledge it takes to program a data store is the syntax of ADO, and the OLE DB provider will translate any calls into understandable form for the ODBC API if the store is a relational database that does not yet have a native OLE DB provider.

When ADO is used with the data provider, it normally works with service components in the OLE DB architecture. The service components encapsulate functionality such as a query preprocessor that prepares SQL statements, cursor engines for viewing data in the store, and support for transactions. Because of the variety of providers and systems of data storage, there is a variety of service components and features given by the data provider to the ADO programming interface. As a resulting side effect, or bonus, the programmer will have two different properties available that define the attributes of ActiveX Data Objects.

Dynamic Properties

As systems vary, so does functionality. A certain data provider might want to add a number of properties and features that are not built into ADO by default. Therefore, dynamic properties must be available to the programmer. Dynamic properties are Property objects that are pushed onto the Properties collection and accessed by $object->Properties("Property").

The Property object has four properties of its own:

- The Name property identifies the Property object.

- Type is represented by a DataTypeEnumerator (see Table 8.11).

- Value represents the value of the type.

- The Attributes property is a PropertySettingsEnumerator (Table 6.7).

The Attributes property of its respective object can be the value of a single constant or it may be the sum of several constants. To see what Property objects have been invoked, the Properties collection can be iterated.

```
# Iterate the Property-objects of the Properties-collection
# in $object. Print value and name formated as "Name: Value"
#
foreach my $property (Win32::OLE::in($object->Properties)) {
    $Response->Write( $property->{Name} );
    $Response->Write( ": " );
    $Response->Write( $property->{Value} );
    $Response->Write( "<BR>" );
    }
```

A perfect example of a data provider that adds a number of dynamic properties is Microsoft Cursor Service for OLE DB (Table 6.8), which is a client-side cursor for viewing a row set of data.

To invoke Microsoft Cursor Service for OLE DB and get the dynamic properties listed in Table 6.8, the CursorLocation property of the Connection or Record Set object must be set to reside on the client side; however, setting the Connection's CursorLocation to the client side means that the dynamic properties are only visible in the created row

Table 6.7 Attributes for Property Object—PropertySettingsEnum

VALUE	CONSTANT	DESCRIPTION
0x0000	adPropNotSupported	The data provider does not support the property.
0x0001	adPropRequired	The property must have a set value.
0x0002	adPropOptional	The property is optional.
0x0200	adPropRead	The property can be read.
0x0400	adPropWrite	The property can be set.

Table 6.8 Dynamic Properties with Microsoft Cursor Service for OLE DB

PROPERTY	DESCRIPTION
Name	A given name for the Recordset object.
Optimize	Reads or writes whether an index is to be created for a Field object. True (1) will create an index and False (0) will delete an index.
Unique Table	Name of a base table where editing, adding, and deleting data are possible.
Unique Schema	Schema of the table or name of the table owner.
Unique Catalog	Catalog or name of the database that holds the table.
Resync	Container of a command string used to refresh the data in a unique table.

set that is the result of a query—the separate row set inherits the current CursorLocation setting of its Connection object.

When moving the cursor from the server side to the client side, it is required that ADO, in one single round trip to the server, fetch all records that match the criteria. From there on, the records are locally cached and accessed. As a result of the local caching, the first time the records are fetched with a client-side cursor, the process will be slower than it would with a server-side cursor because of all the records that have to be retrieved. Afterward, when the records have been retrieved, navigating and manipulating them will be faster than with a server-side cursor.

Built-In Properties

In contrast to provider-specific properties, there are built-in properties that are available directly by $object->{Property}. These are listed in the sections about each object.

In short, the built-in properties are available from the moment the ADO object is created in the Web application and can be accessed as normal properties from the object without referencing through.

The Data Source

The data source functions for OLE DB as the object that knows how to connect to a data store such as a relational database. Each data provider implements a data source to make the connection, and consequently every data consumer must specify the data source to connect to.

A data source is necessary to let the data provider expose data to the consumer. In essence, the provider needs an object that knows how to connect to the data store, and the data source object fills that need. Consequently, the data consumer must specify which data source to connect to, so the first step is to figure out how to establish the initial connection before the data store can be accessed.

Before moving on to the programming, keep in mind that as long as you have a database, it will connect with your application. It is not 10 mystical, magic lines of code that must be written to enable the connection. On the contrary, chronically failing to connect to a data store is like winning the lottery. It could happen, but is likely not to.

The Native Provider

The best way to open a connection is to specify the native OLE DB data provider for the data source. In conjunction with that, a series of arguments are passed. As a placeholder for all the arguments, the ConnectionString property of the Connection object will store the string that is used to embed the arguments, and so will the ActiveConnection property of the Recordset object—they can have the same data as the Recordset implicitly creates a Connection object. However, to call it a connection string is close to the truth—it is a string that connects to a data source.

A connection string is a textual string where the arguments are separated by semicolons. There is no fixed number of arguments; rather, as many arguments as needed or desired are placed in the string, although only two are required for connecting to many data sources.

The text of the connection string will be passed by the application, and then the provider and the data store must determine what the contents of the string mean. It is worth mentioning that when allowed or required, provider-specific commands may be included as they are documented in the native provider's documentation.

Table 6.9 displays a number of common connection strings that can be used for accessing a data source. The number in the connection string is the version number of the provider, and in cases where a newer provider is available, it should always be used. Check with the vendor for a newer native data provider.

Please note that version numbers of the OLE DB providers may vary, and note that specifying the version number of the OLE DB provider may not always be necessary.

As most databases know ODBC, the default provider for ADO is MSDASQL, which is the OLE DB provider for ODBC. However, using the native data provider outweighs the default driver because of the number of services that must be invoked.

Table 6.9 Connection Strings for Accessing a Data Source

DATA PROVIDER	NATIVE CONNECTION STRING
Microsoft Access	Provider=Microsoft.Jet.OLEDB.4.0;Data Source=path
Microsoft SQL Server	Provider=SQLOLEDB.1;Data Source=path to database
Microsoft Indexing Service	Provider=MSIDXS.1;Data Source=path
Oracle	Provider=MSDAORA.1;Data Source=path to database

To illustrate the advantages and disadvantages of native provider versus the ODBC provider, let's compare the routes both providers take in order to get to the data store. The native provider takes two steps before it reaches the data store:

1. Deploy the OLE DB core services.
2. Deploy the OLE DB data provider for the data store.

In contrast, the OLE DB provider for ODBC-compliant databases must take two extra steps because it needs to initialize the ODBC driver. Thus there are four steps for the MSDASQL data provider:

1. Deploy the OLE DB core services.
2. Deploy the OLE DB data provider for ODBC.
3. Deploy ODBC core services.
4. Deploy the ODBC driver.

As can be seen, there are two very good reasons to avoid the default driver. The native data provider avoids the extra layers of the ODBC application programming interface and instead directly interacts with the data store. In all cases where applicable, use the native provider for your data stores.

Universal Data Link

The universal data link is very straightforward. It is a configuration and connection file set up and saved by a wizard. The next few steps will set up a .udl file:

1. Create a new text document.
2. Rename the file extension to .udl.
3. Right-click on the .udl file and choose Properties.
4. Choose a data provider from the Provider tab.
5. Choose a data source from the Connection tab.
6. Alternatively, fill out a user name and password.
7. If desired, test the connection by clicking on Test Connection.
8. If desired, set permissions and network settings from the Advanced tab.
9. If desired, manually edit the values from the All tab.

When the UDL file has been prepared, it is used as the definition of the connection arguments—the path to the file substitutes for the connection string.

Data Source Name

When little time or patience remains, the quickest approach to making your data store accessible through the Web application is to create a data source name (DSN) for the

ODBC-compliant type of data store. From the previous section, however, recall the advantages of the native provider before choosing this option.

A wizard is used to produce DSNs of all types. The wizard automatically generates the arguments needed for the connection instead of making you do all the typing.

Creating a System DSN

The system data source name is stored and accessed in the registry. The wizard will set up the system DSN in eight easy steps:

1. Open the control panel.
2. Locate and start the ODBC 32 application either directly accessible in the control panel or in the Administrative Tools directory as Data Sources from the control panel.
3. Click on the System DSN tab.
4. Click on Add.
5. Select your driver, then click Finish.
6. Click on the Select button, and you will get to browse for and select the file. When that is done, click OK.
7. Type in a data source name in the text field designated Data Source Name. This will be the name by which your application calls the database.
8. Optionally, enter a description of the database.

The system data source name will be visible to all users. For a system DSN to be used as the connection string, only the data source name needs to be passed.

Creating a File DSN

The file DSN is a text file that contains the arguments for a connection. Like the system DSN, it can be set up by the ODBC wizard.

Follow the steps in the previous section, but instead of System DSN choose File DSN as the type of DSN. When completed, the file is saved with the extension .dsn, and, like the .udl file, it must be accessed by passing the file path as a connection string.

Due to the fact that a text file is used to extract the arguments, it will be slower than the other available approaches. First the text file is opened and its contents are extracted, and then the text file is closed. In 9 cases out of 10, a better option than the file DSN can be discovered.

No DSN or DSN-Less

You can save yourself from working with DSNs by establishing a DSN-less connection. This is done by embedding the arguments in a string instead of storing the string either in the registry or a file. This topic was discussed in the section about connection strings, but the term *DSN-less connection* is commonly used, so although there is no real separation between the two, it is portrayed that way here to bring forth the facts.

Example with SQL Server and OLE DB

```
<%
# Open thesource by using the native SQL Server provider
#

$conn->Open(<<EOF);
   Provider=sqloledb;
   Data Source=thesource;
   Initial Catalog=dbs;
   User Id=Admin;
   Password=secret;
EOF
%>
```

<< is an operator in Perl that will treat all text between its starting point and end point as a single string—and we will see a lot of it. It prevents text over multiple lines from being glued together into an unreadable string. The *EOF* used in the example is not a keyword of any kind and is not needed for the code to work. Almost any combination of letters could be used, provided the same combination is used at the beginning and the end.

The OLE DB Consumer

In the architecture that has been described so far in this chapter, the data consumer is physically located between the client application and the data provider (Figure 6.2). The consumer of data is ActiveX Data Objects, since any program call from the Web applications presented here goes through the ADO interface. ADO's only task and purpose is to access the data exposed by the data provider.

Commands passed to the data store are sent by way of the ADO interface to the data provider, then from the data provider to the data store as was presented in the comparison between native data providers and default providers for ODBC-compliant databases.

The ADO Object Model

It is now time to look at the object model that we will be working with for database programming. In the ADO object model, there are seven objects that can be used.

- Connection
- Recordset
- Command
- Parameter

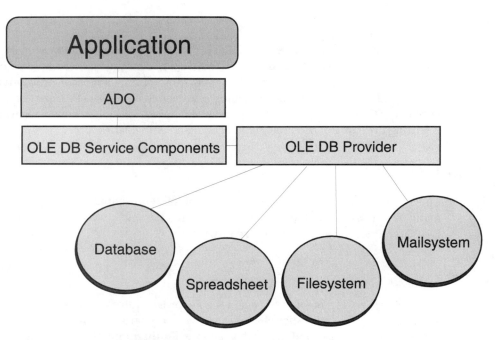

Figure 6.2 Microsoft data access components in the works.

- Field
- Error
- Property

Each object fills a different purpose, and most of the objects are interconnected somehow. The following is a short summary of what the different objects do and how they fit into the world of ADO.

Connection

The Connection is the object that establishes the connection with the data source. It can execute commands such as database queries; retrieve schematic information about a database, such as database tables; and begin and end database transactions.

Recordset

The Recordset is either a row set of records or a non–row set Recordset that can be created from the bottom up by appending columns and data, thus creating a virtual database. In terms of functionality, it provides a cursor for viewing and navigating the records, and the functionality to add, delete, edit, and view records. However, in contrast to the regular flat row sets represented by databases, the Recordset supports hierarchical structures.

Command

The Command object represents a defined command such as a database query that retrieves data from the database. In contrast to a normal query, the command can be precompiled as a parameterized statement or stored procedure, thus preventing recompilation and a loss of performance. Parameters allow the statement of a database query to be written once and dynamically reused with different values without rewriting the query or recompiling the command at the data source.

Parameter

The Parameter is an object used as variable in the represented statement of the Command object. Each Parameter is accessible in the Parameters collection and can have its characteristics defined or be read or written.

Field

The Field object is a column of data in the Recordset. Information about the column such as name, size, and other characteristics can be retrieved, and new values can be set and updated to the underlying data source. Furthermore, the Field object has the ability to work with binary data and long text values against databases.

Error

The Error is the object representation of a single error that has occurred with the data provider. It can be examined for detailed information about the particular error that occurred.

Property

A Property is an object that represents a dynamic property added by the data provider, and its features can be thoroughly examined by using this object.

Record

The Record object is used to work with structures that are naturally hierarchical, such as file systems or e-mail systems. It provides top functionality for two machines at separate locations by URL binding, then remotely works between the machines.

Stream

The Stream object represents a stream of binary or textual data. Reading and writing binary and textual files is a common use for this object.

System and Software Requirements

If you have not done so already, download Microsoft Data Access Components (MDAC) from Microsoft's Internet Web site or install the latest update.

ActiveX Data Objects is included in the MDAC package for systems using operating systems other than Windows 2000. For Windows 2000, ADO is an integrated part of the operating system. In both cases, it is very important to make sure the version is as up to date as possible because of added functionality and bug fixes.

When ADO has been installed, any language that supports the Component Object Model (COM) and Object Linking and Embedding (OLE) Automation can use it. In essence, this means that not only PerlScript but also Perl are qualified languages, leaving a great opportunity open for the development of powerful desktop applications with ADO.

Database Requirements

In the examples, the underlying data store is a Microsoft Access Jet database. The MS Access accompanying the Northwind database will be used where applicable. However, Northwind is also included with SQL Server and Visual Studio.

Microsoft Access is not used because it would be the best possible or most scalable solution for any Web application, but instead to ensure that everyone on any relatively modern Windows operating system can use the examples with minimum hassle.

The ActiveX Data Objects API essentially looks the same regardless of what database system you program against. The connection string does tend to look slightly different, because different providers require different arguments. If you cannot find a suitable connection string in the previous chapter, please see the documentation for the database in question.

Summary

In this chapter we have covered the Universal Data Access (UDA) strategy from Microsoft and its implementation, MDAC. MDAC implements access to all types of data regardless of their natural structure. There are three important technologies contained in MDAC: OLE DB, ADO, and ODBC. OLE DB is the technology that communicates with a data store—for example a relational database, e-mail system, or file system. A scripting language, however, cannot access OLE DB directly, so the scripting language must use the ActiveX Data Objects (ADO) to obtain simplified access to the services of OLE DB. ADO is an application-level programming interface, and it is composed of the Connection, Recordset, Command, Parameter, Field, Error, and Property objects. Also included in MDAC is ODBC, as which is older yet popular technology that provides access to relational databases. Its limitation is that it deals only with relational databases. UDA is much broader in range because it will give you access to programming both relational and nonrelational types of data from the ADO interface. MDAC even encapsulates ODBC and makes it available through the ADO interface. As a result, knowing the interface of ADO will go a very long way in programming various stores of data.

Up next is the Connection object, using the Connection object to establish a link of communication with your data store, and issuing commands through the Connection object.

## CHAPTER 7

Database Programming in ADO

I n the ActiveX object model, the connection is the most important object. It is responsible for opening a link of communication between the client application and the data source, thus enabling database programming in Active Server Pages.

Introduction to the Connection

As the only direct route to the data source, the Connection object is the essential backbone of ADO. Even though an object such as the Recordset, presented in detail in the next chapter, can perform a query and update records just like the Connection, the Connection object is between the Recordset and the data store because it enables the communication. In short, the Connection object is the engine that drives ADO.

The Syntax

To begin, when getting your hands on an external object, recall that any external object can be returned from the CreateObject() method of the Server object—and ActiveX Data Objects is not all that is available. The CreateObject() method takes a Prog ID of a component as its parameter and finds the external library, then returns it—thus the Connection object is created in the following way:

```
$Conn = $Server->CreateObject ("ADODB.Connection");
```

When the object has been created, the Open() method can be called with no parameters—or with any number of parameters, provided that they are in the order given in Table 7.1.

Table 7.1 The Parameters of the Connection's Open() Method

NAME	DESCRIPTION
ConnectionString	The string of arguments used to establish the connection
User ID	A user name to open the connection
Password	A password to open the connection
ConnectOptionEnum	A constant of value either *adConnectUnspecified* (–1) or *adAsyncConnect* (16) which will define whether the connection is opened synchronously or asynchronously

The default value for the ConnectOptionEnumerator is *adConnectUnspecified* (–1). With the parameters from Table 7.1 in mind, the syntax for opening the connection is as follows:

```
$Conn->Open ( ConnectionString, UserID, Password, ConnectOptionEnum );
```

Of all the parameters in Table 7.1, the most important is ConnectionString, because it defines what is needed to find the data source that opens the connection to the data store. A connection string can either be provided with the call to the Open method() or set as a property of the Connection object.

The following example shows how to call Open() with a connection string that is the name of a system DSN:

```
<%@Language=PerlScript%>
<%
# The system DSN is used as parameter
#
$Conn->Open( "A_System_DSN" );
%>
```

Open() can also be called without any parameters when the *ConnectionString* property, which holds information on how to connect to a data source, has been defined.

```
<%@Language=PerlScript%>
<%
# A "DSN-less" connection that uses the native provider and physical
# path to the database file
#
$Conn->{ConnectionString} = (<<EOF);
    Provider=Microsoft.Jet.OLEDB.4.0;
    Data Source=C:\\somepath\\datasource.mdb;
EOF

# Open the connection without using any parameters
#
$Conn->Open();
%>
```

Making the Connection

To make the initial connection, we let the Server object create the Connection object that is required. After its instance is there, the object is used to make the physical connection to the data source by calling its Open() method.

When the object is connected by the Open() call, few actual problems arise—if any! Figure 7.1 shows a connection that uses the native OLE DB provider and not a DSN, which is the preferred way.

Connecting without a DSN

The following example will make a DSN-less connection—preferably known as using the connection string for the native provider. There are numerous reasons why the native provider is better than the DSN. For example, with system DSNs, access either to the registry or to the control panel may not be permitted—or could be very expensive. Moreover, you want the fastest possible connection instead of bothering yourself with file DSNs or risking using the native provider for ODBC and using the excess of both initializing OLE DB services and ODBC services. The DSN-less connection with the Jet provider is as follows.

```
<HTML>
<BODY>
<%@Language=PerlScript%>

<!--#INCLUDE VIRTUAL=/ADOPS.INC"-->

<%
# Create connection object
#
$conn = $Server->CreateObject("ADODB.Connection");

# Set the connection timeout to 15 seconds
#
$Connection->{ConnectionTimeout} = 15;
```

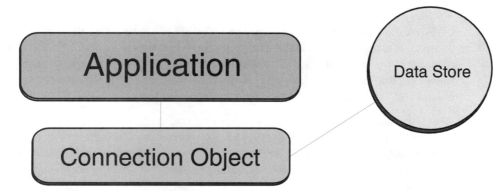

Figure 7.1 Establishing a link to the source.

```perl
# Print the version of ADO being used
#
$Response->Write( "The Current ADO-Version is " );
$Response->Write( $Connection->{Version} );
$Response->Write( "<BR>" );

# Open the connection by using the native provider
#
$conn->Open(<<EOF);
    Provider=Microsoft.Jet.OLEDB.4.0;
    Data Source=C:\\somepath\\datasource.mdb;
    UID=;
    PWD=;
EOF

# If the connection is open, say so, and print a property
# Else if it is closed, say so.
# Any other case is suspect.
#
if( $Connection->{State} == adStateOpen )
{
    $Response->Write( "Connection Established" );
    $Response->Write( $Connection->{"DefaultDatabase"} );
}
elsif( $Connection->{State} == adStateClosed ) {
    $Response->Write( "Connection Not Established" )
    }
    else {
        $Response->Write("Hmmmm");
        }

# Close the connection
#
$conn->Close();

# Undefine the connection object
#
undef $conn;
%>
```

In the example, the constants that are being used are imported as a server-side includes file. *adStateOpen* is used to check if the connection is open. If it is open, a message is printed to the standard output (normally the screen). adStateOpen's numeric value is one (1); if the State property is not equal to 1, we assume that it is closed and print another message to the standard output.

When programming ADO, there are no reasons not to reduce the loading time of the include file by using the numeric values of the constants or selecting only the few constants that you need. However, most examples in the real world will define the constants somehow because it is a kind of standard and it makes the code much more readable.

Checking the Database Session for Errors

The Connection object contains an Errors collection of single Error objects. Each object represents a misoccurrence that originated with one single operation during the database session. The Error object can be examined to locate the cause of the error.

An error will not automatically be detected or signaled, so to detect an error, the Count property of the Errors collection reveals whether or not something has gone wrong during the database session because it contains the number of Error objects. If there are Error objects present in the Errors collection, they can be referenced by index. A very basic example follows:

```
<%
# If there is an error object in the errors collection, print the
# error to the browser windows
#
if( $Conn->Errors->{Count} ) {
    $Response->Write( $Conn->Errors(0) );
    }
%>
```

The feature of detecting errors is very useful for determining whether or not an action should proceed within the application. Furthermore, an Error object is priceless during debugging as it provides very detailed error information and saves hours of frustration.

On the inside, the Error object itself has a number of properties that enable the causes of error to be easily traced where index is an integer. The basic call $Conn->Errors(index); will return a default property of the Error object as specified by the data provider—often a textual description of the error. However, should you wish to specify and customize the output, the properties described in Table 7.2 are available.

Use these properties of the Error object to provide yourself or the user with the available information about the error.

```
<%
# Get the description property of the first error-object
#
my $errorDescription = $Conn->Errors(0)->{Description};
# Get the source property of the first error-object
#
my $errorSource = $Conn->Errors(0)->{Source};
%>
```

The Errors collection will automatically be cleared when a new action that can produce a new error message is run. However, it can also be cleared manually by calling the Clear() method.

Table 7.2   The Properties of the Error Object

PROPERTY	DESCRIPTION
Description	A textual description of the error
HelpContextID	An ID of a certain topic in a help file that concerns the error occurred
HelpFile	The full path to a help file that provides further information on the error
NativeError	An error code from the data source
Number	The constant that represents the error
Source	The name of the object or application that signaled the error
SQLState	An error code of 5 characters from the provider that describes the error of an issued SQL statement

Executing an SQL Query

Most databases have a firm understanding of Structured Query Language (SQL). As a refresher, SQL is a standard command language that databases can operate upon. However, each database tends to have its own features and lack thereof when it comes to SQL—mainly additional features, though.

Making the Selection

When a query returns data, the result is stored as a rowset in a new object: the Recordset. This new object contains not only the data, but also important methods for navigating and manipulating the results.

For example, a member with the log-in Perl forgot the password to some forum so the application has to look up the password in the database and e-mail it to the address specified in the database.

```
<HTML>
<BODY>
<%@Language=PerlScript%>
<%
# Get the Login-value filled out from the form
#
my $Login = $Request->Form('Login')->Item();

# Prepare the SQL statement with the Login-value
#
my $strSQL="SELECT Password,
                  Email
           FROM   MemberTable
           WHERE  Login=\'$Login\'";
```

```
# Create the connection object
#
$conn = $Server->CreateObject("ADODB.Connection");

# Open the database
#
$conn->Open("MemberDatabase");

# Execute the SQL and retrieve the Recordset
#
$rst = $conn->Execute($strSQL);

# If the Recordset is not at End of File, do the following
#    1) Get the value of password and email,
#    2) Pass it to a fictious sendmail
#
if(! $rst->{EOF} )
{
    my $password = $rst->Fields('Password')->{Value};
    my $email = $rst->Fields('Email')->{Value};
    ...
    sendmailRequest($email, $password);
    ...
}
%>
</BODY>
</HTML>
```

In the example, the requested data was returned in a rowset. The rowset is contained in a Recordset object, which will be dealt with shortly, and from the Recordset the columns of rows that were returned are extracted.

Examining an Error

In the previous example, no error checking was done. As previously mentioned, when something fails during the session with the data source, the error messages from the single occasion are stored as Error objects in the Errors collection. When a new error is generated, the collection is cleared and new room is made for the upcoming errors. Let's take a look at how to thoroughly examine an error.

```
<HTML>
<BODY>
<%@Language=PerlScript%>
<%
# "People" is deliberately misspelled so that an error
# will be generated
#
my $strSQL = "SELECT firstname, lastname
              FROM Poeple";

# Create Connection
#
$conn = $Server->CreateObject("ADODB.Connection");
```

```perl
# Open connection
#
$conn->Open("database");

# Execute the query
#
$conn->Execute($strSQL);

# Check for errors
#
scanForErrors();
%>

<%
##########################################################
# Name..........: scanForErrors
# Parameters....: None
# Description...: Counts the errors collection to see if
#                 any errors have occurred. If so, each
#                 object in the collection is presented
#                 and the keys of each object are stored
#                 in a scalar which later is printed to
#                 the screen.
##########################################################

sub scanForErrors
{

    # If count is anything but null
    #
    if($conn->Errors->{Count}) {

        # Declare the scalar to store error-output
        #
        my $errOutput;

        # Iterate the Errors-collection
        #
        foreach my $error (Win32::OLE::in($conn->Errors)) {

            # Loop the hash-keys of the Error-object
            # "add" each key and value (property name
            # and property value) to the errOutput
            # scalar
            #
            foreach my $property (keys %{$error}) {
                $errOutput.=$property.": ";
                $errOutput.=${$error}{$property};
                $errOutput.="<BR>";
                }

            }

        # Output the scalar
        #
        $Response->Write($errOutput);
```

```
                # Exit the application
                #
                exit(1);
                }
}
%>
</BODY>
</HTML>
```

In terms of environments, error checking can and should be applied almost anywhere. When deciding whether or not a database action should proceed or cancel, or during debugging, the Errors collection is priceless.

Performance Tweaking

A Recordset comes in two shapes—a rowset or a non-rowset. When it is a rowset, the object is populated in rows and columns with the data that was retrieved from the data store. For example, we've seen how the rows Email and Password were represented in this object in the last example. A Recordset that is not a rowset will contain everything a regular Recordset does except for the rows. So, what is the point of all this? The point is that a Recordset is returned each time Execute is called by the Connection object. It does not matter what type of query is issued, because any type of query will return a Recordset. For example, the following will return a Recordset:

```
<%
# An action query that deletes the record with the ID number 25
#
$Connection->Execute("DELETE
                FROM    tableStudents
                WHERE   ID=25");
%>
```

Although it is not assigned to a variable, the Recordset's metadata is prepared and the Recordset is returned to ADO. This is an unnecessary performance hit. However, it is easily prevented by specifying that no records are to be returned from the query.

To be verbose about preventing a Recordset from being invoked means telling the ADO object being used that the command performed is an action query that is intended to bear no results. For this purpose, the constant *adExecuteNoRecords* will assure the application that the command does not invoke a Recordset. The constants in Table 7.3 describe how the command is to be executed.

When *adExecuteNoRecords* (0x00000080) is used, it is combined with a Command-Type enumerated constant that describes the type of command that is being executed. You can use adExecuteNoRecords (0x00000080) with either adCmdText (0x0001) or adCmdStoredProc (0x0400) only since all other types of commands should return data by nature.

Table 7.3 The ExecuteOptions Enumerated Constants

VALUE	CONSTANT	DESCRIPTION
−1	adOptionUnspecified	The type of command being sent is not specified.
0x00000010	adAsyncExecute	Executes the command asynchronously.
0x00000020	adAsyncFetch	Any records that are beyond the number of records specified in CacheSize will be fetched asynchronously.
0x00000040	adAsyncFetchNonBlocking	If a row has not been fetched because it is blocked, the current row will move to the position at the end of the file.
0x00000080	adExecuteNoRecords	The executed command is one that does not return rows, so no Recordset will be prepared or returned.

```
<%
# Including the adExecuteNoRecords-constant to prevent a Recordset.
# And including adCmdText to describe the command being issued.
#
$Connection->Execute($dataSQL,
                     undef,
                     adExecuteNoRecords+adCmdText);
%>
```

The constants in Table 7.4 are used to describe what type of command is passed.

Table 7.4 The CommandType Enumerated Constants

VALUE	CONSTANT	DESCRIPTION
0x0008	adCmdUnknown	Default type. The command is unknown.
0x0001	adCmdText	Textual command such as an SQL statement.
0x0002	adCmdTable	Name of a table that ADO generates a SQL query for, to return all rows from.
0x0004	adCmdStoredProc	Stored procedure.
0x0100	adCmdFile	Filepath to a persisted Recordset.
0x0200	adCmdTableDirect	Name of a table whose columns all are returned from the provider.
0x0400	adCmdURLBind	URL to bind.

The following example shows how to describe the type of command that is being executed:

```
<HTML>
<BODY>
<%@Language=PerlScript%>
<!--#INCLUDE VIRTUAL=/ADOPS.INC"-->

<%
# Prepare the ConnectionString with the data source to connect
#
my $connString = "DSN=Budget_system_DSN;UID=Admin;pwd=secret"

# Prepare the SQL statement to delete the record with the ID 12
#
my $dataSQL = "DELETE
               FROM    tableName
               WHERE   ID=12";

# The connection object is instantiated by the ASP Server object
#
$conn = $Server->CreateObject("ADODB.Connection");

# Open the Connection object with the ConnectionString
#
$conn->Open($connString);

# Execute the command, or query, through the connection object and
# let ADO know not to return a Recordset
#
$conn->Execute($dataSQL,
               undef,
               adExecuteNoRecords+adCmdText);

# Close the connection since the query is completed
#
$conn->Close();

# Undefine the connection object
#
undef $conn;
%>

</BODY>
</HTML>
```

In the example, what is undef in the call to Execute() is simply the value of nothing—we need to pass a parameter without value because the constant is the very last parameter in a set of three. In conclusion, the Execute() method is fast because it is the most direct route to the data source, so it is a perfect object to use either to return many populated row sets or to perform single action queries.

Learning the Database Structure

The OpenSchema() method of the Connection object when it is called returns a Recordset object with a rowset that contains schematic information about the underlying database structure in the data store. From this Recordset, certain information such as what tables are in the database, their descriptions, and so forth can be extracted.

```
$conn->OpenSchema(Schema, Criteria, SchemaID);
```

When OpenSchema() has been called and with the Recordset in store, the Count property of the Fields collection within the Recordset is used to automate the loop of the columns. However, in the next case we can safely assume that the schema contains only two columns where both the name and the value of each column are stored in a scalar variable that is outputted at the end of the script.

```
<HTML>
<BODY>

<%@Language=PerlScript%>

<!--#include virtual="/adops.inc"-->

<%
# The connection object is instantiated by the ASP Server object
#
my $conn = $Server->CreateObject("ADODB.Connection");

# The recordset object is instantiated by the ASP Server object
#
my $rst = $Server->CreateObject("ADODB.Recordset");

# The calls to get it started
#
init();

scanForErrors();

loopRows();
%>

<%
############################################################
# Name..........: init
# Parameters....: None
# Description...: Declares and initalizes a string which
#                 is passed in the Open-method of the
#                 Connection object. Next, the OpenSchama-
#                 method of the Connection is called, and
#                 the schematic information is returned
#                 to the Recordset.
############################################################
sub init
{
```

```
    # The connection string that will establish the connection
    #
    my $connString = 'Provider=Microsoft.Jet.OLEDB.4.0;
                        Data Source=C:\nwind.mdb;';

    # Open the connection with the connection string
    #
    $conn->Open($connString);

    # Check and make sure there were no errors that occurred
    #
    scanForErrors();

    # Return the recordset from the OpenSchema-method
    #
    $rst = $conn->OpenSchema(adSchemaTables);

    # Check and make sure there were no errors upon execution
    #
    scanForErrors();
}
%>

<%
##########################################################
# Name.........: loopRows
# Parameters....: None
# Description...: Determines the number of fields
#                 in the Fields-collection. Loops
#                 the Recordset until it reaches
#                 end of file, and stores every
#                 value of each field into a
#                 somewhat formatted string.
#                 Closes the Recordset.
##########################################################
sub loopRows
{
    # Count the number of fields in the Fields-collection
    #
    my $countFields = $rst->Fields->{Count};
    # While EOF is has not been reached
    #
    while (! $rst->{EOF} )
    {

      # For-loop to make sure each field is entered
      #
      for(my $i=0; $i<$countFields; $i++) {
          $output.=$rst->Fields($i)->{Name};
          $output.="="
          $output.=$rst->Fields($i)->{Value};
```

```perl
            $output.='<BR>';
            }

    # Move to the next record in the populated rowset
    #
    $rst->MoveNext;
    }

  # Close the Recordset
  #
  $rst->Close();
}
%>



<%
############################################################
# Name..........: scanForErrors
# Parameters....: None
# Description...: Counts the errors collection to see if
#                 any errors have occured. If so, each
#                 object in the collection is presented
#                 and the keys of each object is stored
#                 in a scalar which later is printed to
#                 the screen.
############################################################
sub scanForErrors
{

    # If any errors were detected, the following routing will log
    # the information on the error
    #
    if($conn->Errors->{Count})
    {
      my $errOutput;

        foreach my $error (Win32::OLE::in($conn->Errors)) {
            foreach my $property (keys %{$error}) {
                $errOutput.=$property.": ";
                $errOutput.=${$error}{$property};
                $errOutput.="<BR>";
                }
            }

        $Response->Write($errOutput);

        exit(1);
    }
}
%>
<%=$output%>
</BODY>
</HTML>
```

It is worthwhile to note that this script will output all available columns that were returned as the schematic information. When the data is dumped to the screen, however, it becomes obvious that the names of the columns are not cryptic. For example, Northwind will output information similar to the following (including more about where the information came from):

```
TABLE_CATALOG=
TABLE_SCHEMA=
TABLE_NAME=Categories
TABLE_TYPE=TABLE
TABLE_GUID=
DESCRIPTION=Categories of Northwind products.
```

This is the actual output from a schema query. What is printed is the name-value pairs of each field separated by a comma. If you want to see only the table names, the following is one way of printing only those:

```
<%
# Display the column with the name "Table_Name"
#
$rst->Fields('TABLE_NAME')->{Value};
%>
```

In the next chapter, many different ways of filtering the data and retrieving the data from the data store will give rise to more ideas on how to extract certain information from a rowset. A number of useful queries that can be used when opening a schema are listed in Table 7.5.

The following example loads the schema values in an array, then prints the results to the screen by looping the name-value pairs of each record set.

```
<HTML>
<BODY
<%@Language=PerlScript%>
<%
# The values of the schematypes to use are defined
#
my @schemas = (22, 30);

# Where to store the output/result
#
my $output;

# The connection object
#
$conn = $Server->CreateObject("ADODB.Connection");

# Open the connection object
#
$conn->Open('Provider=Microsoft.Jet.OLEDB.4.0;
          Data source=D:\northwind.mdb');

# Open the schema of each element in the schemas-array and
# save the results in the output-scalar
```

Table 7.5 Schema Types

VALUE	CONSTANT	DESCRIPTION OF RETURN VALUES
−1	adSchemaProviderSpecific	The provider that has its own schema already defined
0	adSchemaAsserts	The assertions for a catalog
1	adSchemaCatalogs	The attributes for catalogs that can be reached from the DBMS itself
2	adSchemaCharacterSets	The character sets that have been defined
3	adSchemaCollations	The collations in the catalog
4	adSchemaColumns	The columns that are in the tables
11	adSchemaColumnDomainUsage	The columns that are dependent on a domain
12	adSchemaIndexes	The indexes that are in the catalog
13	adSchemaColumnPrivileges	The privileges of columns in the table
14	adSchemaTablePrivileges	The privileges of the tables
15	adSchemaUsagePrivileges	The usage privileges of the objects
16	adSchemaProcedures	The procedures that are available
17	adSchemaSchemata	The schemas
18	adSchemaSQLLanguages	Conformance levels, options, and dialects
19	adSchemaStatistics	The statistics that have been defined
20	adSchemaTables	The tables and views
21	adSchemaTranslations	Character translations
22	adSchemaProviderTypes	The supported data types
23	adSchemaViews	The views
24	adSchemaViewColumnUsage	The columns that viewed tables are dependent on
25	adSchemaViewTableUsage	The tables that viewed tables are dependent on
26	adSchemaProcedureParameters	The parameters and their definitions of the procedures
27	adSchemaForeignKeys	The foreign key columns
28	adSchemaPrimaryKeys	The primary key columns
29	adSchemaProcedureColumns	Definitions of columns returned by procedures
30	adSchemaDBInfoKeywords	Provider-specific keywords

Table 7.5 (Continued)

VALUE	CONSTANT	DESCRIPTION OF RETURN VALUES
31	adSchemaDBInfoLiters	Provider-specific literals used in textual commands
32	adSchemaCubes	Available cubes in a schema or catalog
33	adSchemaDimensions	The dimensions of a cube
34	adSchemaHierarchies	The hierarchies of a dimension
35	adSchemaLevels	The levels of a dimension
36	adSchemaMeasures	The available measures
37	adSchemaProperties	The properties for each level
38	adSchemaMembers	The available members
39	adSchemaTrustees	Information about the trustees

```perl
#
foreach $querySchema (@schemas) {
    printrows( $conn->OpenSchema($querySchema) );
    }

# Print the output from the query to the screen
#
$Response->Write( $output );
%>

<%
##########################################################
# Name:        printrows
# Parameters:  A Recordset
# Description: Stores the data in the name-value pairs of
#              the Recordset in the output-variable
##########################################################
sub printrows
{

    # Get the object
    #
    my ($param) = shift;

    # If the value is defined
    #
    if( $param ) {
        # Loop until End of File
        #
        while(! $param->{EOF} ) {

            # Loop every field object in the fields-collection
            #
            foreach $fld (Win32::OLE::in($param->Fields)){
```

```
                    $output.=$fld->{Name};
                    $output.="=";
                    $output.=$fld->{Value};
                    $output.= "<BR>";
                    }

            # Move to the next record
            #
            $param->Movenext();
            }
        }
    }
%>
```

A number of constraints are available for the call to OpenSchema( ). A constraint restricts the data, and either a single constraint or an array of constraints may be applied when calling OpenSchema( ) (Table 7.6).

Inserting New Records

The SQL Insert clause will add a new row to the specified database table. The Connection object is the ideal object for one-time action operations that are not supposed to return any results. However, remember to use *adExecuteNoRecords* (0x00000080), because in certain environments it can improve the performance of the application.

In the following example, the table into which a row is supposed to be inserted has the columns firstname, lastname, and age. The first two columns take character-based input and the last is an integer column.

```
<%@Language=PerlScript%>
<%
# Declare the constant that will prevent a Recordset
```

Table 7.6 Criteria Constraints for Schema Types

VALUE	CONSTANT	RETURN VALUES
5	adSchemaCheckConstraints	The check constraints
6	adSchemaConstraintColumnUsage	Assertions and columns used by the following constraints: referential, unique, and check
7	adSchemaContraintTableUsage	The same criteria as the one above, but associated with tables instead of columns
8	adSchemaKeyColumnUsage	The columns constrained as keys
9	adSchemaReferentialConstraints	The referential constraints
10	adSchemaTableConstraints	The table constraints

```
#
use constant adExecuteNoRecords => 0x00000080;

# Prepare the SQL statement to use for the new row
#
my $strSQL = (<<EOF);
    INSERT INTO table
                    FIELDS (firstname, lastname, age)
                    VALUES ('Bob', 'Smith', 12)
EOF

# Create the Connection
#
$conn = $Server->CreateObject("ADODB.Connection");

# Open the database
#
$conn->Open('Provider=Microsoft.Jet.OLEDB.4.0;
            Data Source=C:\Friends.mdb;');

# Execute the query
#
$conn->Execute($strSQL, undef, adExecuteNoRecords+adCmdText);

# Close the connection
#
$conn->Close();

# Undefine the connection
#
undef $conn;
%>
```

The rule regarding text-based entries is the same when inserting data as it is when matching data—the value of text fields must be contained within single quotes while numeric values do not require this treatment. If a single quote is missed, no record will be inserted. If the error trapping routine that we saw earlier is used, this will be easily fixed since the error is signaled to the application and describes what was done correctly.

Creating Database Tables

The Create clause creates a new database object in the database that the connection is established with, and in our case a new table in the database. The name of the new table is specified directly after the clause Create Table. After the table is named, two columns are appended. The first column is text based and takes 40 characters, and the second is numeric and takes an integer value.

```
<%@Language=PerlScript%>
<%
# Prepare not to return a recordset
#
use constant adExecuteNoRecords => 0x00000080;
```

```
# Prepare the SQL statement
#
my $strSQL = (<<EOF);
    CREATE TABLE
                myNewTable (
                            city char(40),
                            year int
                            );
EOF

# Create the connection object
#
$conn = $Server->CreateObject("ADODB.Connection");
# Open the database
#
$conn->Open(`Provider=Microsoft.Jet.OLEDB.4.0;
          Data Source=C:\Friends.mdb;');

# Execute the SQL
#
$conn->Execute($strSQL, undef, adExecuteNoRecords+adCmdText);

# Close the connection
#
$conn->Close();
%>
```

Since there are many different databases, there are also different data types and ranges used with each database. Table 7.7 displays a common range for some of these values to give an idea of what type of data they can hold. Be advised, however, that the local database documentation for your system is always the best and most reliable source—Table 7.7 is a generic table.

Table 7.7 gives a general idea of the range of different integer types; from there on it is up to the DBMS where the range begins and ends.

Table 7.7 Some Database Types and Their Generic Values

SYNTAX	TYPE	DESCRIPTION
char(*n*)	character	A string of *n* characters
c*n*	character	A string of *n* characters
varchar(*n*)	character	A string of *n* characters
text(*n*)	character	A string of *n* characters
tinyint	1-byte integer	−128 to +127
smallint	2-byte integer	−32,768 to 32,767
integer	4-byte integer	−2,147,483,648 to +2,147,483,647

Deleting Database Tables

In the previous section, a new database object—a table—was created. The SQL Drop clause will drop (delete) a database object from its source. Consequently, to remove the recently created table, the following code would be used:

```
$Connection->Execute("DROP TABLE myNewTable",
                     undef,
                     adExecuteNoRecords+adCmdText);
```

Database Transactions

An established database connection can be handled as a transaction. A transaction is initiated by calling the BeginTrans() method of the Connection object. You can then make a number of changes to the database and have the ability to either save the changes as final or cancel all changes made within the transaction.

When a series of changes have been made to the database, you can call CommitTrans, which will save your changes as final and end the transaction. In some instances, it may also start a new transaction. On the other hand, should you need to cancel any changes, you call the RollbackTrans method, which will cancel any changes made during the transaction and then end the transaction. Calling this method may also result in initiation of a new transaction.

Characterizing the transaction, the Properties collection of the Connection object must include the Transaction DDL property, or else transactions are not supported by the provider. Whether or not a method call initiates a new transaction is defined in the Attributes property of the Connection object. It can be adXactCommitRetaining (131072), which means that calling CommitTrans starts a new transaction, or it can be adXactAbortRetaining (262144), which starts a new transaction when RollbackTrans is called. The default value for this property is 0. In addition, transactions can be nested. The BeginTrans() method will return a value that indicates the level of nesting. Not all providers support this, but a value of 1 indicates that it is a top-level transaction, a value of 2 indicates that it is the second level, 3 indicates the third level, and so on. Any method calls only affect the transaction you are currently in.

Overview: The Connection

Table 7.8 displays the properties, methods, and collections of the Connection object.

Summary

In this chapter we have discussed database programming in ADO. The ADO Connection object is used to establish a connection to a relational database, and when the connection has been established, it is open to run commands at the database and

Table 7.8 The Connection Object

	DESCRIPTION
Collection	
Errors	Error objects representing errors that occurred from the most recent action.
Properties	Property objects defining the properties of the connection.
Method	
BeginTrans	Begins a new transaction.
CommitTrans	Saves changes made during the transaction, then ends the transaction.
RollbackTrans	Cancels changes made during the transaction, then ends the transaction.
Cancel	Cancels an asynchronous call to Open or Execute.
Close	Closes the Connection object and objects associated with it.
Execute ([CommandText], [Affect Enum], [Options])	Executes one of several types of commands such as SQL query, stored procedure, Command object, URL, and so forth (see beginning of chapter). Returns a Recordset unless specified (see Performance Tweaking).
Open ([ConnString], [User Id] [Password] [ConnectOptionEnum])	Opens a new connection (see beginning of chapter).
OpenSchema (schema, [criteria], [schemaid])	Executes a query for schematic information that is returned from the data source (see Learning the Database Structure).
Property	
Attributes	Attributes of the connection.
CommandTimeout	Number of seconds before a command returns an error.
ConnectionString	String used to connect to the data source.
ConnectionTimeout	Number of seconds before an Open call returns an error.
CursorLocation	Location of cursor. A Recordset caused by the connection inherits this setting.
DefaultDatabase	Default database for the connection.
IsolationLevel	Level of isolation for a transaction.

Table 7.8 (Continued)

	DESCRIPTION
Mode	Permissions for modifying data in the connection.
Provider	Name of the provider.
State	State of the connection.
Version	Version of ADO.

retrieve data about the database objects that make up the database. The Connection object rides on its ability to run commands, so it is extremely important to know how to describe the commands programatically. For example, a stored procedure, table name, or SQL query that is not defined by command type before it is run will result in a series of tests where the command will be tested as each type of command until it is executed successfully. Furthermore, unless defined otherwise, each query that is run at the database results in a Recordset object being prepared and returned. With all this in mind, it is very important to be descriptive when running commands through the Connection object.

Up next is the heart of ADO: the content-rich Recordset object.

## CHAPTER 8

The Heart of ADO

When a database server is queried to send the client data, a set of rows and columns is returned from the server. The rows and columns are called a *rowset*, and this rowset is essentially the heart of the Recordset object. A great object for storing structured data, the Recordset provides its native methods and properties regardless of whether a Connection object to an existing data store is open. It is the perfect object for storing both permanent and temporary data in everything from simple rowsets up to advanced hierarchical rowsets of nested Recordsets, on everything from floppy disks to ASP objects.

Introduction to the Recordset

A Recordset contains not only the rowset, but also a number of properties that define how the rowset and the underlying data store can be worked with in terms of update-ability and navigation. A Recordset does not have to contain a rowset, but instead the rowset can be built programmatically and hierarchical structures can be defined by using a special language called the Shape language.

The Syntax

Like the Connection object, the Recordset is created in Active Server Pages by using the CreateObject() method of the Server object:

```
<%
$rst = $Server->CreateObject("ADODB.Recordset");
%>
```

After the instance of the Recordset has been created, the Open() method is called to establish the connection. At that point, the call will go out either with or without parameters. If parameters are used, they must be passed in the order defined in Table 8.1.

The syntax for the Open() method, with all parameters included, is as follows:

```
$rst->Open( Source, ActiveConnection, CursorType, LockType,
Options )
```

The Open() method does not directly open the Recordset object and provide the magic functionality for navigation and manipulation of the contained records in the rowset. Instead it opens a cursor that enables and defines the navigation and manipulation of the rowset. The following sections discuss the cursor and the locktype of the Recordset.

Perfecting the Recordset

As seen in the call with all parameters to the Open() method, there are many properties that define the Recordset. The two most important, however, are the CursorType and LockType properties, because these control to what extent the navigation and manipulation of the records is permitted. It is most necessary to know these properties when it comes to opening the right cursor for the right needs.

The Cursor Type Property

The *cursor* is a software device that controls how the records can be traversed and how up to date the records are in relation to the underlying data store. In memory, the device keeps track of the current record and the position of the next record to return. Furthermore, the cursor property defines how up to date the records are by specifying how the records are viewed.

Table 8.1 The Parameters of the Recordset's Open() Method

NAME	DESCRIPTION
Source	The command issued at the data source; a Command object, SQL statement, table name, stored procedure, URL, or the name of a file or Stream object of which either contains a persisted Recordset
ActiveConnection	Either a connection string to a data provider or a Connection object
CursorType	The type of cursor used for navigating the Recordset
LockType	The type of lock applied to updateability of the Recordset
Options	CommandTypeEnum and/or ExecuteOptionsEnum (see Chapter 7)

The Right Type of Cursor

Choose a cursor that does not exceed the needs of the application. For example, an application that moves only forward through the record set should use a forward-only cursor, and an application that does not require the data to be up to date should use a cursor that promotes static data. Cursor types are detailed in Table 8.2.

The forward-only cursor is the default cursor. With both the forward-only and static cursors, no changes made to the records by other users are visible. The forward-only cursor is the fastest cursor because it requires only one position for the next record in memory as it only navigates in one direction. The apparent trade-off is the navigation, and, as a side effect, the inability to count the number of records with the Record-Count property.

The key set cursor will only make changes to the records visible and will be assigned an accurate RecordCount by some, but not all, providers. However, additions are not recognized, and deletions are only recognized when trying to access a deleted record. The dynamic cursor will support all types of navigation and provide an accurate RecordCount. Furthermore, it is fully up to date. The downside is that it is the slowest cursor.

When the type of cursor has been chosen, it can be set either with a call to the Open method or as a property. It cannot, however, be set after the Recordset has been opened.

```
<%@Language=PerlScript%>
<%
...
# Define some constants
...
```

Table 8.2 The CursorTypes

VALUE	CONSTANT	DESCRIPTION
0	adOpenForwardOnly	Forward-only navigation. No alterations, additions, or deletions in the underlying data store are made visible.
1	adOpenKeyset	Full navigation. Alterations of records are visible, deletions will not be able to be accessed, and additions are not visible. Supports bookmarks.
2	adOpenDynamic	Provides the most current information. However, this is also the slowest cursor because all changes are visible. Bookmarks are supported by the provider.
3	adOpenStatic	Full navigation. No changes, additions, or deletions in the underlying data store are visible.

```
# Create the Recordset object
#
$rst = $Server->CreateObject("ADODB.recordset");

# Set the cursortype
#
$rst->{CursorType} = adOpenKeySet;

...
# Do some more stuff
...

# Open the Recordset
#
$rst->Open();
%>
```

Alternatively, pass it as a parameter:

```
<%
$rst->Open(query, connection, adOpenForwardOnly, locktype);
%>
```

On a final note, every provider may not support every listed CursorType, and in those cases the CursorType will be set to the default. It is always worth exploring a little further what features the existing providers support.

The LockType Property

The LockType defines what types of alterations may be performed on the data in the records within the Recordset. There are several types of locks, and each has its special attributes (Table 8.3).

The Right Type of Lock

Is your data static or constantly updated? How many clients are expected to update the database? Do you want the ability to update the records? How many records are

Table 8.3 LockTypes

VALUE	CONSTANT	DESCRIPTION
1	adLockReadOnly	Default. Allows read-only access to the data. No updates are possible.
2	adLockPessimistic	Locks the affected record immediately upon editing the record.
3	adLockOptimistic	Locks the affected record when the Update() method is called.
4	adLockBatchOptimistic	Batch optimistic locking is required for batch-update mode.

updated at a time? These are some of the questions that must be answered before the LockType is set on the Recordset.

In cases where you are not going to be updating records, the default read-only Lock-Type is the best. However, if you do intend to update, then most providers support the Optimistic LockType. As mentioned, the optimistic lock will lock when the Update() method is called, while a pessimistic lock will safeguard data from the second the editing begins. When updating a group of records, use batch optimistic locking if supported by the data provider.

The LockType property can be set in the call to the Open() method or simply as a property. However, properties must be set before Open() is called.

```
<%@Language=PerlScript%>
<%
...
# Define some constants
...

# Create the Recordset object
#
$rst = $Server->CreateObject("ADODB.Recordset");

# Set the locktype
#
$rst->{LockType} = AdLockOptimistic;

...
# Do some more stuff
...

# Open the Recordset
#
$rst->Open();
%>
```

Or, alternatively:

```
$rst->Open(query, connection, adOpenForwardOnly, locktype);
```

Rows and Columns

Each record in the rowset has its own special properties and methods, which can be accessed through the Fields collection.

A column is represented by a Field object contained in the Fields collection (Figure 8.1). Through the Fields collection, you access the records that were returned from the database. Single objects can be accessed either by name or by index. The name is the same name the object has in the underlying data source, and the index is an integer value starting at 0.

Table 8.4 shows the properties of the Field object. To illustrate the properties, return either the name property or the value property of the first fictitious field, named country.

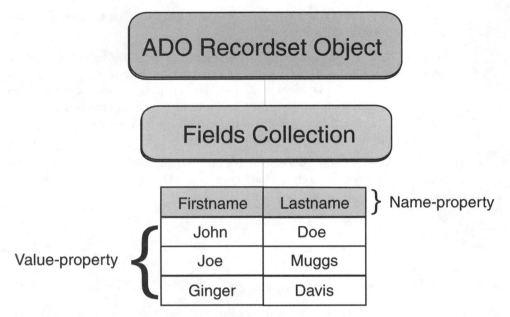

Figure 8.1 Field objects in the Fields collection.

```
<%
# Get the value-property of a field by the index of the field
# object
#
$valueOfField = $Recordset->Fields(0)->{Value};
%>

<%
# Get it by the keyname of the column
#
```

Table 8.4 The Properties of the Field Object

PROPERTY	DESCRIPTION
Value	Value of the column of data that is in the field
Name	Name of the column of data that is in the field
Type	DataTypeEnum constant that defines the type of data
Precision	Degree of precision for numeric values
NumericScale	Scale of numeric values
DefinedSize	Declared size of the field
ActualSize	Size of data in the declared field
OriginalValue	Restores the field to the value it had before it was modified
Underlying Value	Restores the field to the value in the data source

```
$valueOfField = $Recordset->Fields("country")->{Value};
%>

<%
# Get the name-property of a field-object
#
$nameOfField = $Recordset->Fields(0)->{Name};
%>
```

Working with binary data in a database, such as images in SQL server or large text values, there are two methods of the Field object that are directly responsible for reading and writing (Table 8.5).

How to Create the Recordset

There are three possible ways of creating a record set.

1. A Connection object executes a query and returns a default Recordset with an open cursor. For example:

```
$Rst = $Conn->Execute("SELECT Firstname FROM Friends");
```

2. A Command object executes and returns a default Recordset with an open cursor. For example:

```
$Rst = $cmd->Execute();
```

3. A Recordset is explicitly created.

There are four different ways to open a Recordset. However, if not explicitly designated, the Recordset will be a default set object. So, let's look at what makes the default Recordsets different.

The Everyday Recordset

When a Recordset is returned from the Connection or Command object, either object executes and returns a default Recordset with an open cursor.

Table 8.6 shows the methods for navigating the Recordset. The default record set allows the cursor to move forward only in the rowset, and the data cannot be updated. On the bright side, when it comes to displaying data in a single loop, this type of Recordset offers state-of-the-art performance.

Table 8.5 Field Object's Methods for Working with Binary or Long Text Data

METHODS	DESCRIPTION
AppendChunk(*data*)	Appends *data* to the field
GetChunk(*byte*)	Gets specified number of bytes from the field

Table 8.6 Methods for Navigating the Recordset

METHOD	DESCRIPTION
Move(n, bookmark)	Move *n* records where *n* is a positive or negative integer. On a forward-only cursor, backward movement works within the locally cached records. Use a bookmark to set the starting point of the number of records to move if the current record is not desirable.
MoveFirst()	Move to the first row in the Recordset.
MoveLast()	Move to the last row in the Recordset.
MoveNext()	Move one row forward in the Recordset.
MovePrevious()	Move one row backward in the Recordset.

```
<%@Language=PerlScript%>
<%
# Create the SQL statement
#
my $sqlStmnt = 'SELECT Firstname, Lastname FROM tablename';

# Create the connectionstring
#
my $connString = 'Provider=Microsoft.Jet.OLEDB.4.0;
                  Data Source=C:\nwind.mdb;';

# Create the connection object
#
my $Connection = $Server->CreateObject('ADODB.Connection');

# Open the connection object
#
$Connection->Open($connString);

# Execute the query and get the Recordset
#
my $Recordset = $Connection->Execute($sqlStmnt);

# While the Recordset is not at End of File
# Print the values of the fields "Firstname" and "Lastname"
# Then move to the next record
#
while ( ! $Recordset->{EOF} )
{
%>
        <%=$Recordset->Fields('Firstname')->{Value}%>
        <%=$Recordset->Fields('Lastname')->{Value}%>
<%
$Recordset->MoveNext();
}
```

```
# Close the Recordset
#
$Recordset->Close();

# Close the connection
#
$Connection->Close();

# Undefine the Recordset
#
undef $Recordset;

# Undefine the connection
#
undef $Connection;
%>
```

When looping a Recordset, the Beginning of File (BOF) and End of File (EOF) properties (Table 8.7) are used to make sure the loop does not go out of range and return an error.

A Better Recordset

In contrast to the result of an operation, the next example will explicitly open a Recordset. When you want a Recordset that you can move in directions other than forward and perform updates against, then you need to create it explicitly. This is not much different from the previous example except that the CursorType and LockType are defined in the Open() method or set as properties before Open() is called.

```
<%@Language=PerlScript%>
<%
# Create the SQL statement
#
my $rsSource = "SELECT Firstname, Lastname FROM tablename";

# Create the connectionstring
#
my $rsActiveConn = 'Provider=Microsoft.Jet.OLEDB.4.0;
                    Data Source=C:\nwind.mdb;';


# Create the Recordset object
#
$rst  = $Server->CreateObject ("ADODB.Recordset");
```

Table 8.7 The Properties for Deleting the Beginning and End of File

PROPERTY	DESCRIPTION
BOF	Position before the first row in the Recordset
EOF	Position after the last record

```
# Open the Recordset with a dynamic cursor,
# pessimistic locking, and the CommandType
# as a texual command
#
$rst->Open($rsSource,
        $rsActiveConn,
        adOpenDynamic,
        adLockPessimistic,
        adCmdText);

# The familiar while-loop
#
while (! $rst->{EOF} )
{
%>
    <%=$rst->Fields("Firstname")->{Value}%>
    <%=$rst->Fields("Lastname")->{Value}%>
    <BR>
<%
    $Rst->MoveNext;
}

# Close the Recordset
#
$rst->Close();

# Undefine the Recordset
#
undef $rst;
%>
```

When multiple Recordsets returned from a single data store are used, it is helpful to create a Connection object instead of sending a connection string for each Recordset, thus preventing an excess of Connection objects.

Examples of How To . . .

The following sections show various examples covering areas such as paging a Recordset, tweaking performance, converting PerlScripts to Perl, and using the properties and methods of the Recordset object.

Escape the While Loop and Catch Up on Speed

There is a faster way of presenting all the retrieved records. Until now, the applications have looped the Recordset until it signaled that it had reached the end of file. By that time, the entire contents of the Recordset had had plenty of time to be outputted. However, because it is very common to present data this way, there is an alternative method for formatting the layout and blasting the records to the screen. It does not require a loop, and it does not require a single call to Movenext. The only thing we need to do is to call the GetString() method, which will then prearrange all of the records and return the formatted string—provided that we send the right arguments in our parameters.

```
$Recordset->GetString ( StringFormat,
                        NumRows,
                        ColumnDelimiter,
                        RowDelimiter,
                        NullExpr );
```

The adClipString constant is used to format the string. The number of rows is left undefined because by default all the records returned to the open Recordset are included. The column delimiter and row delimiter will contain the white space, text, or the HTML tags that will be used to separate the fields from the database and each row from the database in the layout in the resulting string.

The following example will separate columns by tab (\t) and records by new line (\n). When the string has been prepared, it is saved to a text file on the local disk.

```
<%@Language=PerlScript%>

<!--#INCLUDE VIRTUAL="/ADOPS.INC"-->

<%
# Define the SQL statement
#
my $rsSource = "SELECT Firstname, Lastname FROM tablename";

# Define the connectionstring
#
my $rsActiveConn = 'Provider=Microsoft.Jet.OLEDB.4.0;
                    Data Source=C:\nwind.mdb;';


# Define the filepath to store the result
#
my $filepath = $Server->MapPath("/PSdatabase.txt");

# Create the Recordset object
#
my $RS = $Server->CreateObject("ADODB.Recordset");

# Open the Recordset object
#
$RS->Open( $rsSource,
           $rsActiveConn,
           adOpenForwardOnly,
           adLockReadOnly,
           adCmdText );
# Call GetString to return the prepared string
#
my $String = $RS->GetString(adClipString, undef, "\t", "\n");
```

```
# Open a file in the specified path
#
open (F, ">$filepath");

# Print the value of $String to the filehandle
#
print F $String;

# Close the filehandle
#
close (F);

# Close the Recordset
#
$RS->Close();
%>
```

As we will see, instead of the full contents of the rowset being outputted to either the screen or a file, the records can be divided into pages, and we can page through the Recordset by following links to the other pages. This allows a more intuitive way of moving between the records in the set. All this is made possible only by setting a number of properties. For each page, we define the number of records that we want displayed, and of course the links to the other pages of the Recordset will be provided.

Splitting the Recordset into Book Pages

Again, we will avoid using a while loop to display our records. And although several records are retrieved, the need for Movenext() is eliminated as the Recordset is divided into pages by the GetRows() method (Table 8.8).

Table 8.9 shows the properties used when paging a Recordset. The following example divides the Recordset into a series of logical pages, and presents a simple HTML interface for choosing what page to display.

```
<%@Language=PerlScript%>
<HTML>
<HEAD>
<TITLE> Paging Recordsets Using the GetRows-method </TITLE>
</HEAD>
<BODY BGCOLOR="WHITE" TEXT="BLACK">
<!--#INCLUDE VIRTUAL="/ADOPS.INC"-->
<TABLE WIDTH="100%" BORDER="1" CELLSPACING="0" CELLPADDING="2">

<%
# Create a connection object
#
my $conn = $Server->CreateObject("ADODB.Connection");

# Create a Recordset object
#
my $Rset = $Server->CreateObject("ADODB.Recordset");
```

Table 8.8   The GetRows( ) Method

DESCRIPTION
The GetRows( ) method will get a number of rows from the Recordset object. The records are returned in a two-dimensional array that represents the fields of the Recordset. Unless the number of rows is specified, the default is adGetRowsRest (−1), which returns the number of records from the starting point, which defaults to the current position. However, a bookmark can be used. A certain field, or an array with specified fields, can be returned. If omitted, all fields are returned.

PARAMETERS
Number of rows to return (optional). A bookmark or a BookmarkEnum of adBookmarkCurrent (value:−1; meaning: the current record), adBookmarkFirst (value: 1; meaning: the first record), or adBookmarkLast (value: 2; meaning: the last record) to start fetching from (optional), fields to fetch (optional).

RETURN VALUE
A 2-dimensional array. To divide a Recordset into pages, there are a number of properties that need to be set. First, the *CursorLocation* property must be set to adUseClient when using MS Access. As a result, all records will be fetched from the database in one single trip, then cached and accessed locally. However, more powerful database servers such as SQL Server and Oracle normally permit a server-side cursor location. Next, the properties that define the size of each page, the current page, and the results in number of pages must be read and written.

```
# Declare a variable where to store the results
#
my $output;
# Get the value of the querystring Page-variable
#
my $queryString = $Request->QueryString("Page")->Item();

# If querystring is undefined, set it equal to 1
#
$queryString=1 if (! $queryString );

# Call main
#
```

Table 8.9   The Properties Used When Paging a Recordset

PROPERTY	DESCRIPTION
PageSize	Set this property to the number of records that should fit on each logical page in the Recordset.
AbsolutePage	Set this property to the page that will be displayed.
PageCount	Read this property for the number of logical pages in the Recordset.

```perl
main($queryString);
%>

<%
###########################################################
# Name.........: main
# Parameters....: The logical page to display
# Description...: Controlling subroutine which calls init
#                 to fetch the logical page to display,
#                 and then calls printRows to display the
#                 retrieved records.
###########################################################
sub main
{

    # Get the pagenumber, logical page, to show
    #
    my $pageToShow = shift;

    # Initialize the Recordset
    #
    init($pageToShow);

    # Print the rows
    #
    printRows();
}
%>

<%
###########################################################
# Name.........: init
# Parameters....: The logical page to display
# Description...: Opens the Recordset, calls scanForErrors
#                 and printHeaders, sets the position
#                 of the cursor to the logical page that
#                 should be displayed.
###########################################################
sub init
{
    # Get the page to show
    #
    my $requestedPage = shift;

    # The connectionstring
    #
    my $dsn = 'nwind';

    # The number of records to display per logical page
    #
    my $rowsPerPage = 15;

    # The query to execute to get the Recordset
    #
```

```perl
    my $query = (<<EOF);
SELECT ProductID,
    ProductName,
    UnitPrice,
    UnitsInStock
FROM Products
EOF

    # Open the connection
    #
    $conn->Open($dsn);

    # Set the cursorlocation of the Recordset to client
    # Set both pagesize and cachesize to 15
    #
    $Rset->{CursorLocation} = 3;
    $Rset->{PageSize} = $rowsPerPage;
    $Rset->{CacheSize} = $rowsPerPage;

    # Open the Recordset
    #
    $Rset->Open($query, $conn, 3, 1, 0x0001);

    # Check for errors
    #
    scanForErrors();

    # Print the column-names by the fieldnames
    #
    printHeaders();

    # Set the logical page
    #
    $Rset->{AbsolutePage} = $requestedPage;
    }
%>

<%
############################################################
# Name..........: printHeaders
# Parameters....: None
# Description...: Counts the number of fields and sets the
#                 cellwidth per tablecell in percentage
#                 according to the calculated value. Loops
#                 each field and concatenates it to $output
############################################################
sub printHeaders
{
    # Estimate a cellwidth for the HTML table
    my $cellWidth = ( 100/$Rset->Fields->{Count} );


    # The first row in the HTML-table
    #
```

```perl
    $output.='<TR>';
    # Foreach field, put the name of the field in a cell
    #
    for(my $i=0; $i<$Rset->Fields->{Count}; $i++) {
        $output.='<TD WIDTH="';
        $output.=$cellWidth;
        $output.='%">';
        $output.=$Rset->Fields($i)->{Name};
        $output.='</TD>';
        }

    # Close the first table row
    #
    $output.='</TR>';
}
%>

<%
############################################################
# Name..........: printRows
# Parameters....: None
# Description...: Counts the number of fields and sets
#                 cellwidth per tablecell in percentage
#                 according to the calculated value.
#                 Loops each field and outputs the
#                 fieldnames as tableheaders.
############################################################
sub printRows
{
    # Get the rows from the resulting records
    #
    my $rowSet = $Rset->GetRows();

    # Loop the returns array
    #
    for($i=0; $i<$Rset->{PageSize}; $i++) {
        # Begin a new HTML-row
        #
        $output.='<TR>';

          # Get the values of each field in a cell each
          #
          for($j=0; $j<$Rset->Fields->{Count}; $j++) {
              $output.='<TD>';
              $output.=$$rowSet[$j][$i];
              $output.='</TD>';
              }

        # Close the HTML-rot
        #
        $output.='</TR>';
        }
```

```
}
%>

<%
############################################################
# Name..........: scanForErrors
# Parameters....: None
# Description...: Counts the errors collection to see if
#                 any errors have occurred. If so, each
#                 object in the collection is presented
#                 and the keys of each object are stored
#                 in a scalar which later is printed to
#                 the screen.
#
############################################################
sub scanForErrors
{
    # If there is an error object in the Errors-collection
    #
    if($conn->Errors->{Count})
    {
      # Declare a variable to store the output
      #
      my $errOutput;

        # Loop the errors-collection
        #
        foreach my $error (Win32::OLE::in($conn->Errors)) {

          # Get all properties of the error-object
          #
          foreach my $property (keys %{$error}) {
            $errOutput.=$property.": ";
            $errOutput.=${$error} {$property};
            $errOutput.="<BR>";
            }
            }

        # Print the error output
        #
        $Response->Write($errOutput);

        # Exit the script
        #
        exit(1);
        }
    }
    %>

    <%=$output%>
    </TABLE>

    <CENTER>
```

```
      <FONT SIZE="+1">
      <%
        # Output a link for each logical page
        #
        for(1..$Rset->{PageCount}) {
      %>

        <A HREF="PagingRecordset.asp?Page=<%=$_%>"><%=$_%></A>

      <%
        }
      %>

      </FONT>
     </CENTER>
    </BODY>
    </HTML>
```

The properties set for paging a Recordset are used only to define the actual size of the pages. In detail, the PageSize property is told how many records should fit on each page. When this value has been set, the number of records is divided by the PageSize property to set a PageCount value. The PageCount simply states how many logical pages there are in the Recordset. With the query string, the page number of the records to display is passed. This will be known as the logical page, and setting the page number in the Absolute Page property causes the cursor to make the first record in the logical page its current record.

A caveat with using GetRows and the paging properties is that a call to GetRows will invalidate the AbsolutePosition property and set it to –3. Because the example can display only one page at a time, this is not a problem. Furthermore, an Internet solution would require Dynamic HTML, which hides and shows the layers on the screen, and for efficiency even such an application would load all records at once and divide into layers. Very large databases tend not to be divided into logical pages collected on one page (especially not on the Internet, as it would become slow), but instead let the user click on the number of the page to show. In such cases, the most efficient database servers support the server-side cursor, thus preventing it from storing all the records locally.

Using GetRows with CacheSize

In many cases, fetching data from the server becomes costly in terms of performance. A major reason for this is that ADO by default fetches records one at a time from the data store. Instead of allowing this, use the CacheSize property when retrieving data. CacheSize controls how many records are fetched each time the data store is accessed, and then locally caches that number of records.

```
<%
$rst->{CacheSize} = 20;
%>
```

By applying a CacheSize greater than the default setting 1, you can make some serious improvement in the application. For example, retrieving 100 records from a database requires 100 round trips to the database server. However, if the cache size value is changed to 20, only 5 round trips to the server are necessary for all the records to be displayed. The result is a greatly decreased pressure on the server.

The catch with using CacheSize is that you need to test different values on the type of database server that is being used. This is because each server has an undetermined cache size that works best on its current machine. In short, there is no universal CacheSize value that will improve performance on all database servers, but if you try different values, you will quickly get everything you need for the best possible performance of the ADO application.

Searching for a Record

Whenever you need to match a column with a value, the Find() method is a prominent solution. On the one hand, it is very simple, and it matches only one record at a time. The record specified by the criteria will be set as the current record for the cursor to display. On the other hand, the limitation is that this method is designed to work with only one record at a time.

```
<%@Language=PerlScript%>
<%
# Create a connection object
#
$conn = $Server->CreateObject("ADODB.Connection");

# Create a Recordset object
#
$rst = $Server->CreateObject("ADODB.Recordset");
...
# Set the active connection of the Recordset to the connection object
#
$rst->{ActiveConnection} = $conn;

# Set the source of the command to execute to some tablename
#
$rst->{Source} = "tablename";

# Open the Recordset
#
$rst->Open();

# Find the record with the ID-number 2 in the rowset
#
$rst->Find("ID = 2");
%>
```

What the Find() method essentially does is alert the programmer to define a select where query on the row set that has already been returned and then set the cursor's position at the result. For matching groups of data, the Recordset should be filtered by utilizing the Filter property, which also uses an inline select where query when filtering out the group of records requested.

Features You May Access

When a rowset is made available through the Recordset object, the CursorType and LockType specify what permissions for altering and navigating the rowset are available. The available types may vary from provider to provider because although ADO was meant to be a universal interface, the provider may prevent some functions. There is a method, however, for determining the functionality (Table 8.10). The Supports() method will return true(1) or false(0) whether a specified function given by the constants in Table 8.10 is supported by the provider. The Recordset must consequently have a cursor before functionality can be checked—it must have been opened.

```
<%@Language=PerlScript%>

<!--#include virtual="/ADOPS.INC"-->

<%
# Create the Recordset object
#
my $rst = $Server->CreateObject("ADODB.Recordset");
```

Table 8.10 Constants for Determining Supported Functionality

VALUE	CONSTANT	DESCRIPTION
0x1000400	adAddNew	Supports the AddNew() method.
0x00004000	adApproxPosition	Supports AbsolutePosition and AbsolutePage properties.
0x00002000	adBookmark	Supports bookmarks.
0x0100800	adDelete	Supports the Delete() method.
0x00080000	adFind	Supports the Find() method.
0x00000100	adHoldRecords	
0x0080000	adIndex	Supports the Index property.
0x200	adMovePrevious	Supports MoveFirst and MovePrevious and Move or GetRows for backward movement.
0x00040000	adNotify	The data provider supports notification and so may support the Recordset events.
0x00020000	adResynch	Supports the Resynch() method.
0x200000	adSeek	Supports the Seek() method.
0x1008000	adUpdate	Supports the Update() method.
0x00010000	adUpdateBatch	Supports batch processing by Update-Batch() and CancelBatch() methods.

```
# Open the Recordset object
#
$rst->Open("Name", "PersonDB", adOpenDynamic,
adLockOptimistic);

# If the Recordset supports updating of its rowset, then do something
#
if ( $rst->Supports(adUpdate) ) {
   doSomething();
   }

   # Otherwise, kindly notify the lack of updateability
   #
   else {
%>
   Do not have the permissions to update the rowset
<%
   }
%>
```

A New Group of Records with Filter

Previously the Find() method was presented as a solution for finding individual records. When a large group of records must be found, the Filter property fits the bill.

The Filter property is made for finding a certain group of records within the rowset. It simply will force specification of all records matching the criteria in the method call as the visible rowset to the cursor.

For example, filtering the rowset according to the query State="FL" would alter the current cursor to display only those records that have FL in their State fields. When you are finished looking through those records and ready to restore the Recordset to its original state, you can set the filter *adFilterNone* as the current query without destroying the original rowset.

```
<%@ Language=PerlScript %>
<%
...
# Filter the rows to display only those where the state column is
# 'FL' and nothing else
#
$rst->{Filter} = "State='FL'";
...
%>
```

Three more constants for manageability may be applied to the Filter property. *adFilter-PendingRecords* makes visible the records altered within your Recordset prior to a batch update call. *adFilterAffectedRecords* makes visible the records affected by the last Delete(), Resync(), UpdateBatch(), or CancelBatch() call. *adFilterFetchedRecords* displays the records in the cache memory.

Ordering the Records

The Sort property enables the Recordset to be sorted in either ascending or descending order. To use it, set the cursor to *adUseClient*, then set the value of sort to the field name(s) and how you want it sorted:

```
<%@Language=PerlScript%>
<%
# Create the Recordset object
#
$rst = $Server->CreateObject("ADODB.Recordset");

# Set the cursorlocation to use a client-side cursor
#
$rst->{CursorLocation} = adUseClient;

# Open the Recordset
#
$rst->Open("Name", "PersonDB");

# The names of two columns in the rowset
#
$FieldA = "Firstname";
$FieldB = "Lastname";

# Sort the Recordset in ascending order by the $fieldA column
#
$rst->{Sort} = "$FieldA ASC";
%>
```

ASC will sort the Firstname fields in ascending order. Exchanging ASC for DESC would enable sorting in descending order. To restore the rowset to its original order and remove any indexes created, set Sort to an empty string.

Deleting Records

The Delete() method is the most basic method of manipulation. It takes one of two constants as its parameter. The first constant, *adAffectCurrent*, is also the default constant, and it deletes the current record. The second constant, *adAffectGroup*, will affect the group of records that are sorted by the value of the Filter property.

```
<%@Language=PerlScript%>
<%
# Delete the current record
#
  $Recordset->Delete();

    # $Recordset->Delete is equivalent to
    # $Recordset->Delete(adAffectCurrent);
    #
%>

<%@Language=PerlScript%>
<%
```

```
# Delete the filtered group
#
$Recordset->Delete (adAffectGroup);
%>
```

Adding New Records

To add brand-new records, AddNew() must be called. The record will be added, followed by Update() to make the changes to the data source. The Update() method accepts parameters for data addition as well.

```
<%@Language=PerlScript%>
<%
# Create the Recordset
#
my $rst = $Server->CreateObject ("ADODB.Recordset");

# Create the connection string
#
my $connString = 'Provider=Microsoft.Jet.OLEDB.4.0;
                  Data Source=C:\nwind.mdb;';

# Open the Recordset
#
    $rst->Open("tbl36", $connString, adLockOptimistic,
adOpenDynamic);

# The fieldnames of the current Recordset
#
my $Fields = ["Name", "City", "State"];

# A set of values that are not yet entered into the database
#
my $Values = ["Tom", "Miami", "Florida"];
# Add the new values into the database
#
$rst->AddNew($Fields, $Values);

# Update the Recordset
#
$rst->Update();

# Close the Recordset
#
$rst->Close();

# Destroy it
#
undef $rst;
%>
```

The following example shows how to set a single field in one operation.

```
<%@Language=PerlScript%>
    <%

# Add a new empty record
#
$rst->AddNew();

# Then update a column in the record
#
$rst->Update("FieldName", "FieldValue");
%>
```

The next example uses only Update.

```
<%@Language=PerlScript%>
    <%

# Update all fields and columns at once
#
$rst->Update($Fields, $Values);
%>
```

The following example shows how to set the Value property.

```
<%@Language=PerlScript%>
<%
# Add a new empty record
#
$rs->AddNew();

# Set the values of each column
#
$rs->Fields(0)->{Value} = "Text";
$rs->Fields(1)->{Value} = "Text";
$rs->Fields(2)->{Value} = "Text";

# Update the underlying database
#
$rs->Update();
%>
```

Both the AddNew() method and the Update() method can receive the arrays of the values needed for creating the new record in the database.

ADO from Command Line Perl

ActiveX Data Objects is available to Perl and not at all limited to the Active Server Pages environment. As OLE Automation objects, any one of the ADO objects can be easily instantiated within Perl applications that run in a graphical user interface or from the command line. From there on, all native methods, properties, and collections in ActiveX Data Objects follow the same rules they do in Active Server Pages.

Back and Forth—Script Conversion

The most prominent reason for converting an ASP PerlScript to command-line Perl is because its purpose is to be seated in a regular Windows application. Whether the script will be used in a business solution or for automating a task on the personal computer, ADO provides a most efficient way of managing data on either one of the machines, and the code is virtually interchangeable.

For conversion, the practical example that has been chosen is the PerlScript that divides a Recordset into logical pages. In that task, it is a matter of loading the data from the database, then taking a request from the client for a page to display and presenting the requested records to the standard output while maintaining the state of the database records. There are a number of reasons why this is more suitable in Perl, and each reason is worth discussing—however briefly—before beginning the actual conversion.

To begin with, when the script is run in Perl, it will only have to be loaded into memory and run once, as will the database records that are fetched from the underlying database. This eliminates the Web's stateless protocol of requesting a new page and instance of the ASP document for each logical page to display. Moreover, the database does not maintain state on the Web because it can be altered by another client between each page display. The interface for choosing pages becomes more intuitive and responsive than it is on the Web. The Web application's limit of interactivity is to use Dynamic HTML, store each logical page in its own layer, and only show the layer when the page is requested. The reasons for avoiding that approach, however, are countless. Perl, on the other hand, can build a very intuitive and interactive user interface—even if it is plain text based—and it can do everything in one single request, whereas the Web application would require a new request for each action before it could perform the work. The real issue comes down to why a desktop application is more appropriate than an Internet application—but, more importantly, it is also a matter of mastering both tools, because in addition to Internet application in PerlScript, there is a another common methodology of programming that provides custom solutions—COM.

Many programming solutions turn to COM components and find answers. When writing a COM component in Perl, with all its capacity, it is necessary to know some of the basics of how Perl works in the OLE territories outside the world of Active Server Pages; for this reason, the natural starting point is the Perl module for OLE automation—Win32::OLE.

Accessing ADO from Perl

Perl uses a module named Win32::OLE to enable OLE automation. The *Win32* in the module name indicates that it is a Windows 32-bit–specific module, and the *OLE* is the functionality it provides.

ActiveX Data Objects is accessible from the OLE module in the form of components. As a result, instead of using $Server->CreateObject(), which is only available from

Active Server Pages, an external COM object such as an ADO Connection object can be instantiated with the constructor for automation objects of Win32::OLE.

```
# Import the Win32::OLE module
#
use Win32::OLE;

# Create a new OLE automation object - an ADO connection object
#
$conn = Win32::OLE->new("ADODB.Connection");
```

This script basically instantiates the ADO object into Perl. The object is still the same old object, regardless of what language is using it. This means that it has the same capability in Perl that it does in the Internet applications, and that no knowledge so far has been wasted knowledge.

Win32::OLE holds numerous methods that should be examined further while developing Perl applications. If you would like to use the ADO constants employed in the Internet examples, the following will work:

```
# Use the ActiveX constants
#
use Win32::OLE::Const ('Microsoft ActiveX Data Objects');
```

Const will import a type library, and the constants for ActiveX Data Objects are but one drop in the bucket. The same is true regardless of where the application takes place. Nothing in the architecture of Universal Data Access prevents the ADO constants from being imported in a similar fashion into the Active Server Pages documents. The same statement will function properly in the Internet applications as well.

```
<%@Language=PerlScript%>
<%
# Use the ActiveX constants
#
use Win32::OLE::Const ('Microsoft ActiveX Data Objects');

# Print out the value of the adUseClient constants
#
$Response->Write(adUseClient);
%>
```

The methods displayed so far are essentially the only requirements for converting an Active Server Pages PerlScript into Perl; in the next section we will finally convert the example of logical paging of the records in a Recordset.

Splitting a Recordset with Perl

As previously seen, the properties required for paging a Recordset, and the methodology for doing so, have been thoroughly covered. This time, however the Recordset will be split into pages in a Perl environment.

The following example is a rewritten and improved version of the PerlScript that pages a Recordset within the Web application. The following should be run from a command prompt and accepts a logical page number as the argument for which page to display. A command-line argument may as well be omitted, and it will result in the first logical page in the Recordset being displayed.

```
# Import the "in"-method
#
use Win32::OLE ('in');

# Import the ActiveX Data Objects constants version 2.5
#
use Win32::OLE::Const ('Microsoft ActiveX Data Objects 2.5');

# And use strict
#
use strict;

# Variables for the output of a formatted header and body
#
my ($output, $header);

# The length of each "column"
#
my (@length);

# Let's create the objects we will need
#
my ($conn) = Win32::OLE->new("ADODB.Connection");
my ($rst) = Win32::OLE->new("ADODB.Recordset");

# Check for command-line arguments
#
my $cmdargv = @ARGV == 1 ? shift @ARGV : 1;

# Initialize the script
#
init();

# Format the given logical page
#
FormatPage($cmdargv);

# Enter the controlling subroutine
#
main();

############################################################
# Sub: main
# Description: Controlling subroutine
############################################################
sub main
{
    while(<STDIN>) {
        # Get the input from the user
        #
        my ($param) = $_;
```

```perl
        # Remove the newline
        #
        chomp($param);

        # Exit the script if the input was the character
        # "q"
        #
        last if ($param eq "q");

            # Control that the input is within valid range
            #
            if( IsOutOfRange($param) ) {
                print "\n", "Please enter a valid pagenumber: ";
                }
            else {
                FormatPage($param);
                }
    }
}

##########################################################
# Sub: init
# Description: Initialize the Recordset
##########################################################
sub init
{
    my ($delimiter, $titles, $connString,
        $sqlQuery, $fldCnt, @names);

    # The database connection string - an Access database
    #
    $connString = (<<EOF);
        Provider=Microsoft.Jet.OLEDB.4.0;
        Data Source=C:\\nwind.mdb;
EOF

    $sqlQuery = (<<EOF);
            SELECT ProductID,
                   ProductName,
                   UnitPrice,
                   UnitsInStock
            FROM   Products
EOF

    # Open or show us the errors
    #
    $conn->Open($connString) || ScanForErrors();
    # Number of records per logical page
    #
    $rst->{PageSize} = 15;

    # The command to generate the Recordset
    #
```

```perl
    $rst->{Source} = $sqlQuery;

    # The connection to send the query
    #
    $rst->{ActiveConnection} = $conn;

    # The location of the cursor
    #
    $rst->{CursorLocation} = adUseClient;

    # Open or show us the errors
    #
    $rst->Open() || ScanForErrors();

    # Count the number of fields
    #
    $fldCnt = $rst->Fields->{Count};

    # Get the name and fieldsize for each column/field
    #
    for(my $i=0; $i<$fldCnt; $i++) {
        my $name = $rst->Fields($i)->{Name};
        my $size = $rst->Fields($i)->{DefinedSize};

    # Push the column name onto the names-array
    #
    push @names, $name;

    # Quite a long comment . . .
    # Test if the length in characters of the name of
    # the column is longer than the defined size of
    # the data it can hold - cosmetic purposes for
    # the layout on the screen. If the string-length
    # is greater than the size, use the stringlength
    # as the "virtual" cell for the field-value when
    # printed to the screen. Otherwise, use the defined
    # size for the "cell".
    #
    push @length, length($name)>$size
                  ? length($name)
                  : $size;
    }

    # Create the header for each column
    #
    for(my $a=0; $a<$fldCnt; $a++) {
        $titles.=sprintf("%-".$length[$a]."s ",
        $names[$a]);
    }

    $delimiter = '-'x(length($titles));
    $header.="$delimiter\n$titles\n$delimiter\n";
}
```

```perl
###########################################################
# Sub: FormatPage
# Description: Sets the pagenumber, prints header, the
# records on the page, and the footer (number of pages to
# choose from)
###########################################################
sub FormatPage
{
    # Get the number of the logical page to view
    #
    my ($param) = shift @_;

    # Set the current page to $param
    #
    $rst->{AbsolutePage} = $param;

    # Print the field-names that are composed as a header
    #
    print $header;

    # Print the records that make up the rows to display
    #
    PrintRows();

    # Print the "links" to the available pages to view
    #
    PrintLinks();
}

###########################################################
# Sub: PrintRows
# Description: Prints the records in current page to the
# standard output
###########################################################
sub PrintRows
{
    my (@values, $max, $index, $fldCnt);

    # The position of the last record of the current page
    #
    $max = ($rst->{PageSize} + $rst->{AbsolutePosition});

    # The position of the current record
    #
    $index = $rst->{AbsolutePosition};

    # Set max equal to the number of records, or in other words
    # the last record, if the position of the last record would
    # override the number of total records in the set
    #
    $max = $rst->{RecordCount} if ($max>$rst->{RecordCount});

    # Count the number of fields
    #
    $fldCnt = $rst->Fields->{Count};
```

```perl
    while( $index<=$max )
    {
        # Demonstrate push once again by pushing the
        # field-values onto the values-array
        #
        for($a=0; $a<$fldCnt; $a++) {
            push @values, $rst->Fields($a)->{Value};
        }

        # Print out a neatly laid out row of the values
        #
        for($b=0; $b<$fldCnt; $b++) {
            printf("%-".$length[$b]."s ", $values[$b]);
        }

        # Add a newline
        #
        print "\n";

        # Increment the index counter
        #
        $index++;

        # Move to the next record in the set
        #
        $rst->MoveNext();

        # Undefine the values-array so that it does not
        # keep the values that were stored in it during
        # this first trip in the loop
        #
        undef(@values);
    }
}

##########################################################
# Sub: PrintLinks
# Description: Prints the pagenumbers available
##########################################################
sub PrintLinks
{
    # Print the pagenumbers to choose from by the client
    #
    print "\n\nSelect Page To Display: | ";
    print "$_ | " for( 1..$rst->{PageCount} );
}

##########################################################
# Sub: IsOutOfRange
# Description: Validates the pagenumber
##########################################################
sub IsOutOfRange
{
    # Get the requested pagenumber and the number of
```

```perl
    # logical pages in the rowset
    #
    my ($param, $pages) = (shift @_, $rst->{PageCount});

    # Return 1 if the pagenumber is more than the number of
    # logical pages in the rowset or less than 1
    #
    return 1 if ($param>$pages || $param<1);
}


##########################################################
# Sub: scanForErrors
# Description: Checks for errors
##########################################################
sub ScanForErrors
{
    if($conn->Errors->{Count})
    {
    my $errOutput;
        foreach my $error (Win32::OLE::in($conn->Errors)) {
            foreach my $property (keys %{$error}) {
                $errOutput.="$property: ";
                $errOutput.=${$error}{$property};
                $errOutput.="\n";
            }
        }
    print $errOutput;
    exit(1);
    }
}
```

The Disconnected Recordset

Yet another feature of ActiveX Data Objects is the ability to handle a Recordset that is not associated with a database session or connection. Essentially, such a disconnected Recordset does not need to be connected to an underlying database to work. In terms of functionality, it provides an alternative as a data store and can be used for temporary storage of batch-process updating of an underlying database.

No Connections

A Recordset is disconnected when it does not have an active connection. The active connection defines the Connection object that is holding the database session open to a data store. What this means is that the Recordset must be held in storage somewhere, such as in the client cache by a client-side cursor or as an object in the ASP Application object. With this in mind, there are two approaches to obtaining a disconnected Recordset:

- Query a database, then set the ActiveConnection Properties to nothing.
- Create a Recordset object from the ground up.

The two approaches are different and have different intents. In short, the first method is used to return an actual result from the database, which normally concerns populating a rowset in the Recordset object before returning it. The second approach will let you add the fields manually to the Recordset and is used when you want to create a Recordset from scratch and define its structure from the ground up. Ideally, this is a portable Recordset, but it is also good for storage in the ASP Application object.

Hanging Up on the Data Source

For any disconnected Recordset, the provider must support its disconnected state. The easiest way to achieve this is to always set the CursorLocation property to a client-side cursor so that the Microsoft OLE DB cursor service is invoked. This cursor supports disconnected Recordsets. However, there are a few things to keep in mind when using the client-side provider.

As previously mentioned, when the client-side cursor is used, all data are fetched at once in one single trip to the server. Then the local cache makes it seem as if the database is being navigated when it reads the locally stored rowset.

```
<%
# Set the constant for the cursorlocation
#
use constant adUseClient=>3;

# Create the Recordset
#
$rst = $Server->CreateObject("ADODB.Recordset");

# Set the client-side cursor
#
$rst->{CursorLocation} = adUseClient;
%>
```

To disconnect from the data source generally means to get a set of records from a command, perform some local additions, modifications, and deletions to the records, and then update them as a group to the underlying database—that is, to perform a batch update.

```
<%@Language=PerlScript%>
<%
# Create the recordset
#
$rst = $Server->CreateObject("ADODB.Recordset");
# Set the cursor-location to use the OLE DB client-cursor service
#
$rst->{CursorLocation} = adUseClient;

# The source to run as a command is the name of a table
#
$rst->{Source} = "Test";

# The connection string that will invoke a connection object
#
$rst->{ActiveConnection} = 'Provider=Microsoft.Jet.OLEDB.4.0;
                            Data Source=C:\nwind.mdb;';
```

```perl
# The description of the "Source"-property to speed it up a little
#
$rst->{CommandText} = adCmdTableDirect;

# The type of cursor is open and static
#
$rst->{CursorType} = adOpenStatic;

# A Locktype that supports batch-updates
#
$rst->{LockType} = adLockBatchOptimistic;

# Open the Recordset
#
$rst->Open();

# Undefine the Active Connection; disconnect the Recordset
#
$rst->{ActiveConnection} = undef;

# Add three new records to the locally cached rowset
#
$rst->AddNew( [0,1], ['Hello', 'There'] );
$rst->AddNew( [0,1], ['Guten', 'Tag'] );
$rst->AddNew( [0,1], ['Bon', 'Jour'] );

# Define the ActiveConnection
#
$rst->{ActiveConnection} = 'Provider=Microsoft.Jet.OLEDB.4.0;
                            Data Source=C:\nwind.mdb;';

# Perform a batch-update where the three added records are updated in
# the underlying data store.
#
$rst->UpdateBatch();

# Move to the first record in the rowset
#
$rst->MoveFirst();

# Loop the rowset
#
while( ! $rst->{EOF} )
{
    $Response->Write( $rst->Fields(0)->{Value} );
    $Response->Write( $rst->Fields(1)->{Value} );
    $Response->Write( $rst->Fields(2)->{Value} );

    $Response->Write( "<BR>" );

    $rst->MoveNext();
}
%>
```

The key in the previous example is the client-side cursor. However, the ActiveConnection property is manually undefined in the program, and the added records are inserted into the locally cached rowset. Afterward, the ActiveConnection is set to a Connection object, and then the call to UpdateBatch() will perform all updates in the underlying database.

Creating the Recordset Programmatically

Unlike a Recordset that has deliberately been disconnected from its data source, detailed in the next section, a programmatically built Recordset does not require an active connection in order to work. However, a Recordset that is connected to a data source and that does perform a database query also gets a structured rowset. For this to work, a structure (or fields) must be appended to the Recordset. The syntax to append a Field object onto the Fields collection is as follows:

```
<%
$rst->Fields->Append( Name, Type, DefinedSize, Attributes, Value );
%>
```

The set Name for the appended field will be the key to access the field by, the type is the data the field holds, the DefinedSize is the size of the field, the Attributes refer to the field itself, and the Value is what it sounds like. The required parameters are the Name and Type properties. The types to choose from are shown in Table 8.11, but bear in mind that the ranges of the data types normally differ from database to database.

Achieving functionality is a matter of plugging in a few constants and numbers here and there. For example, let's create three fields:

```
<%@Language=PerlScript%>
<%
# A field of thirty characters
#
$rst->Fields->Append("greetingOne", adChar, 30);

# Another field of thirty characters
#
$rst->Fields->Append("greetingTwo", adChar, 30);

# An integer field
#
$rst->Fields->Append("anyInteger", adInteger);
```

The complete code for this is as follows:

```
# Create the Recordset
#
$rst = $Server->CreateObject("ADODB.Recordset");

# Append the following fields:
# "greetingOne": field for a 30 character string
# "greetingTwo": field for a 30 character string
# "anyInteger": field for an integer
#
$rst->Fields->Append("greetingOne", adChar, 30);
$rst->Fields->Append("greetingTwo", adChar, 30);
$rst->Fields->Append("anyInteger", adInteger);
```

Table 8.11   A Number of Data Types a Field Object Can Contain

VALUE	CONSTANT	DESCRIPTION
20	adBigInt	8-byte signed integer
128	adTypeBinary	Type for binary data
11	adTypeBoolean	Boolean value of either true or false
8	adBstr	Null-terminated Unicode character string
136	adChapter	Chapter column in a hierarchical Recordset
129	adChar	String of characters
6	adCurrency	Currency type
133	adDBDate	Date in format year/month/day (yyyy/mm/dd)
134	adDBTime	Time in format hour/minute/seconds (hh/mm/ss)
135	asDBTimeStamp	Time stamp in format year/month/day/hour/minute/seconds (yyyy/mm/dd/hh/mm/ss)
14	adDecimal	Decimal value
6	adDouble	Floating point that has a value that is of double precision
0	adEmpty	No value
72	adGUID	Global Unique Identifier
3	adInteger	Four-byte signed integer
131	adNumeric	Numeric value
4	adSingle	Floating point that has a value that is of single precision
2	adSmallInt	2-byte signed integer
16	adTinyInt	1-byte signed integer
21	adUnsignedBigInt	8-byte unsigned integer
19	adUnsignedInt	4-byte unsigned integer
18	adUnsignedSmallInt	2-byte unsigned integer
17	adUnsignedTinyInt	1-byte unsigned integer
132	adUserDefined	Type defined by the user
12	adVariant	Variant
130	adWChar	Null-terminated Unicode character string

```
# Then open the recordset with a static cursor and batch-update mode
#
$rst->Open(undef, undef, adOpenStatic, adLockBatchOptimistic);

# Add a few records
#
$rst->AddNew( [0,1,2], ['Hello', 'There', 10] );
$rst->AddNew( [0,1,2], ['Guten', 'Tag', 20] );
$rst->AddNew( [0,1,2], ['Bon', 'Jour', 30]);

# The changes will remain pending until UpdateBatch is called
#
$rst->UpdateBatch();

# Loop the Recordset from the last record to BOF since the new
# records place the cursor at the end where it last was to add
# a record
#
while( ! $rst->{BOF} )
{
    $Response->Write( $rst->Fields(0)->{Value} );
    $Response->Write( $rst->Fields(1)->{Value} );
    $Response->Write( $rst->Fields(2)->{Value} );

    $Response->Write( "<BR>" );

    $rst->MovePrevious();

}
%>
```

Persisting a Recordset

Saving or *Persisting* a Recordset simply means that its current state is stored. As a state, this includes the data and the metadata, preserving not only the existing records but also the permissions and pending changes applied to the Recordset. There are a number of ways to persist a Recordset.

Saving It as a File

The most common way of persisting a Recordset is as a file. The result is that its state is stored to disk. In the application, the Save() method writes the Recordset to disk, and the stored file can later be opened by the Open() method. A Recordset can be stored to disk for a variety of reasons.

- A Recordset is portable, or easily transferable, on a floppy disk. It can be brought to many places and provides an easy access to data.

- Recordsets are automatically generated and temporarily stored on the server for processing. The application for processing a Recordset can be easily reused and extended or interfaced with a database system.

- A Recordset can be easily e-mailed between parties who rely on exchanging information. The interface for accessing the Recordset can be a simple standard application, either online or on the desktop, and the data store can easily be entered into a database.

In addition, in every scenario the primary reason for storing data as a Recordset is the structured and easy-to-access format the Recordset provides. When persisting the Recordset as a file, there are two formats to choose from.

- Extensible Markup Language (XML)
- Advanced Data Tablegram Format (ADTG)

When a format has been selected, the syntax of the method call is $rst->Save($path, format); now that the theory and background are in place, the following sections will show how to save and open with Recordset persistence.

As an XML Document

At first glance, XML is a markup language that resembles HTML. XML is plain ASCII, and contrary to HTML, which describes how the text or content is presented, the XML elements describe the data that is presented.

In both XML and HTML, the elements are enclosed within tags that describe them. XML, however, is not only used on the Internet. It makes information more transferable and deployable because it explains how the information should be handled. To begin with the persistence in XML, the data and the metadata will be saved to an XML document in the following example:

```
<%@Language=PerlScript%>
<%
# The command
#
my $source = 'SELECT * FROM Customers';

# The native provider connection-string
#
my $activeconnection = 'Provider=Microsoft.Jet.OLEDB.4.0;
                        Data source=C:\NWIND.mdb';

# The destination of persisted file
#
my $destination = 'c:\Persisted.xml';

# Create the Recordset
#
$rst = $Server->CreateObject("ADODB.recordset");

# Open the cursor
#
$rst->Open($source, $activeconnection);
```

```
# Save/Persist the Recordset as an XML-file
#
$rst->Save($destination, adPersistXML);
%>
```

In the call to Save(), what defines the file format is the constant *adPersistXML*(1). This constant will result in the file being saved as an XML document. On an important note, since the metadata is saved, if the Recordset is a read-only Recordset, it cannot be opened and modified by hand and then resaved without causing an error the next time it is opened by the ADO application.

In the Binary ADTG Format

The Advanced Data Tablegram format is a binary format from Microsoft. ADTG is a not an open format such as XML, but instead proprietary to Microsoft. In MDAC, it can also be found in Remote Data Services (RDS).

When working with persisting Recordsets, the format is *adPersistADTG* (0) and the following saves a file in the binary format:

```
<%@Language=PerlScript%>
<%
# The command
#
my $source = 'SELECT * FROM Customers';

# The native provider connection-string
#
my $activeconnection = 'Provider=Microsoft.Jet.OLEDB.4.0;
                        Data source=C:\NWIND.mdb';

# The destination of persisted file
#
my $destination = 'c:\Persisted.adtg';

# Create the Recordset
#
$rst = $Server->CreateObject("ADODB.Recordset");

# Open the cursor
#
$rst->Open($source, $activeconnection);

# Save/Persist the Recordset as an ADTG-file
#
$rst->Save($destination, adPersistADTG);
%>
```

For hierarchical Recordsets, the Recordset in the hierarchy that calls Save() will be the top-level Recordset when saving the Recordset to file. As a result, its parents are not saved.

Reading a Persisted Recordset from File

Until the Recordset is reopened from where it has been stored, it maintains state—as long as it remains unaltered.

In order to open a persisted Recordset, the file path must be passed as the source parameter to the Open() method. Furthermore, in the ActiveConnection property, the OLE DB provider for Recordset persistence is required. To prevent the Open method from guessing what type of source is sent, the application will tell it that there is a file by using *adCmdFile*.

```
<%@Language=PerlScript%>
<%
# Filepath to where the file to read is found
#
my $file = 'C:\Persisted.xml';
# The provider needed to read a persisted Recordset
#
my $provider = 'PROVIDER=MSPERSIST';
# Create the Recordset object
#
$rst = $Server->CreateObject("ADODB.Recordset");
# Open the Recordset

#
$rst->Open( $file,
            $provider,
            undef,
            undef,
            adCmdFile );
%>
```

In the same application, when Save() has been called once with the location and file to which to save the data, exclusive write permission on that file is given to the calling Recordset. For that reason, further calls to Save() will not require a destination to be set. However, if needed, a new file can be set to store the Recordset. In such situations, exclusive write permissions are put on both files by the Recordset, although in all cases another Recordset can read either file.

Persisting a Recordset to the ASP Response Object

As an alternative to writing the Recordset to a file, it can be sent to the ASP Response object, which will result in it printing directly to the screen.

```
<%@Language=PerlScript%>
<%
# Set the content-type for the browser to receive XML
#
$Response->{ContentType} = "text/xml";

# Create the Recordset object
#
```

```
$rst = $Server->CreateObject("ADODB.Recordset");

# The query and Active Connection
#
$rst->Open("SELECT * FROM Customers",
           "Provider=Microsoft.Jet.OLEDB.4.0;
            Data Source=D:\\northwind.mdb");

# Persist it as the format defined by the value 1
(adPersistXML) to
# the Response object of the built-in ASP objects
#
$rst->Save($Response,1);
%>
```

Shaped Hierarchical Recordsets

The OLE DB provider for data shaping enables work with hierarchical Recordsets. The name says it all yet says nothing, so let's look twice at what a hierarchical Recordset is. In essence, a hierarchy in this context describes the ability to store Recordsets within Recordsets, structure Recordsets by grouping, or perform aggregate calculations on child Recordsets. This allows for natural yet complex data structures. From the previous chapter, you may recall that joins were used to query two separate tables. The join, however, will store all returned columns as one relational table, or a flat rowset. Data shaping does not have the same limitation—its limitation is measured purely in RAM on the box executing the script.

The Shape Language

The Shape language is used to describe a relationship between a series of commands, which in general are SQL queries. It is called the Shape language because it has its own syntax, which is interpreted by the data shape provider. It will use the commands to translate the queries into the hierarchy and the type of hierarchy that was described in the Shape command. The most common types of hierarchies are the following:

- Relation-based hierarchy
- Parameterized command hierarchies
- Commuted or grouped hierarchies

To use the Shape language, the Provider property or provider argument must stipulate that MSDatashape is going to be used, or else the database will return a message saying that it does not understand the language being spoken, since it generally expects SQL to be issued and Shape is unknown to anyone but the provider for data shaping.

```
<%
# Example 1: We define MSDataShape in the provider property
#
$conn = $Server->CreateObject("ADODB.Connection");
```

```
$rst = $Server->CreateObject("ADODB.Recordset");

...

# Set the DataShape provider
#
$conn->{Provider} = 'MSDataShape';

...

# We imagine that $shapeCommand has been defined between
# the lines, and open the Recordset.
#
$rst->Open($shapeCommand, $conn);
%>

<%
# Example 2: We define MSDataShape in the ActiveConnection
#            property
#
$rst = $Server->CreateObject("ADODB.Recordset");

...

# Imagine that a shape-command has been created
#
$rst->{Source} = $shapeCommand;

# A connection to the SQL Server Northwind database
#
$rst->{ActiveConnection} = (<<EOF);
    Provider=MSDataShape;
    Data Provider=SQLOLEDB;
    Integrated Security=SSPI;
    Persist Security Info=False;
    Initial Catalog=Northwind;
EOF

$rst->Open();
%>
```

Although the provider is set to MSDatashape, that does not mean that it works alone—the records must come from somewhere.

In an active connection with a data source, the DataShape provider will function together with one or more data providers for data stores.

In the next section, the Shape language will be expanded by introducing the first type of hierarchy—the relation-based hierarchy.

A Relation-Based Hierarchy

When the data shaping provider has been set to be used, it is invoked when it sees the SHAPE command in the command. The SHAPE command works with a series of statements to prepare the hierarchy that later makes up the Recordset, and the syntax is as follows:

```
SHAPE { <Command to create parent recordset> }

    [ AS [<Alias for parent recordset>] ]

APPEND ( { <Command to create child recordset> }

    [ AS <Alias for childrecordset> ]

RELATE [Parent-field] to [Child-field])

    [ AS <Alias for the chapter column> ]
```

The SHAPE command invokes the OLE DB provider for data shaping, and the query that follows within curly braces is the query that created the root node, also called the *parent Recordset*. For example, using the SQL command SELECT * FROM tblProducts would set all fields of the tbleProducts table as the fields of the parent. After the query, an (optional) alias is given to the parent. Next, in the SHAPE statement, APPEND is called and the Recordset it results in is given an alias by the AS <alias for the child recordset> if desired. Lastly, a RELATE statement is set to define two identical fields within both tables that will relate the parent and child Recordsets. The alias that follows RELATE is also called the chapter alias. This is a reference to the chapter column that was added by the APPEND command. If this reference omitted, an alias such as Chapter n, where n is a positive integer such as 1, 2, 3, 4, and so on, will be automatically generated. From its parent, the chapter Recordset is available to the application as a field. The chapter alias that is given is created as a field within the parent Recordset. However, in contrast to regular data fields, the value property of the chapter field contains the child Recordset, so to make it easier to work with the child Recordset it must be dropped as follows:

```
<%
# If the chapter-alias used was called "Friends," then the child
# Recordset is accessed by the value property of it.
#
$childRecordset = $parRst->Fields('Friends')->{Value};
%>

<%
# However, the above statement is equal to the longer version
# which follows
#
$parRst->Fields('Friends')->{Value}->Fields('FirstName')-
>{Value};
%>
```

The relational bond between the two Recordsets is described by the RELATE command. For example, the parent query is SELECT * FROM tblProducts and the child query is SELECT * FROM tblSales. In both tables, a product identification number could be used to recognize the product because it is available in both fields. As a fictitious example, tblSales defines the amount of sales for the product during the time span of a month at a time and tblProducts keeps updates on price, quantity, and so forth—although price is the most relevant issue in a real example. To create the relation between the tables, the relational bond could be between the product identification number. The statement would then look as follows:

```
SHAPE {SELECT * FROM tblProducts}
    AS parentQuery
APPEND ({SELECT * FROM tblSales}
    AS childQuery
RELATE ProductID to ProductID) AS SalesStats
```

As a result, the chapter Recordset will be named SalesStats. To illustrate the point in a real-world example, the next listing will demonstrate the use of a parent and child Recordset in a basic way. It will function with the Northwind database that comes with MS Office and Developer studio; for other databases it is a matter of exchanging the field names to get things running. However, just reading the example illustrates the point very well.

```
<%@Language=PerlScript%>
<HTML>
<BODY>

<!--
This HTML above sets up the layout for a table in which the
records we will retrieve are displayed.

OrderID, Freight, and ShipCountry are all fields in the child recordset.
-->

<TABLE WIDTH="100%">
<TR>

<TD WIDTH="20%" ALIGN="LEFT" BGCOLOR="#7777bb">
    <FONT FACE="ARIAL" COLOR="#ffffff"><B>Company Name</B></FONT>
</TD>

<TD WIDTH="20%" ALIGN="LEFT" BGCOLOR="#7777bb">
    <FONT FACE="ARIAL" COLOR="#ffffff"><B>Contact Name</B></FONT>
</TD>

<TD WIDTH="20%" ALIGN="LEFT" BGCOLOR="#7777bb">
    <FONT FACE="ARIAL" COLOR="#ffffff"><B>Order ID</B></FONT>
</TD>

<TD WIDTH="20%" ALIGN="LEFT" BGCOLOR="#7777bb">
    <FONT FACE="ARIAL" COLOR="#ffffff"><B>Freight</B></FONT>
</TD>

<TD WIDTH="20%" ALIGN="LEFT" BGCOLOR="#7777bb">
    <FONT FACE="ARIAL" COLOR="#ffffff"><B>Ship country</B></FONT>
</TD>

</TR>
<%
# Create the Recordset
#
$rst = $Server->CreateObject("ADODB.Recordset");

# Set the connectionstring that will invoke the OLE DB provider
# for datashaping, and the OLE DB provider for Microsoft Jet
```

```
# databases that will connect to the Northwind Jet database
#
$rst->{ActiveConnection} = (<<EOF);
        PROVIDER=MSDataShape;
        Data Provider=Microsoft.Jet.OLEDB.4.0;
        Data source=C:\\NWIND.mdb;
EOF
# The command that will generate our shaped Recordset. The
# following fields will be read from the Customers table
# and be contained in the parent Recordset:
#     CustomerID
#     CompanyName
#     ContactName
#
# The child Recordset will be named "OrderScheme" and from
# the Orders table contain the following fields:
#     CustomerID
#     OrderID
#     Freight
#     ShipCountry
#
# The relational bond is the CustomerID
#
$rst->{Source} = (<<EOF);
SHAPE {SELECT CustomerID,
                      CompanyName,
                      ContactName
    FROM Customers} AS parentCusts
          APPEND({SELECT CustomerID,
                                 OrderID,
                                 Freight,
                                 ShipCountry
          FROM Orders} AS childOrders
      RELATE CustomerID to CustomerID) AS OrderScheme
EOF

# Open the Recordset
#
$rst->Open();

# Loop the Recordset until we reach the End Of File
#
while( ! $rst->{EOF} )
{

    # Print out the values for the parent Recordset
    # with exception for the CustomerID field since
    # we only used it to create the relation between
    # parent and child
    #
%>
```

```
      <TR>
      <TD><%=$rst->Fields('CompanyName')->{Value}%></TD>
      <TD><%=$rst->Fields('ContactName')->{Value}%></TD>

<%
      # Drop the child Recordset into $childRst
      #
      $childRst = $rst->Fields('OrderScheme')->{Value};
      # Then print the selected fields
      #
%>

      <TD><%=$childRst->Fields('OrderID')->{Value}%></TD>
      <TD>$<%=$childRst->Fields('Freight')->{Value}%></TD>
      <TD><%=$childRst->Fields('ShipCountry')->{Value}%></TD>
      </TR>
<%
      # Move to the next record
      #
      $rst->MoveNext();
}
%>

</TABLE>
</BODY>
</HTML>
```

The command that is used as parent query or child query can contain a table name followed by the TABLE keyword, a name that identifies an already-created shaped Recordset, or an inline SHAPE command. The RELATE keyword shows the association between the queries, and although any given field returned from the query is accepted, something that is the same in both queried tables, such as two ID numbers, is what will show the relation—otherwise a true relationship will not be established. The chapter alias that is the result of RELATE is a Field object identified by its type being the constant *adChapter* (136)—thus the data type is a chapter, not ordinal data.

As expected, the hierarchies allow a rather full depth to the number of children that can be appended to a parent and the number of children that can be appended to children. Because of this functionality, the SHAPE statements tend to become complex very quickly. The next example uses the Northwind database to create a hierarchy of categories, products that belong to the categories, and the suppliers of the products. It calls for an inline SHAPE command, and this will create a child within the child. The statement looks as follows:

```
SHAPE {SELECT CategoryName, CategoryID FROM Categories} AS
Parent

APPEND((
        SHAPE {SELECT ProductName,
                   UnitPrice,
                   SupplierID,
                   CategoryID
```

```
                          FROM Products}
            APPEND ({SELECT CompanyName,
                            Address,
                            City,
                            Country,
                            SupplierID
                    FROM Suppliers} AS SupplierInfo

            RELATE SupplierID TO SupplierID))

RELATE CategoryID TO CategoryID) AS ChildRS
```

The first child relates to the parent by CategoryID. Then the inline SHAPE command creates the child of the child where the two are related by SupplierID. In effect, the code would be similar to the next example.

```
<%@Language=PerlScript%>
<%
# Create the Recordset object
#
$rst = $Server->CreateObject("ADODB.Recordset");

# Create the Connection object
#
$conn = $Server->CreateObject("ADODB.Connection");

# Open the connection by providing a full connection string
#
$conn->Open(<<EOF);
    PROVIDER=MSDataShape;
    Data Provider=Microsoft.Jet.OLEDB.4.0;
    Data source=C:\\NWIND.mdb;
EOF

# Put the Connection object to use by the Recordset
#
$rst->{ActiveConnection} = $conn;

# Write the shape command
#
$rst->{Source} = (<<EOF);
SHAPE {SELECT CategoryName,
              CategoryID
       FROM   Categories} AS Parent
    APPEND(( SHAPE {SELECT ProductName,
                           UnitPrice,
                           SupplierID,
                           CategoryID
                    FROM   Products}
                APPEND ({SELECT CompanyName,
                                Address,
                                City,
                                Country,
                                SupplierID
```

```
                        FROM   Suppliers} AS SupplierInfo
              RELATE SupplierID TO SupplierID))
       RELATE CategoryID TO CategoryID) AS ChildRS
EOF

# Open it up
#
$rst->Open();

# Loop until End Of File
#
while( ! $rst->{EOF} ) {
%>
     <FONT FACE="ARIAL">
     <B><%=$rst->Fields("CategoryName")->{Value}%></B>
     </FONT>

<%
     # Get the child Recordset
     #
     $crst = $rst->Fields('ChildRS')->{Value};

     # Get the grandchild Recordset
     #
     $ccrst = $crst->Fields('SupplierInfo')->{Value};

     # Loop the child and the grandchild
     #
     while( ! $crst->{EOF} ) {
%>

     <BR> Product:
     <%=$crst->Fields('ProductName')->{Value}%>

     <BR> Price: $
     <%=$crst->Fields('UnitPrice')->{Value}%>

     <BR>  Supplier:
     <%=$ccrst->Fields('CompanyName')->{Value}%>

     <BR>  Address:
     <%=$ccrst->Fields('Address')->{Value}%>,
     <%=$ccrst->Fields('City')->{Value}%>
     <BR>
       
     <%=$ccrst->Fields('Country')->{Value}%>

     <BR>
     <BR>

     <%
     # Get the next child record
     #
     $crst->MoveNext();
     }
```

```
# Get the next parent record
#
$rst->MoveNext();
}
%>
```

Parameterized Shape Statements

Although the name is similar to the ADO parameter object, there is no relation between this and the parameters that are used in SHAPE commands. The previous example could have been rewritten to use a parameterized SHAPE command as follows:

```
SHAPE {SELECT CustomerID,
            CompanyName,
            ContactName
      FROM Customers} AS parentCusts

APPEND({SELECT CustomerID,
             OrderID,
             Freight,
             ShipCountry
       FROM Orders WHERE CustomerID = ?} AS childOrders

RELATE CustomerID to PARAMETER 0) AS OrderScheme
```

In a normal data shape relation scenario, the rowsets of both the parent query and the child query are fetched when the SHAPE command is translated and executed, so the process can become rather slow.

On the other hand, the SHAPE command is run once, and then there the data is—no additional queries are needed. A parameterized hierarchical Recordset works a bit differently. Instead of executing the child query at once to fetch all records that match its criteria, this type of Recordset is executed each time a row from the parent Recordset is requested to be read into memory. So, in contrast to the regular hierarchical Recordset, the parameterized version will execute a child query only when it needs to. In short, the initialization process is faster than that for the normal SHAPE-RELATE command, but there will be more queries during the lifetime of the application than there otherwise would.

A Computed or Grouped Hierarchy

The syntax changes somewhat when a computed or grouped hierarchy is being entered. Again all records are fetched when a grouped hierarchy is established. First, let's look at the syntax before explaining how it operates.

```
SHAPE {query for child recordset}

    AS <Alias for child recordset>

COMPUTE <Child recordset alias>
      [,Aggregate function
```

```
            Command-field-list
      ]

[BY group-field-list]
```

Instead of including a parent query, the child query will create a parent whose columns are references to the Recordsets and field values that resulted from queries or other valid commands in the SHAPE command. Aggregate functions, detailed in Table 8.12, are frequently used in these situations.

To begin with aggregate functions, let's look at an example that uses the Northwind database. It will be very basic to get the right syntax up front. The following illustrates a SHAPE command that uses COMPUTE to find the maximum freight cost that is entered in the database.

```
SHAPE {SELECT
            OrderID,
            Freight
      FROM   Orders} AS childRst

COMPUTE
      childRst, MAX(childRst.Freight) AS MaxFreight
```

Indeed, this code can probably be used more effectively by a regular SQL statement, but the issue is closer to clarifying the syntax of the grouped hierarchy, although the command produces no hierarchy. Instead, it creates a parent that includes a rowset named childRst and a field named MaxFreight. MaxFreight is the result of the aggregate function and it includes only one value, which is the maximum cost for freight that was found in the database. childRst contains each OrderID and freight cost from the Orders table in the Northwind database. Besides using the aggregate functions previously listed, dynamic calculations can be performed by using the CALC function. The CALC function is provided by Jet Expression Service.

For a hierarchy to be group based, we are looking at a parent Recordset that is the result of the child query. The following example is simple but illustrative. We use the COMPUTE statement to group the records by what country they are from.

Table 8.12 Aggregate Functions Called with Parameters
Function(Chapter, Column)

FUNCTION	DESCRIPTION
ANY	Field value that is the same for each row
AVG	Calculated average
COUNT	Number of rows in either chapter only or column
MAX	Maximum value in a specified column
MIN	Minimum value in a specified column
STDEV	Standard deviation of a column
SUM	Sum of each row in a column

```
<%@Language=PerlScript%>
<HTML>
<BODY>
<TABLE WIDTH="640" ALIGN="CENTER">
<%
# Create the Recordset object
#
$rst = $Server->CreateObject("ADODB.Recordset");

# Set the shape command
#
$rst->{Source} = (<<EOF);
    SHAPE   {SELECT CompanyName,
                    Country
            FROM    Customers} AS childRS
    COMPUTE childRS BY Country
EOF

# Set the connectionstring
#
$rst->{ActiveConnection} = (<<EOF);
    PROVIDER=MSDataShape;
    Data Provider=Microsoft.Jet.OLEDB.4.0;
    Data source=C:\\NWIND.mdb;
EOF

# Open the Recordset
#
$rst->Open();

# Loop the Recordset
#
while( ! $rst->{EOF} ) {
    $fldValue = $rst->Fields('Country')->{Value};

    $html .= (<<EndHTML);
    <TR>
    <TD WIDTH="640" BGCOLOR="#FFFFEE">
    <B>$fldValue</B>
    </TD>
    </TR>
EndHTML

    my $childRst = $rst->Fields('childRS')->{Value};

    while(! $childRst->{EOF} ) {
        $fldValue = $childRst->Fields('CompanyName')->{Value};
        $html.=(<<EndHTML);
        <TR>
        <TD WIDTH="640" BGCOLOR="#EEEEEE">
        $fldValue
        </TD>
        </TR>
EndHTML
```

```
        $childRst->MoveNext();
        }

    $html.= '<TR><TD HEIGHT="5"></TD></TR>'; # HTML spacer

    $rst->MoveNext();
}
%>

<%=$html%>

</TABLE>
</BODY>
</HTML>
```

In essence, COMPUTE creates the parent Recordset in a group-based hierarchy. Although it can take more parameters, the only required parameter is the child alias, as seen in the preceding example. Commands regarding shape are shown in Table 8.13.

Aggregate calculations can be grouped for one statement. The following example uses a series of aggregate calculations and prints the computed value to the standard output.

```
<%@Language=PerlScript%>
<%
# Create the Recordset object
```

Table 8.13 The Shape Command Language

COMMAND	ARGUMENTS	EXAMPLE	DESCRIPTION
SHAPE	{ <sql-statement> } (<shape-command>) "<shaped recordset>" TABLE "tablename"	SHAPE { SELECT Firstname, ID FROM tblPeople } AS ParentRowset	Parent command, or node, for a parent Recordset where child Recordsets can attach as subnodes.
APPEND	Same as SHAPE; see above	APPEND({ SELECT * FROM tblOrders } AS ChildRowset RELATE ID TO ID) AS ChapterAlias	Appends a child Recordset, or subnode, to the parent as the value of a field by the name in AS *name*. The RELATE clause defines the relation between parent and child, thus the Chapter column.
COMPUTE	<Existing-Rowset-Alias> [, aggregate function calculated expression] [BY <group-of-fields>]	COMPUTE ChildRS, AVG (ChildRS.Purchase) BY ID	Creates a parent Recordset with possibly appended columns. Where there is a BY statement, it is specified how to group the rows of childRS and the column(s) specified are added to the parent created.
NEW	AS Fieldname <DataType>[Attributes]	NEW adChar(60) AS Firstname	Appends a new field to the rowset.

```
#
$rst = $Server->CreateObject("ADODB.Recordset");

# Create the command to execute
#
$rst->{Source} = (<<EOF);
    SHAPE {SELECT * FROM [Order Details]} AS childRS
    COMPUTE childRS,
    COUNT(childRs.OrderID) AS numOrdr,
    SUM(childRS.UnitPrice) AS sumPrice,
    MAX(childRS.Quantity) AS maxQty,
    MIN(childRS.Quantity) AS minQty
EOF

# Set the activeconnection
#
$rst->{ActiveConnection} = (<<EOF);
    PROVIDER=MSDataShape;
    Data Provider=Microsoft.Jet.OLEDB.4.0;
    Data source=C:\\NWIND.mdb;
EOF

# Open the Recordset
#
$rst->Open();
%>

<BR>Number of orders: <%=$rst->Fields('numOrdr')->{Value}%>
<BR>Sum of orders: $<%=$rst->Fields('SumPrice')->{Value}%>
<BR>Max quantity ordered: <%=$rst->Fields('maxQty')->{Value}%>
<BR>Min quantity ordered: <%=$rst->Fields('minQty')->{Value}%>
```

Disconnected Hierarchical Recordsets

As with regular rowsets, a hierarchical structure can make up a disconnected rowset. You will need to understand the data type identifiers and know how to use the shape language to create the Recordset.

The approach is the same as creating the hierarchical disconnected Recordset. The provider must still be set to use MSDataShape. However, the data provider must not be specified.

```
Provider=MSDataShape;Data Provider=NONE;
```

Next, the SHAPE command is used with the keyword NEW.

```
SHAPE
    APPEND
        NEW adChar(50) AS Model,
        NEW adInteger AS Year
```

This only creates a flat rowset. As with an inline SHAPE command, the same technique must be applied for creating a hierarchical Recordset instead of a flat rowset. Notice that SHAPE is appended like the other fields that are created with NEW.

```
SHAPE
    APPEND NEW adInteger As ID,
           NEW adVarChar(10) As Model,
         ((SHAPE
               APPEND NEW adInteger As ID,
                      NEW adVarChar(10) As Colour)
    RELATE ID TO cID) AS Child
```

In essence, building hierarchical Recordsets either by function or by hand is not very complicated. However, the SHAPE statements themselves become complicated. Error checking by using a Connection object is a must when writing SHAPE statements, or else it is easy to go insane.

When accessing the children, the child Recordset cannot just be set to a variable. The reason is that it needs in turn to be initialized with data before the object and its metadata are made available. Initializing the Recordset is as simple as calling AddNew and then deleting the record. It's a bit ugly, but it is readable and it works. The following example does this to initialize the child Recordsets.

```
<%@ Language=PerlScript %>
<%
# Create a connection object
#
$conn = $Server->CreateObject("ADODB.Connection");

# Create a Recordset for parents and children
#
$rs1 = $Server->CreateObject("ADODB.Recordset");
$rs2 = $Server->CreateObject("ADODB.Recordset");
$rs3 = $Server->CreateObject("ADODB.Recordset");

# The fields of the parent Recordset
#
my @table_parent = qw(id model make);

# The fields of the child Recordset
#
my @table_orders = qw(id customerid price);

# The fields of the grandchild Recordset
#
my @table_customers = qw(customerid firstname lastname);

# The variable that will contain what is printed to the
# screen when the script is done
#
my $output;

# Open the connection
#
$conn->Open(<<EOF);
    PROVIDER=MSDataShape;
    Data Provider=Microsoft.Jet.OLEDB.4.0;
    Data source=C:\\NWIND.mdb;
```

```
EOF

# Set some familiar properties
#
$rs1->{ActiveConnection} = $conn;
$rs1->{LockType} = 3;
$rs1->{CursorType} = 3;
$rs1->{Source} = (<<EOF);
SHAPE
   APPEND new adInteger AS $table_parent[0],
          new adVarChar(10) AS $table_parent[1],
          new adInteger AS $table_parent[2],
     ((SHAPE
        APPEND new adInteger AS $table_orders[0],
               new adInteger AS $table_orders[1],
               new adInteger AS $table_orders[2],
          ((SHAPE
             APPEND new adInteger AS $table_customers[0],
                    new adChar(30) AS $table_customers[1],
                    new adChar(30) AS $table_customers[2])
                RELATE $table_orders[1] TO $table_customers[0])
                AS OrderInfo)
         RELATE $table_parent[0] TO $table_orders[0])
         AS AutoListing
EOF

# Open the Recordset or show us the errors
#
$rs1->Open() || scanForErrors();

# Initialize the children of the parent Recordset
#
init();

# Add a record by passing three array references
#
addrecord([1, 'Volvo', 1975],
          [1, 3423000, 99],
          [3423000, 'John', 'Smith'] );

# And add another record
#
addrecord([2, 'Volvo', 1985],
          [2, 2342, 199],
          [2342, 'Andy', 'Smith'] );

# Move the current position to the first record
#
$rs1->MoveFirst();

# Start looping and call addoutput with all three
# Recordset objects until we have reach the end of
# file
#
```

```perl
while(!$rs1->{EOF})
{
    addoutput($rs1, $rs2, $rs3);
    $rs1->MoveNext();
}

%>

<%
############################################################
# Name:        Init
# Description: Adds a new record to the parent, hence
#              initialized the autoListing child. In turn
#              the child calls AddNew, and does the same
#              to its child, which adds yet another
#              record. Then after having initialized the
#              metadata for these Recordsets in this
#              cumbersome way, the record is deleted.
############################################################
sub init
{
    $rs1->AddNew();
    $rs2=$rs1->Fields("AutoListing")->{Value};
    $rs2->AddNew();
    $rs3=$rs2->Fields("OrderInfo")->{Value};
    $rs3->AddNew();
    $rs1->Delete(1);
}
%>

<%
############################################################
# Name:        addrecord
# Parameters:  Array references
# Description: Adds a record to the whole hierarchy. The
#              fields are set  in  the  array  references
#                  table_parent
#                  table_orders
#                  table_customers
#              The parameters passed are the ones that
#              represent the value-fields ion the calls
#              to the AddNew-method of the Recordset
#              object. Level1 is the parent, Level2 is
#              the child, and so forth
############################################################
sub addrecord
{
    my ($level1, $level2, $level3) = @_;
    $rs1->AddNew( \@table_parent, $level1 );
    $rs2->AddNew( \@table_orders, $level2 );
    $rs3->AddNew( \@table_customers, $level3 );
}
```

```
%>


<%
###########################################################
# Name:        addoutput
# Parameters:  The objects which contents to output
# Description: One or more Recordsets are passed to this
#              subroutine for having the names and values
#              of the fields stored in the variable that
#              will have its contents printed to the
#              screen when the script is done.
###########################################################
sub addoutput
{
    my (@param) = @_;
        foreach my $recordset (@param) {
            foreach my $fld(Win32::OLE::in($recordset->Fields)) {
                $output.=$fld->{Name};
                $output.="=";
                $output.=$fld->{Value};
                $output.="<BR>";
            }
        }
}
%>


<%
###########################################################
# Name:        scanForErrors
# Description: The standard error-check routine
###########################################################
sub scanForErrors
{
    if($conn->Errors->{Count})
    {
        my $errOutput;
            foreach my $error (Win32::OLE::in($conn->Errors)) {
                foreach my $property (keys %{$error}) {
                    $errOutput.="$property: ";
                    $errOutput.=${$error}{$property};
                    $errOutput.="<BR>";
                }
            }

    $Response->Write($errOutput);
    exit(1);
    }
}
%>

<%=$output%>
```

In the preceding example, probably the most confusing part is the shape statement. The parent call looks as follows:

```
SHAPE
     APPEND new adInteger      AS $table_parent[0],
            new adVarChar(10) AS $table_parent[1],
            new adInteger      AS $table_parent[2],
```

The SHAPE command is creating three fields: 2 of integer type, and 1 of the type character with space for 10 characters. The parent table has the following columns, as specified in the table_parents array:

- id
- model
- make

The first column is used to identify the item, and also to create the relationship to the child Recordset, whose fields are:

- id
- customerid
- price

Id relates to the parent, while customerid relates to the grandchild and represents the person who has purchased the car. The grandchild is made up of three fields:

- customerid
- firstname
- lastname

This structure is very easy to read, as the first column of each Recordset has been made to relate to the next Recordset, or in this case to relate to the child Recordset.

```
SHAPE
     APPEND new adInteger      AS id,
            new adVarChar(10) AS model,
            new adInteger      AS make,

     ((SHAPE
          APPEND new adInteger      AS id,
                 new adInteger      AS customerid,
                 new adInteger      AS price,
          ((SHAPE
               APPEND new adInteger      AS customerid,
                      new adChar(30)     AS firstname,
                      new adChar(30)     AS lastname)

               RELATE customerid
               TO     customerid) AS OrderInfo)

          RELATE id TO id) AS AutoListing
```

Table 8.14 The Recordset Object

	DESCRIPTION
Collection	
Fields	Fields collection of Field objects in the Recordset.
Properties	Property objects of the Recordset: for example, dynamic properties that were added by the data provider to the Recordset.
Method	
AddNew([fieldnames], [fieldvalues])	Adds a new, empty record to the Recordset or an array reference of one or more field names in the underlying database and the field values of the new record.
Cancel() CancelBatch ([AffectEnum])	Cancels an asynchronous call to Open. Cancels pending batch updates in a Recordset opened in batch mode. The records are affected differently depending on which constant is used: adAffectCurrent (1) will affect the current record only. adAffectGroup (2) is used when records have been filtered with the filter property and the operation should affect only the filtered group. adAffectAll (3) will deal with all records unconditionally. adAffectAllChapters (4) affects all chapters in a Recordset such as a hierarchical Recordset.
CancelUpdate()	Cancels the changes applied to the current record or a recently added record.
Clone([LockType])	Returns a clone of the current Recordset. It will either inherit the LockType of the current Recordset, or it can be set to read only by specifying that in the parameter. The criterion for cloning a Recordset is that it supports bookmarks, and Requery() must be called to desynchronize the clone and the original Recordset.
Close()	Closes the Recordset.
CompareBookmarks (Bookmark1, Bookmark2)	Compares bookmark1 to bookmark2 when associated with the same Recordset or closed Recordset. A CompareEnum will be returned to indicate how their position is compared. It can be one of the following, where first bookmark is the left value that it compares to: adCompareLessThan (0)—positioned before the second. adCompareEqual (1)—equal. adCompareGreaterThan (2)—greater than. adCompareNotEqual (3)—not equal to. adCompareNotComparable (4)—cannot be compared.
Delete([AffectEnum])	Deletes the current record or records defined by the parameter. *Continues*

Table 8.14   *(Continued)*

	DESCRIPTION
Find(Criteria, [Offset], [Direction], [start])	Finds a record by the specified criteria. Optionally specifies an offset from the current record or bookmark or sets the start parameter to a bookmark where the search should start. Direction determies whether it should search for the record forward (default) or backward. adSearchForward (1) will search until EOF, and adSearchBackward (−1) will search until BOF.
GetRows([Start], [Fields])	By default uses the GetRowsOptionEnum adGetRowsRest (−1) to retrieve [GetRowsOption-Enum], all records in the rowset. Start is a bookmark or a BookmarkEnum and fields can be a single field name or index or an array of field names or indexes. The return value is a two-dimensional array.
GetString (see page 144)	Returns a formatted string of the records.
Move(n, [start])	Moves *n* records from the current record and optionally sets a bookmark for the starting position.
MoveFirst()	Moves to the first record.
MoveLast()	Moves to the last record.
MoveNext()	Moves to the next record.
MovePrevious()	Moves to the previous record.
NextRecordset(	Executes the next command that has been defined in the command text. For example, SELECT * FROM Products; SELECT * FROM Orders.
[AffectEnum])	Returns a Recordset, or may set the current Recordset to the result of the query.
Open (see beginning)	Opens a cursor.
Requery ([ExecuteOptionEnum])	Runs the original command text against the underlying data store to update the records in the current Recordset.
Resynch ([ResynchValues])	Resynchronizes the records with the underlying data base without running the [AffectEnum] command text. An affect enum can be used to define the records to be affected, and resynchvalues defines two values: adResynchAllValues (2)—the underlying values are overwritten by the new and all pending updates are cancelled. This is the default. AdResynchUnderly-ingValues (1)—Will not overwrite or cancel pending updates.

Table 8.14 *(Continued)*

	DESCRIPTION
Save([destination], [PersistEnum])	Persists the Recordset to destination in format PersistEnum.
Seek(KeyValues, SeekOptions)	Seeks an index for KeyValues, which represents columns, and SeekOptions to define how the search is performed. The SeekOptions are the following. When matching a key to Keyvalues: adSeekFirstEQ (1)—first equal to. adSeekLastEQ (2)—last equal to. adSeekAfterEQ (4)—either equal to or right after a match. adSeekAfter (8)—after a match. adSeekBeforeEQ (16)—equal to or right before a match. adSeekBefore (32)—before a match.
Supports (CursorOptions)	Returns whether a function is supported or not.
Update([fieldnames], [fieldvalues])	Updates array field names with array field values in the current record.
UpdateBatch ([Affect Enum])	Performs the pending batch updates.
Property	
AbsolutePage	Current page in the Recordset.
AbsolutePosition	Position of the current record.
ActiveCommand	Command object that created the Recordset.
ActiveConnection	Connection object used by the Recordset.
BOF	Position before the first record.
Bookmark	Bookmark.
CacheSize	Number of records to fetch from the data store per round trip.
CursorLocation	Location of the cursor service.
CursorType	Type of cursor used by the Recordset.
DataMember	Named data member to retrieve from DataSource.
DataSource	Data that will embody the Recordset. Used with the data environment.
EditMode	EditModeEnum that describes the editing mode of the current record. adEditNone (0)—none. adEditInProgress (1)—the record has been edited, but changes are not updated to the underlying data store. adEditAdd (2)— the current record is a new record not yet updated to the underlying data store. adEditDelete (4)—the current record has been deleted.

Continues

Table 8.14   (Continued)

	DESCRIPTION
Filter	Filters a group of records.
Index	Name of the index.
LockType	Type of lock put on the records.
MarshalOptions	MarshalOptionsEnum that defines how records are marshaled back to the server. adMarshalAll (0)—all rows are returned (default). adMarshalModifiedOnly (1)—only those rows modified are returned.
MaxRecords	Maximum number of records to retrieve with a query.
PageCount	Number of logical pages.
RecordCount	Number of returned records.
Sort	One or more field names by which to sort the Recordset in ascending or descending order.
Source	Text that resulted in the Recordset, for example an SQL query.
State	Current state of the object.
Status	Current status of the object in batch update mode and similar operations.
StayInSync	Boolean for whether the children in a hierarchical rowset should move when a parent changes the current record.

The previous SHAPE command looks somewhat clustered, but it follows a logical flow. The first SHAPE command creates the parent, and all the columns therein are separated by commas. The next SHAPE statement, too, is included as part of the parent Recordset. It is placed into the statement after a comma, and after it has added its own columns, the third shape is added the very same way. Next, the innermost relationship is represented by the first Relate clause, and the outermost by the second clause.

Reshaping the Hierarchy

Hierarchical Recordsets support reshaping. For this to be reality, the names that are given to Recordsets will become important. As a name can be specified in a SHAPE command, several already-shaped Recordsets can become part of new hierarchies. The name of a Recordset is given by the AS clause, but is also available in the Name property of the Recordset.

Overview: The Recordset

Table 8.14 displays the properties, methods, and collections of the Recordset object.

Summary

In this chapter we saw the many faces of the Recordset object. We have discussed the difference between a default Recordset and a tailor-made Recordset, and several examples have been used to display the Recordset's flexibility. In most cases, a Recordset embodies data that was requested from a data store. For example, the Recordset can contain records that were returned from a database. However, there are also Recordsets that do not need an active connection such as a database. These *disconnected Recordsets* can be created either without any external data stores, which means they are created from nothing, or they can have had an active connection to a database, for example, and can simply have disconnected from that database after the database returned records that were queried. When a disconnected Recordset has been created from nothing, it may be stored in the ASP Application object, for example, and collect information about statistics on the server. Later, the Recordset can be persisted to a file in either XML format or a binary ADTG format. If the disconnected Recordset has had an active connection, it may perform local updates to the Recordset and then reconnect to the database and upload the changes. The reason for this could be to minimize the number of concurrent connections. In addition to all this, we have learned how hierarchical Recordsets, or nested Recordsets, can be created, manipulated, and navigated by using the Shape language that comes with the OLE DB provider for data shaping.

In the next chapter, we will see how ADO can be used to precompile queries with the Parameter object, and in that way improve the performance of a database application.

## CHAPTER 9

Fast Queries with the Command Object

W hen a query is issued, the database does not immediately respond. At the destination, the query is compiled into a form understandable to the database server. When this process is completed, the compiled query is executed. Use of the Command object, however, eliminates having to go through this cycle.

Introduction to the Command

The Command object can represent a precompiled version of a query that has been issued at the database. As a result, the very first query will be somewhat slower than normal because the provider must store the command. Afterward, though, the query is never recompiled, which affords ADO an increase in performance.

Preparing a Fast Query

The basic process of using the Command object does not differ much from how the Connection object is used. You must instantiate the Command object, set the necessary properties, and then execute. The main difference is that this object represents a command that is issued against the data source. It sounds silly, but it is practical.

In the case of a query, a Recordset is returned unless the *adExecuteNoRecords* (0x00000080) constant specifies that a Recordset should not be created. However, before the Command can represent a query, for example, a number of properties must be defined. The properties will define what the provider requires to compile your command so that a precompiled version of the command can be stored. First, the CommandText property contains the actual command that will be issued, and the CommandType property describes CommandText. The ActiveConnection property is the string necessary to open a connection. The Prepared property is either set to compile the statement or left alone if compiling is not desired.

For example, CommandText can be a regular SQL statement that returns a Recordset containing a rowset of data from the source. To describe the SQL statement in the CommandType property, the constant *adCmdText* is used.

```perl
<%@Language=PerlScript%>
<%
# Create the Command object
#
$cmd = $Server->CreateObject('ADODB.Command');

# Set the command text
#
$cmd->{CommandText} = "SELECT * FROM Test";

# The type of command that was defined
#
$cmd->{CommandType} = adCmdText;

# The connection object is is associated with
#
$cmd->{ActiveConnection} = (<<EOF);
    Provider=Microsoft.Jet.OLEDB.4.0;
    Data Source=C:\\nwind.mdb;
EOF

# Create a prepared version of the command
#
$cmd->{Prepared} = 1;

# Execute it
#
$rst = $cmd->Execute();

# Loop the result
#
while( ! $rst->{EOF} )
{

    foreach $fld (Win32::OLE::in($rst->Fields)) {
        $Response->Write( $fld->{Name} );
        $Response->Write( ': ' );
        $Response->Write( $fld->{Value} );
        $Response->Write( '<BR>' );
        }

    $Response->Write( '<BR><BR>' );

    $rst->MoveNext();
}
```

```
# Close the recordset
#
$rst->Close();
# Close the command
#
$cmd->Close();
%>
```

The problem with the previous command is that it is static. Unless it is going to be issued many, many times, there is no reason to use it as a command. However, it does represent a precompiled command. In contrast, the command could have been rewritten to use parameterized queries, which we will talk about next.

Parameters

The command object is very useful when utilizing the parameter. Let's compare two statements to see what they look like syntactically.

```
<%
# The following sql query is a static select query
#
$sql = "SELECT Firstname, Lastname, State, Country WHERE ID=12";
%>

<%
# The following sql query is a parameterized select query
#
$sql = "SELECT Firstname, Lastname, State, Country WHERE ID=?"
%>
```

Whether or not the previous statement is precompiled, the question mark (?) represents a parameter that can be substituted for a variable by the application. Not that the previous example is very useful when using only one parameter, but the feature of parameters is appreciated when dealing with very long SQL queries. However, the last bit of code was only an SQL statement. Next, let's take a look at how to create Parameter objects that will represent the value.

Creating the Parameters

To enable parameters in the application, a Parameter object for each must be created. The next example displays the process of using parameters more in detail. The standard constants are imported as usual, and for the sake of detail two objects instead of one are now used to perform the command.

```
<%@Language=PerlScript%>
<!--#include virtual="/adops.inc"-->
<%
# Instantiate the connection object and the command object
#
$conn = $Server->CreateObject("ADODB.Connection");
$cmd  = $Server->CreateObject("ADODB.Command");
```

```perl
# The following sql query inserts a new record into a table
# where city and year are the only two fields and the only
# two parameters.
#
my $sql = "INSERT INTO myNewTable (city, year) VALUES (?, ?)";

# Use the connection object to open northwind
#
$conn->Open(<<EOF);
    Provider=Microsoft.Jet.OLEDB.4.0;
    Data Source=C:\\nwind.mdb;
EOF

# Set the connection object as the ActiveConnection property
# of the Command object. This will be where it executes the
# query at.
#
$cmd->{ActiveConnection} = $conn;

# Set the CommandText and Prepare the statement
#
$cmd->{CommandText} = $sql;
$cmd->{CommandType} = adCmdText;
$cmd->{Prepared} = 1;

# In the Parameters collection of the Command object,
# Append (create on-the-fly) the following parameters
# of the following types and lengths.
#
$cmd->Parameters->Append(
                    $cmd->CreateParameter
                        ('city', adVarChar, adParamInput, 255)
                    );

$cmd->Parameters->Append(
                    $cmd->CreateParameter
                        ('year', adVarChar, adParamInput, 255)
                    );


# The parameters above are now available as properties of the
# Properties-collection, and they can be written to. Here they
# are set to the values that will be used in the new record
# created in the database table.
#
$cmd->Parameters->{city} = 'Sometown';
$cmd->Parameters->{year} = 1986;


# Execute the Command
#
$cmd->Execute(undef, undef, adExecuteNoRecords);
```

```
$rst=$conn->Execute("myNewTable", adCmdTable);

while( ! $rst->{EOF} )
{

    $Response->Write($rst->Fields(0)->{Value});
    $Response->Write($rst->Fields(1)->{Value});
    $Response->Write("<BR>");

    $rst->MoveNext();

}
%>
```

This should be fairly self-explanatory from the previous sections up to the appending of parameters. Let's get back to that shortly. But first, the two parameters that were defined in the SQL statement are added to the Parameters collection and then given their values. Since the Command object is executed with a specific notation, it should not return any records. When finished, to check and make sure something was added, the two fields of the database they was added to are looped.

We now return to the appending of parameters. A parameter is an object, and the Append() method appends an object to the Parameters collection.

```
<%
$cmd->CreateParameter( Name, Type, Direction, Size, Value );
%>
```

In essence, the name Parameter sets the name property of the object. Coincidentally, in this case the same name as the field in the underlying database was chosen, but just about any name can be used. The type used is *adVarChar* (10), which means that we are passing a string value. The direction parameter sets the Direction property which is the type of parameter object used, and here it is used for input to the database, so *adParamInput* (0x0001) is the right constant. Table 9.1 details the constants.

Table 9.1   Constants for the Direction of Parameter Objects

VALUE	CONSTANT	DESCRIPTION
0x0000	adParamUnknown	The parameter direction is unknown.
0x0001	adParamInput	The parameter is an input parameter.
0x0002	adParamOutput	The parameter is an output parameter.
0x0003	adParamInputOutput	The parameter is both an input and output parameter.
0x0004	adParamReturnValue	The parameter is a return value.

Lastly, Size defines the maximum size in characters or bytes for the input. The value of the object can be set as a property during runtime of the application or when the parameter is created.

An Overview of the Parameter Object

Table 9.2 displays the properties, methods, and collections of the Parameter object.

Overview: The Command

Table 9.3 displays the properties, methods, and collections of the Command object.

When working with the Command object, some useful methods for handling the Parameter objects belong to the Parameters collection. This collection is summarized in Table 9.4.

Table 9.2   The Parameter Object

	DESCRIPTION
Collection	
Properties	The property objects that belong to the Parameter object.
Method	
AppendChunk(*data*)	Appends a large amount of binary or character *data* to the Parameter object.
Property	
Attributes	Contains certain characteristics of the Parameter object—can be read or written.
Direction	See Table 9.1 for details.
Name	Reads or writes the name of the parameter object.
NumericScale	The number of decimal places to the right of the values of the object—read and write.
Precision	The number of digits for representing values.
Size	Read/Write property determining the size in bytes or characters of the data in the value property.
Type	Reads or writes the type of data used in the value of the parameter object.
Value	Reads or writes a value of the data type specified in the Type property.

Table 9.3 The Command Object

	DESCRIPTION
Collection	
Parameters	Parameter objects associated with the current Command object.
Properties	Property objects of the command.
Method	
Cancel ()	For asynchronous mode only, cancels the last call to the Execute method.
CreateParameter ([*Name*], [*Type*] [*Direction*], [*Size*], [*Value*])]	Creates and returns a new parameter object that later can be appended to the Parameters collection. Name is the name of the parameter, type is a DataTypeEnum constant that specifies the data type of the object's value. Direction is discussed in Table 9.1. Size specifies the maximum amount of bytes or characters that can be stored in the object, and value will set a value of the parameter object.
Execute ([Affected records], [Parameters], [Options])	When calling Execute, the CommandText query will be executed. To prevent a row set from being returned, specify one or several CommandTypeEnums or ExecuteOptionEnums. Affected Records is a variable for which the data provider returns a long value for the number of records that were affected by either an action query or a stored procedure that embodies the Command object.
Property	
ActiveConnection	Connection object that uses the command.
CommandText	Command that the Command object will execute.
CommandTimeout	Number of seconds the command will be executed before returning an error—default is 30 seconds.
CommandType	Describes the type of command in the CommandText property—thus improves performance. Can be one or several CommandTypeEnums and ExecuteOptionEnums.
Name	Reads or writes the name of the Command object.
Prepared	The Prepared property can be set to TRUE when an active connection is open and it will store a precompiled version of the CommandText if the data provider supports precompiled commands—thus improves performance.
State	Current state of the object.

Table 9.4   The Parameters Collection

	DESCRIPTION
Methods	
Append()	Appends a Parameter object to the Parameters collection.
Delete(*index*)	Deletes the Parameter object *index* from the Parameters collection.
Item(*index*)	Returns item *index* from the collection.
Refresh()	When a parameterized query or stored procedure is the essence of the Command object, Refresh can be used to retrieve information from the provider regarding the query. When not available, it returns nothing.
Property	
Count	Counts the number of Parameter objects in the collection.

Summary

In this chapter the Command object has been presented. The purpose of the Command object is simple. When a query is issued against a database, the query is compiled before being executed. This induces a delay in the process, which is where the Command object comes into the picture. The Command object can be used to represent a precompiled version of a query and thus improve performance. A precompiled query will execute somewhat more slowly than normal the first time it is run because it has to be stored, but after that it will execute more quickly than normal. Ideally, the situation for the Command object is the best when the same query is executed multiple times. In addition, the Command object can represent parameterized queries, which enables a flexible reuse of the same queries.

In the next chapter, we will look at the Record object, which is used to represent natural hierarchies such as file systems or e-mail systems.

## CHAPTER 10

A Natural Systems Record

Although hierarchical Recordsets can be shaped, the Recordset was originally designed for tabular and relational data such as a relational database where data is contained in tables. The flat rowset is the core structure for the types of data that will populate the Recordset. Consequently, there is a need for an object where the core is hierarchical—the Record object.

Introduction to the Record

When first encountering the Record object, forget about the Recordset. The Recordset was not designed to pay attention to hierarchical data—the Record was.

- A file system stores files in a hierarchical structure—the directory tree.
- An e-mail system stores messages in a hierarchical structure—the message folders.

The Record object can represent these structures easily. For example, a directory can be loaded into the Record, and it can be manipulated by using built-in methods and properties.

Getting Your Hands on a Record

Each different provider will delineate different uses for the Record object. However, with the OLE DB provider for Internet publishing, a record can be opened and manipulated or moved to a remote machine, for example. The syntax of the Open() method is always Open(*Source, ActiveConnection, Mode, CreateOptions, Options, UserName, Password*);

The OLE DB provider for Internet Publishing works in particular with documents served by the Web Distributed Authoring and Versioning protocol of IIS or by Microsoft FrontPage's Web Extender Client. The provider takes advantage of something known as the root binder, which allows you to use a URL as a connection string without knowing what provider services the source. The Source property can be used together with the ActiveConnection, or either one can be used separately. Furthermore, the ActiveConnection can be represented by a Connection object that has specified a URL as its data source. The options for opening a Record are to specify one of the following:

- An absolute URL
- A relative URL
- An open Recordset object

In example, the root binder would set the root node to the location sharedDirectory on a remote server as follows:

```
<%
# Create a new Record object
#
$rec = $Server->CreateObject("ADODB.Record");

# Create a new connection implicitly by opening a URL
#
$rec->Open("sharedDirectory", "URL=http://www.someplace.org/");
%>
```

As seen in the preceding example, the directory is specified in the Source property and the URL is specified in the ActiveConnection property. The result is that a Connection object is implicitly created, and the type of usage is classified as opening a relative URL. It is similar to opening the Connection object explicitly before opening the record.

```
<%
# Create a new connection object
#
$conn = $Server->CreateObject("ADODB.Connection");

# Let the rootbinder open a new URL
#
$conn->Open("URL=http://www.someplace.org/");
%>
```

If you want to be more specific when opening a record, there are several modes in which the Record object can be opened. These modes are listed in Table 10.1. The mode will take the place of the Mode parameter seen in the Open() method of the Record object, and the default value is adModeUnknown (0).

Table 10.1 The Modes for Connecting—ConnectModeEnum

VALUE	CONSTANT	DESCRIPTION
0	adModeUnknown	The mode is not yet set or it cannot be determined what mode is currently set.
1	adModeRead	Read only.
2	adModeWrite	Write only.
3	adModeReadWrite	Read/write.
4	adModeShareDenyRead	Shares the connection, but denies read access to anyone but the current user.
8	adModeShareDenyWrite	Shares the connection, but denies write access to anyone but the current user.
0xc	adModeShareExclusive	Does not share the connection because the current user has exclusive access and therefore no one can open a connection.
0x10	adModeShareDenyNone	Shares the connection, and lets anyone open a connection using any type of access preferred without limitations.
0x400000	adModeRecursive	Used only with adModeShareDenyNone, adModeShareDenyWrite, or adModeShareDenyRead to determine sharing of the children of a record.

Furthermore, the CreateOptions parameter in the Open() method of the Record object enables you to define whether the record that should be opened already exists, or if the record that should be opened needs to be created. The values are listed in Table 10.2. The default value is adFailIfNotExists (−1), and values can be combined by using the bitwise AND operator, which is represented by the ampersand character (&).

The Options parameter in the Record object's Open() method allows you to specify certain values for options for opening the record or combine several values in Table 10.3 by using the bitwise OR operator, which is represented by the pipe character (¦). The default value if adOpenRecordUnspecified (−1).

When a root node has been set, the files and subdirectories of the location, which the record is representing, can be returned as a Recordset. From there on, this can be traversed as any other Recordset.

```
<%
# Create a new Record object
#
$rec = $Server->CreateObject("ADODB.Record");
```

Table 10.2 The Options for Creating a Record—RecordCreateOptionsEnum

VALUE	CONSTANT	DESCRIPTION
0x00002000	adCreateCollection	Creates a new record. If the entity specified in the source already exists, you must combine this with adOpenIfExists or adCreateOverwrite to prevent an error.
0x80000000	adCreateStructDoc	Creates a new record of type adRecordStructDoc.
0x00000000	adCreateNonCollection	Creates a new record of type adSimpleRecord.
0x02000000	adOpenIfExists	Modifies the meaning of adCreateStructDoc, and adCreateNonCollection when OR is used with this value, so that if the source property of the record points to an existing entity, it will try to open it. Cannot be used with adCreate Overwrite.
0x04000000	adCreateOverwrite	Modifies the meaning of adCreateCollection, adCreateStructDoc, and adCreateNonCollection when OR is used with this value, so that if the source property of the record points to an existing entity, it overwrites it. Cannot be used with adOpenIfExists.
−1	adFailIfNotExists	Open fails if the entity pointed to by the source property does not exist.

```
# Open the Record
#
$rec->Open("shareDir", "URL=http://www.sopmeplace.org");

# Return a Recordset of the files and directories at the URL
#
$rst = $rec->GetChildren();
%>
```

If enabled by the provider, the returned Recordset will contain the names of the files and subdirectories that were in the scope of the root node. In summary, there are three ways to invoke the OLE DB provider for Internet publishing:

Table 10.3   The Options for Opening a Record—RecordOpenOptionsEnum

VALUE	CONSTANT	DESCRIPTION
−1	adOpenRecordUnspecified	The type of record is not specified.
0x00800000	adOpenSource	Opens the source of an executable script such as an .asp document instead of reading the executed result.
0x00001000	adOpenAsync	Opens the record in asynchronous mode.
0x00004000	adDelayFetchStream	The default stream associated with the record does not need to be fetched immediately.
0x00008000	adDelayFetchFields	The fields associated with the record do not need to be fetched until access is attempted.

- Use the keyword URL in the connection string, that is, URL=http://localhost/.
- Define the Provider property of the Connection object used to MSDAIPP.DSO.
- Combine both of these in one connection string Provider=MSDAIPP.DSO;Data Source=http://localhost/.

When a record has been opened, the RecordType property must be used to determine what type of Record has been opened. This property can return an enumerator that reveals whether the Record is a file, directory, or a special collection (see Table 10.4).

When returned, the Record will have a Fields collection with two special types of fields. *adDefaultStream* (−1) points to the field that is the default Stream object for the Record, and *adRecordURL* (−2) points to the field with the absolute URL for the Record object.

Table 10.4   RecordType for Data Contained in a Record

VALUE	CONSTANT	DESCRIPTION
0	adSimpleRecord	A single record without any nodes such as subdirectories—for example, a file
1	adCollectionRecord	A record that contains subnodes—for example, a directory with subdirectories
2	adStructDoc	A collection that contains specific OLE structured documents

Moving, Deleting, and Copying

Each operation that results in manipulation of the fields in the Record object can be either synchronous or asynchronous. The latter means that the program continues executing regardless of whether or not the previous call was completed. For example, when you open a connection in normal instances, you are aware that it is open before you call Execute(). However, if the operation is asynchronous, it is necessary to determine by an If statement or something similar that the connection is open and the Execute() call can be run.

When performing operations with the Record, the last call can be cancelled provided that it was an asynchronous call of the type CopyRecord(), DeleteRecord(), MoveRecord(), or Open().

CopyRecord()

To copy a Record from one location to the other, CopyRecord() will transfer the contents of the Record. The syntax is:

```
$Record->CopyRecord( Source, Destination, UserName, Password,
CopyRecordOptionsEnum, Async )
```

Either omit the Source parameter to let the current Record be copied to the destination specified by a URL, or specify both Source and Destination Parameters by URL. The UserName and Password parameters are fully optional and depend on the configuration, while Async should be specified as either asynchronous—which allows Cancel(), for example—or synchronous (however, it is not necessary). The CopyRecordOptionsEnum can be one of the values shown in Table 10.5.

Table 10.5 The Constants for Copying Records—CopyRecordOptionsEnum

VALUE	CONSTANT	DESCRIPTION
1	adCopyOverWrite	Overwrites existing data of the same name
2	adCopyNonRecursive	Omits subdirectories of the current record in the operation
4	adCopyAllowDataLoss	Allows a loss of data as result of download and upload operations because record is copied to a location served by a different data provider that exposes the functionality

DeleteRecord()

The DeleteRecord() will remove the physical representation of the Record object. For example, if a directory is represented, DeleteRecord() deletes it. The syntax is very simple.

```
$Record->DeleteRecord( Source, Async )
```

However, if the Source parameter is a URL for the data to be deleted, deletion will occur at the location referenced by the URL.

MoveRecord()

As the name indicates, you can for example move what a Record represents from the current machine to a remote machine.

```
$Record->MoveRecord (Source, Destination, UserName, Password,
                  MoveRecordOptionsEnum, Async)
```

The parameters can have the same values as those for the CopyRecord() method. The MoveRecordOptionsEnum is displayed in Table 10.6.

Overview: The Record

Table 10.7 shows the collections, methods, and properties of the Record object described in this chapter.

Table 10.6   The Constant for Moving a Record—MoveRecordOptionsEnum

VALUE	CONSTANT	DESCRIPTION
1	adMoveOverWrite	Overwrites existing data of the same name.
2	adMoveDontUpdateLinks	Will not update hypertext links of the source record.
4	adMoveAllowEmulation	If the move fails because the destination is at a different location than the calling point or uses a different data provider, emulate it by downloading and uploading, and possibly deleting records at the destination.

Table 10.7 The Record Object

	DESCRIPTION
Collection	
Fields	The Field objects that belong to the Record.
Properties	The Property objects that belong to the Record.
Method	
Cancel()	In asynchronous mode, the last call to either CopyRecord(), DeleteRecord(), MoveRecord(), or Open() is cancelled.
Close()	Closes the Record and releases any exclusive locks placed on files or other data while the record was open.
CopyRecord() ([Source], Destination, [Username], [Password], [Options], [Asynch])	Copies Record from source, a Record object, or a URL to the destination URL. User name or password is specified if needed, and Options is set to CopyRecordOptionsEnum. Asynch is set to TRUE to perform the operation asynchronously.
DeleteRecord() ([Source], [Asynch]) GetChildren	Deletes either the current Record or specifies a Record by URL in the Source parameter and the Record it points to. Set Async to TRUE if you want to perform the operation asynchronously. This method will return a Recordset of the current contents and subnodes within the Record object— for example, files and subdirectories.
MoveRecord()	Moves Record from source, a Record object, or a URL to the destination URL.
[Source], Destination, [Username], [Password], [Options], [Asynch])	User name or password is specified if needed, and Options is set to MoveRecordOptionsEnum. Async is set to TRUE to perform the operation asynchronously.
Open() ([Source], [ActiveConnection], [Mode], [CreateOptions], [Options], [Username], [Password])	Opens a new, empty Record object, or specifies the parameters of what you want to embody the Record object. Source is either a URL or row of an open Recordset. ActiveConnection is the Connection object or Connection-String that points to the content that will embody the Record object. Mode is a ConnectModeEnum that sets the access permissions to the content. CreateOptions is a RecordCreateOptionsEnum that specifies whether to open an existing or create a new source of content. Options specifies how to open a Record, and user name and password are used only if needed.

Continues

Table 10.7 *(Continued)*

DESCRIPTION	
Property	
ActiveConnection	The current connection object or connection string
Mode	Access permissions
ParentURL	The URL of the parent Record for the current Record
RecordType	The type of Record (see Table 10.4)
Source	The content of the source property—for example, a URL or RecordSet object reference
State	The current state of the Record

Summary

In this chapter we have discussed the Record object. It is designed for working with natural hierarchical structures such as e-mail systems or file systems. The record can connect to an entity such as a file or a directory by pointing to an absolute URL, a relative URL, or an open Recordset object. After a connection to the entity has been established, the entity embodies as the record and the record can be accessed and manipulated by calling the native methods of the Record object.

The next chapter will cover the Stream object, which is used when working binary and textual data.

## CHAPTER 11

Working the Stream of Data

When working with files, input and output are generally spoken of in terms of *streams*. That terminology has survived for a very long time, and when binary and textual data is accessed from ADO, it is through an object with a familiar ring to its name—the Stream object.

Introduction to the Stream

Whether the source is e-mail in a folder, a file on the system, or another type of data supported and exposed by the provider, there are a number of ways to initialize the stream of data with its contents:

- Opening the Stream object with a URL where the data is
- Explicitly creating a new, empty Stream object
- Utilizing the default Stream object of a Record

After the data has populated the Stream object or an empty Stream object has been explicitly created, there will be a number of methods and properties available for modifying the data.

Opening the Stream

As previously mentioned, the Stream can take a variety of forms, although it is limited to binary data or text. The Open() method is similar to the other Open() methods of ADO: Open(*Source, Mode, StreamOpenOptions, UserName, Password*).

User name and password are considered minor parameters because they may or may not be called for, depending on how the requested stream of data is configured. Let's look at the enumerators for opening the Stream (Table 11.1).

The default value is adOpenStreamFromURL. However, since the constants are very specific, the data source the Stream connection will connect to is either an absolute URL or an already-opened Record object where that object's own default stream can be initialized. When neither is defined, a new, empty Stream will be opened that can be read and written to depending on what permissions are set in the Mode parameter of the Open() method. The default value is *adModeUnknown*(0), and either constant is valid for the Mode property of the Connection, Record, and Stream objects. In essence, a Stream object could be opened as follows:

```
<%@Language=PerlScript%>

<!--#INCLUDE VIRTUAL="/ADOPS.INC"-->

<%
# Create a new Stream object
#
$str = $Server->CreateObject("ADODB.Stream");

# Open the stream object
#
$str->Open('URL=http://www.someplace.org/myfile.txt',
           adModeReadWrite,
           adOpenStreamFromURL);
%>

<%
. . .
# Close the stream object
#
$str->Close();

# Destroy it
#
undef $str;
%>
```

Table 11.1 The Constants for Opening a Stream—StreamOpenOptionsEnum

VALUE	CONSTANT	DESCRIPTION
1	adOpenStreamAsync	Stream will be opened asynchronously.
4	adOpenStreamFromRecord	Source parameter is an open Record object used to access the stream of data.
8	adOpenStreamFromURL	Source parameter is the absolute URL to the location of the stream of data.

When opened asynchronously, the Cancel() method may be applied to cancel the Open() method, but no other methods can be affected by asynchronous mode.

Overview: The Stream

Table 11.2 shows the methods and properties of the Stream object presented in this chapter.

Table 11.2 The Stream Object

	DESCRIPTION
Method	
Cancel()	In asynchronous mode, the Open() method is cancelled.
Close()	Closes the stream object and releases exclusive access permissions to any content it has locked.
CopyTo([Destination],[n])	Copies n number of characters to another open destination Stream object. If n is not specified, everything from the current position to the end will be copied.
Flush()	Flushes the buffer of the Stream object to its underlying object.
LoadFromFile(file)	In an open Stream, will load the file specified in the parameter.
Open([Source], [Mode], [OpenOptions], [Username], [Password])	Either omits source to open a new, empty Stream object, or specifies it by absolute URL or reference to an open Record object. Mode is a ConnectModeEnum that defines the access permissions. OpenOptions describes how to open the Stream by use of a StreamOpenOptionsEnum, and user name and password should be specified only if needed.
Read(n)	Reads n number of bytes, or the value of a StreamReadEnum: adReadAll (−1), adReadLine (−2). By default it will read the whole Stream object.
ReadText(n)	Reads n number of characters from a Stream object; StreamReadEnum.
SaveToFile (Filename, SaveOptions	Specifies location to which to save the file, and a SaveOptionsEnum whether a new file should be created if it does not exist or if a current file with the same name should be overwritten. Default is adSaveCreateNotExist (1), which creates a new file if it does not already exist, and the other possible value is adSaveCreateOverWrite (4), which will overwrite an existing file with the same name.

Continues

Table 11.2 *(Continued)*

	DESCRIPTION
SetEOS()	Makes the current position in the stream the end of the Stream.
SkipLine()	Skips a line when reading text.
Write(*b*)	Writes an array of bytes to the Stream.
WriteText(s,[*Options*])	Writes the text content of scalar *s* to the Stream. As an option, can set whether a line separator is appended after the string by adWriteChar (0) or adWriteLine (1). adWriteChar ignores line separator and is the default setting.
Property	
CharSet	Used with a text stream that specifies the character set with which to read the Stream.
EOS	Current position is at end of the stream.
LineSeparator	Character used to separate lines as specified in the LineSeparatorEnums. Could be adCRLF (– 1), the default carriage return line feed separator, adLF (10), which is a line feed, or adCR (13), which is a carriage return.
Mode	Access permissions mode. The Stream may have inherited the mode from the source if the property does not have a set value.
Position	Current position in number of bytes from the beginning of the Stream.
Size	Total size of the stream in number of bytes.
State	State of the Stream object.
Type	A StreamTypeEnum describing the type of stream that is open. Either adTypeBinary (1) for binary data or adTypeText (2) for text.

Summary

In this chapter we have discussed the Stream object. This object should be used when working with binary and textual data. You can initialize the stream with data by opening a URL that represents a valid entity, using the default Stream object of a Record object, or creating a new, empty Stream object. Several methods can be used for reading or writing to the stream or for performing operations such as copying or saving the stream.

With the end of this chapter, the book concludes its material on Active Server Pages and ActiveX Data Objects. You have come a long way and are now prepared to blend and use Perl, ASP, or ADO for future applications. As we have seen, the trio blends easily together and enables powerful applications to be developed, but it is equally important to note that these technologies are strong individually as well.

A Windows developer can use Perl for great Windows applications because it is a very rich language that has been around to mature for a long time. Perl's community support is great and knowledgeable as well, and there are modules that will save you time on almost any imaginable task. It is natural that when technologies such as ASP emerge, a scripting language of Perl's caliber is adapted to work together with such technologies. It is also natural to learn these new technologies because they can exert many positive effects on the current paradigm of programming.

A unified and centralized programming model has evolved and come to fruition with ASP and ADO in which essentially everything that is needed for applications development is available from a machine running the Perl scripting language. In this programming model on Windows, it is no longer necessary to know a multitude of programming languages to write strong applications, and it is not necessary to know the details of how to access every type of data store to write a useful tool. Perl, ASP, and ADO support the fundamental idea that programming should be simple. As a result, it is simple, and that enables a greater number of people to find a way to express themselves through the computer—which is the essential purpose of this book. Until next time, I hope that this journey has been a natural and enjoyable process.

Bag of Scripts

I n this section, a number of commonly used scripts are provided. The scripts answer frequently asked questions regarding common tasks in Internet development, and they are written in PerlScript and ready to be used in Active Server Pages, although in most cases the code is virtually interchangeable between Perl and PerlScript.

How Do I Send e-mail?

This is a common question. The underlying reason is often that some e-mail functionality is desired on the Web page so that the clients can communicate and relay feedback to the administrators of the server. As a matter of fact, it is easy to send e-mail when using the Net::SMTP module of Graham Barr's Libnet collection. Before running the script, install Libnet by following these two steps:

1. Enter the command prompt.

2. Type ppm install libnet.

The following script presents an HTML form that is used to fill out the information that goes directly into an e-mail message and is sent to the given recipient.

```
<%@Language=PerlScript%>
<%
if ($Request->Form->Item) {
    use Net::SMTP;
```

```
      my($subject,
          $mailto,
          $mailbody) = ($Request->Form('MailSubject')->Item,
                         $Request->Form('MailTo')->Item,
                         $Request->Form('MailBody')->Item);

      my($mailserver, $mailsender) = ('Mail.YourSMTP.com',
                                      'account@YourSMTP.com');
      $smtp = Net::SMTP->new($mailserver);

      $smtp->mail($mailsender);
      $smtp->to($mailto);

      $smtp->data();
      $smtp->datasend("Subject: $subject\n");
      $smtp->datasend("To: $mailto\n");
      $smtp->datasend("From: $mailsender\n\n");
      $smtp->datasend($mailbody);


      $smtp->dataend();
      $smtp->quit;
}
%>

<FORM ACTION="smtp.asp" METHOD="POST">
<TABLE WIDTH="340" ALIGN="CENTER">
<TR>
  <TD COLSPAN=2 ALIGN= "CENTER" BGCOLOR="BLACK">
      <FONT FACE="ARIAL" COLOR="WHITE"><B>MAILFORM</B></FONT>
  </TD>
<TR>
  <TD WIDTH="100">Subject:</TD>
  <TD WIDTH="240" ALIGN = "RIGHT">
      <INPUT TYPE="Textfield" Name="MailSubject">
  </TD>
</TR>
<TR>
  <TD WIDTH="100">Mail to:</TD>
  <TD WIDTH="240" ALIGN = "RIGHT">
      <INPUT TYPE="Textfield" Name="MailTo">
  </TD>
</TR>
<TR>
  <TD WIDTH="100">Short Greeting:</TD>
  <TD WIDTH="240" ALIGN = "RIGHT">
      <INPUT TYPE="Textfield" Name="MailBody">
  </TD>
</TR>
<TR>
  <TD COLSPAN = "2" ALIGN = "RIGHT">
      <INPUT TYPE="SUBMIT" VALUE="Send Email">
  </TD>
```

```
</TR>
</TABLE>
</FORM>
```

How Do I Retrieve e-mail?

Less common than sending e-mail, retrieving e-mail from a POP account either for personal or public use can come in handy. Again, with Graham Barr's Libnet, it is as easy to retrieve e-mail as it is to send it. If you have not yet installed Libnet, follow these two steps:

1. Enter the command prompt.
2. Type ppm install libnet.

Next, let's look at how to retrieve e-mail using the Net::POP3 module. All you need to do is define a few variables, such as the mail server to use, and your username and password on the mail server.

```perl
<%@Language=PerlScript%>
<%
    use Net::POP3;
    my($mailserver,
        $user,
        $pass) = ('mail.YourPOP3.com',
                  'username',
                  'password');

    my $srv = Net::POP3->new($mailserver);

    my $get = $srv->login($user, $pass);
    my $msg = $srv->list();

    foreach $message ( keys(%{$msg}) ) {
        $read = $srv->get($message);

        for( @{$read} ) {
            $output .= $_;
            $output .= '<BR>';
        }

        $output .= '<BR>';
    }

    $srv->quit();
%>

<%=$output%>

<BR>
<BR>
--
Mailbox checked
```

How Do I Draw Graphics on the Fly?

Whether you are producing up-to-the minute, accurate graphs from a database, displaying weather maps, or manipulating images on request of the user, Lincoln D. Stein's Perl-port of Thomas Boutell's GD graphics library makes drawing graphics a simple task. Before moving on, follow these two steps if you have not installed GD:

1. Enter the command prompt.

2. Type ppm install GD.

Early versions of GD draw GIFs, so please update your system if you have one of those versions because this example creates an image in the PNG format. In summary, GD supports methods for generating color palettes, drawing primitives with or without brushes, and using TrueType fonts when drawing strings.

In this example, we draw a string in a built-in font that ships with GD, and it includes the generated image in a somewhat different manner than ordinary. Instead of including an image, the image tag includes an ASP file that contains the code for generating an image using GD. The whole example is divided into two files, and this is the HTML file:

```
<%@ Language=PerlScript %>
<CENTER>This is the generated image:
<BR>
<BR>
<IMG SRC="drawimage.asp?name=<%=$Request->QueryString("name")-
>Item()%>">
<BR>
<BR>
<FORM ACTION="graphics.asp" METHOD="GET">
Please type your name: <INPUT TYPE="textfield" NAME="name">
<INPUT TYPE="SUBMIT">
</FORM>
</CENTER>
```

This is the ASP that draws the image:

```
<%@Language=PerlScript%>
<%
    use GD;
    use Win32::OLE::Variant;

    my $name = $Request->QueryString("name")->Item();

    my $img = new GD::Image(150,20);
    my ($white,
        $red) = ($img->colorAllocate(255,255,255),
                 $img->colorAllocate(255,0,0));

    $img->transparent($white);
    $img->string(gdLargeFont,0,0,"Hello $name", $red);

    my $output = Win32::OLE::Variant->new(VT_UI1, $img->png);
```

```
$Response->{ContentType} = "image/PNG";
$Response->BinaryWrite($output);
%>
```

How Do I Get the Dimensions of an Image?

It often becomes necessary to figure out the original height and width of an image. For this purpose, you can read the dimensions of an image simply by using the Image::Size module. Credit for this module goes to Alex Knowles and Andrew Tong for writing the original, and to Randy J. Ray for providing the Perl module interface. Do the following to install the module:

1. Enter the command prompt.
2. Type ppm install Image-Size.

Some of the image formats that can be used are GIF, JPG, PNG, TIF, XBM, and PPM.

```
<%@Language=PerlScript%>
<%
    use Image::Size;

    # Inspect the "$error" variable if nothing appears
    #
    my($x_width,
       $y_height,
       $error) = imgsize($Server->MapPath("/win2000.gif"));
%>

The dimensions of the image are:
<BR>X: <B><%=$x_width%></B>
<BR>Y: <B><%=$y_height%></B>
```

How Do I Read a Spreadsheet Using ADO?

To read a spreadsheet using ADO, you will need to specify what cells to return when calling the Execute() method, and in the connection string you must both define the file to use and include the Excel properties.

```
<%@Language=PerlScript%>
<%
    my $output;

    $conn = $Server->CreateObject("ADODB.Connection");

    $conn->Open('Provider=Microsoft.Jet.OLEDB.4.0;Data
Source=D:\TheWorkbook.xls;Extended Properties=Excel 8.0;');

    $rst = $conn->Execute('[A1:C10]');

    while(! $rst->{EOF} ) {
```

```
        foreach $field (Win32::OLE::in($rst->Fields)) {
            $output .= $field->{Name}.": ".$field->{Value}."<BR>";
        }
    $rst->MoveNext();
    }
%>

<%=$output%>
```

How Do I Graphically Pie-Chart the System Resources for System Administration?

Perl latently has strong system administrative capabilities. In this example, we will tap into its power. To begin, three pie charts will be drawn to represent the accurate free space, used space, and total space of the following:

- The hard disk
- The random access memory (RAM)
- The virtual memory

In order to do this, we first need a module for drawing the pie chart, and PNGgraph from Martien Verbruggen and Steve Bonds will let us do this easily. It uses the GD graphics library, and it can be used to graph line charts, bar charts, pie charts, and more. Install it by following these two steps:

1. Enter the command prompt.
2. Type ppm install PNGgraph.

In addition to the pie charts, the following information is gathered and presented:

- Version of Windows
- Type of file system, sectors, and clusters
- Number and type of processor(s)
- Length of time the computer has been running
- Present Windows services and their status (started, stopped, paused, and so on)

Dave Roth's Win32::AdminMisc module will provide some good methods for accessing information about the system resources.

1. Enter the command prompt.
2. Type ppm install Win32-AdminMisc.

This example uses two files as well. One ASP file is used to draw a pie chart from the parameters passed in a QueryString to the file, and the main file is used to get the system information and pass these parameters. This is the main file:

```
<%@ Language=PerlScript %>
<%
```

```perl
use Win32;
use Win32::AdminMisc;
use Win32::Service;

Win32::Service::GetServices($hostname,\%services);

my %windows = Win32::AdminMisc::GetWinVersion();
my %memory = Win32::AdminMisc::GetMemoryInfo();
my %cpu = Win32::AdminMisc::GetProcessorInfo();
my %config = ('ActivePerl Build' => Win32::BuildNumber(),
              'Filesystem' => scalar(Win32::FsType()),
              'Uptime' => Win32::GetTickCount(),
              'Domain' => Win32::DomainName(),
              );

my($sectors,
   $bytes,
   $freeclusters,
   $totalclusters)= Win32::AdminMisc::GetDriveGeometry("C:\\");

my($disk_total,
   $disk_free) = Win32::AdminMisc::GetDriveSpace("C:\\");

my($disk_used) = ($disk_total - $disk_free);
my($ram_used) = ($memory{RAMTotal}-$memory{RAMAvail});
my($virtual_used) = ($memory{VirtTotal} - $memory{VirtAvail});


sub check_status {
    my($service) = @_;
    Win32::Service::GetStatus('', $service, \%status_pairs);
    my($status) = $status_pairs{'CurrentState'};
    if($status == 1) { return "Stopped"; }
    if($status == 2) { return "Start pending"; }
    if($status == 3) { return "Stop pending"; }
    if($status == 4) { return "Running"; }
    if($status == 5) { return "Continue pending"; }
    if($status == 6) { return "Pause pending"; }
    if($status == 7) { return "Paused"; }
}
%>


<TABLE WIDTH = "600" border=0 ALIGN="CENTER" CELLPADDING="3">
<TR>
  <TD WIDTH="200" BGCOLOR="#aaaaff" ALIGN="CENTER" VALIGN="TOP">
    <FONT FACE="Verdana" SIZE="+1"><B>Disk space</B></FONT>
  </TD>
  <TD WIDTH="200" BGCOLOR="#aaaaff" ALIGN="CENTER" ALIGN="TOP">
    <FONT FACE="Verdana" SIZE="+1"><B>RAM</B></FONT>
  </TD>
  <TD WIDTH="200" BGCOLOR="#aaaaff" ALIGN="CENTER" VALIGN="TOP">
    <FONT FACE="Verdana" SIZE="+1"><B>Virtual Memory</B></FONT>
  </TD>
```

```
</TR>
<TR>
  <TD WIDTH="200" ALIGN="CENTER" VALIGN="TOP">
    <IMG SRC="piechart.asp?SliceInUse=<%=$disk_used%>
                      &SliceFree=<%=$disk_free%>">
    <BR>
    <TABLE WIDTH="150" ALIGN="CENTER">
      <TR>
      <TD WIDTH="50" ALIGN="LEFT">
        <FONT FACE="VERDANA, ARIAL" SIZE="-2">Total:
        </FONT>
      </TD>
      <TD WIDTH="100" ALIGN="RIGHT">
        <FONT FACE="VERDANA, ARIAL" SIZE="-2">
        <%=$disk_total%>
        </FONT>
        </TD>
      </TR>
      <TR>
        <TD WIDTH="50" ALIGN="LEFT" BGCOLOR="blue">
          <FONT FACE="VERDANA, ARIAL" SIZE="-2" COLOR="white">
          Used:
          </FONT>
        </TD>
        <TD WIDTH="100" ALIGN="RIGHT" BGCOLOR="blue">
          <FONT FACE="VERDANA, ARIAL" SIZE="-2" COLOR="white">
          <%=$disk_used%>
          </FONT>
        </TD>
      </TR>
      <TR>
        <TD WIDTH="50" ALIGN="LEFT" BGCOLOR="yellow">
          <FONT FACE="VERDANA, ARIAL" SIZE="-2">
          Free:
          </FONT>
        </TD>
        <TD WIDTH="100" ALIGN="RIGHT" BGCOLOR="yellow">
          <FONT FACE="VERDANA, ARIAL" SIZE="-2">
          <%=$disk_free%>
          </FONT>
        </TD>
      </TR>
    </TABLE>
  </TD>
  <TD WIDTH="200" ALIGN="CENTER" VALIGN="TOP">
    <IMG SRC="piechart.asp?SliceInUse=<%=$ram_used%>
                      &SliceFree=<%=$memory{RAMAvail}%>">
    <BR>
    <TABLE WIDTH="150" ALIGN="CENTER">
      <TR>
        <TD WIDTH="50" ALIGN="LEFT">
          <FONT FACE="VERDANA, ARIAL" SIZE="-2">
```

```
           Total:
           </FONT>
         </TD>
         <TD WIDTH="100" ALIGN="RIGHT">
           <FONT FACE="VERDANA, ARIAL" SIZE="-2">
           <%=$memory{RAMTotal}%>
           </FONT>
         </TD>
       </TR>
       <TR>
         <TD WIDTH="50" ALIGN="LEFT" BGCOLOR="blue">
           <FONT FACE="VERDANA, ARIAL" SIZE="-2" COLOR="white">
           Used:
           </FONT>
         </TD>
         <TD WIDTH="100" ALIGN="RIGHT" BGCOLOR="blue">
           <FONT FACE="VERDANA, ARIAL" COLOR="white" SIZE="-2">
           <%=$ram_used%>
           </FONT>
         </TD>
       </TR>
       <TR>
         <TD WIDTH="50" ALIGN="LEFT" BGCOLOR="yellow">
           <FONT FACE="VERDANA, ARIAL" SIZE="-2">
           Free:
           </FONT>
         </TD>
         <TD WIDTH="100" ALIGN="RIGHT" BGCOLOR="yellow">
           <FONT FACE="VERDANA, ARIAL" SIZE="-2">
           <%=$memory{RAMAvail}%>
           </FONT>
         </TD>
       </TR>
     </TABLE>
     </TD>
<TD WIDTH="200" ALIGN="CENTER" VALIGN="TOP">
   <IMG SRC="piechart.asp?SliceInUse=<%=$virtual_used%>
                       &SliceFree=<%=$memory{VirtAvail}%>">
   <BR>
   <TABLE WIDTH="150" ALIGN="CENTER">
     <TR>
       <TD WIDTH="50" ALIGN="LEFT">
         <FONT FACE="VERDANA, ARIAL" SIZE="-2">
         Total:
         </FONT>
       </TD>
       <TD WIDTH="100" ALIGN="RIGHT">
         <FONT FACE="VERDANA, ARIAL" SIZE="-2">
         <%=$memory{VirtTotal}%>
         </FONT>
       </TD>
     </TR>
```

```
      <TR>
        <TD WIDTH="50" ALIGN="LEFT" BGCOLOR="blue">
          <FONT FACE="VERDANA, ARIAL" SIZE="-2" COLOR="white">
          Used:
          </FONT>
          </TD>
        <TD WIDTH="100" ALIGN="RIGHT" BGCOLOR="blue">
          <FONT FACE="VERDANA, ARIAL" COLOR="white" SIZE="-2">
          <%=$virtual_used%>
          </FONT>
          </TD>
        </TR>
        <TR>
        <TD WIDTH="50" ALIGN="LEFT" BGCOLOR="yellow">
          <FONT FACE="VERDANA, ARIAL" SIZE="-2">
          Free:
          </FONT>
          </TD>
        <TD WIDTH="100" ALIGN="RIGHT" BGCOLOR="yellow">
          <FONT FACE="VERDANA, ARIAL" SIZE="-2">
          <%=$memory{VirtAvail}%>
          </FONT>
          </TD>
    </TABLE>
  </TD>
</TR>
<TR>
  <TD HEIGHT="10"></TD>
</TR>
<TR>
  <TD WIDTH="600" COLSPAN="3" BGCOLOR="#aaaaff">
    <FONT FACE="Verdana, Arial" size="+1">
    <B>System Setup</B>
  </TD>
</TR>
<TR>
  <TD WIDTH="600" COLSPAN="3">
    <FONT FACE="Verdana, Arial" SIZE="-2">
    <%
    $Response->Write(<<EOF);
    $windows{Platform} $windows{Major} Build $windows{Build}
    with ActivePerl $config{'ActivePerl Build'} that has been
    running for $config{Uptime} milliseconds without reboot on
    $cpu{ProcessorNum} processor(s) a $cpu{ProcessorType}
    revision $cpu{ProcessorRevision} at a filesystem of
    $config{Filesystem} filesystem with $sectors sectors a
    $bytes bytes where there are $freeclusters free clusters of
    $totalclusters total clusters
EOF
    %>
    </FONT>
    <BR>
```

```
    </TD>
  </TR>
</TABLE>

<TABLE WIDTH="600" ALIGN="CENTER">
<TR>
  <TD WIDTH="300" BGCOLOR="#aaaaff">
    <FONT FACE="ARIAL" SIZE="+1"><B>Windows Service</B></FONT>
  </TD>
  <TD WIDTH="300" BGCOLOR="#aaaaff">
    <FONT FACE="ARIAL" SIZE="+1"><B>Status</B></FONT>
  </TD>
</TR>
<%
  foreach my $service (keys %services) {
%>
  <TR>
    <TD WIDTH="300">
      <%=$service%>
    </TD>
    <TD WIDTH="300">
      (<%=check_status($services{$service})%>)
    </TD>
  </TR>
<%
  }
%>
<TR>
</TABLE>
```

The next file is the ASP file that is used to draw the pie chart of the system resources:

```
<%@ Language=perlscript %>
<%
    use PNGgraph::pie;
    use Win32::OLE qw(in);
    use Win32::OLE::Variant;

    my($resource_use) =
        $Request->QueryString("SliceInUse")->Item();
    my($resource_free) =
        $Request->QueryString("SliceFree")->Item();

    my($resource_total) = ($resource_use - $resource_free);
    my(@data) = (["",""], [$resource_use, $resource_free]);

    $my_graph = new PNGgraph::pie(100, 100);
    $my_graph->set('dclrs' => [ qw(blue lyellow) ],
                   'pie_height' => 0);

    $Response->ContentType("image/png");
    $Response->BinaryWrite(Win32::OLE::Variant->new(
                              VT_UI1,
                              $my_graph->plot(\@data)) );
%>
```

What's on the CD-ROM

I n addition to the ActivePerl software bundle, the CD-ROM contains scripts as presented in the book and also a number of additional scripts. It is divided into three sections. First, the ASP section contains PerlScript files that should be run on the Web server; next, the ADO section has both PerlScript files for ASP and regular Perl files that are ready to be run from the command line; finally, the Common Scripts section is a series of various scripts useful for Internet productivity.

Hardware Requirements

To use this CD-ROM, your system must meet the following requirements:

Windows 95/98/NT/2000

Intel 80486 Processor

8/16/32/32 Mb RAM

232 Kb for the scripts on the CD, and 20 MB for ActivePerl.

Installing the Software

To install the software, follow these simple steps:

1. Start Windows on your computer.
2. Place the CD-ROM into your CD-ROM drive.

3. From Program Manager, select Programs, then Windows Explorer. Locate X:\ (where X is the correct letter of your CD-ROM drive).

4. Select the scripts that you want to copy to your hard disk by either clicking once on a single script or holding down CTRL while selecting several scripts.

5. Choose Edit on the toolbar and click on Copy.

6. Locate C:\ (where C is the correct letter of your hard disk) and click on the directory to which you want to copy the files.

7. Choose Edit on the toolbar and click on Paste.

Using the Software

When using a script that is available on the CD-ROM, there are two ways to execute it depending on whether it is an Active Server Pages file or a Perl file.

First, if the file is an Active Server Pages file, it must be run on a Web server that supports Active Server Pages and executed by accessing the file through the Web service. Copy the Active Server Pages file from the CD-ROM and place it in the root directory of your Web server. Next, open and steer your browser to the location of the copied file. For example, if your domain is http://localhost/ and the file is named Logical-Pages.asp, then in the Web browser you would open the address http://localhost/LogicalPages.asp.

However, if you copied a Perl file with the file extension .pl from the CD-ROM to the hard disk, then you need to use the Perl interpreter to execute the script. Assuming that the file was named shape1.pl, in order to do this, enter the command prompt and locate the directory where shape1.pl is located, then type perl shape1.pl.

Please note that a script that uses ADO will apply either to a Microsoft Access database or a Microsoft SQL Server database. Every example that is a Perl file with the extension .pl will attempt to connect to the Microsoft SQL Server and query the Northwind database if not modified. Every example that is an Active Server Pages file will attempt to load the Northwind Access database with the file extension .mdb. Both examples can be easily modified to suit your needs. For example, if you do not have Microsoft SQL Server, you can copy the connection string from an Active Server Pages file and paste it into the Perl file in which you want to use the Access database. To do this you should follow these easy steps:

1. Open an .asp file that either is located in the ADO section of the CD-ROM or has been copied from the ADO section of the CD-ROM.

2. Locate the following text: Provider=Microsoft.Jet.OLEDB.4.0;Data source=C:\ NWIND.mdb.

3. Highlight text in the script by clicking on the first letter without releasing the left mouse button, then drag the mouse to the last letter.

4. Copy the highlighted text into memory by pressing CTRL+c on the keyboard.

5. Open a .pl file that was copied from the CD-ROM to the hard disk and locate the line(s) with the text Provider=SQLOLEDB;Integrated Security=SSPI;Persist Security Info=False;Initial Catalog=Northwind;.

6. Highlight the text that you located in step 5.

7. Paste the text copied into memory in step 4 by pressing CTRL+v on the keyboard.

8. Save the .pl file.

9. Run the .pl file by typing perl scriptname.pl.

In the same manner, if the Access database, for example, is not located in the same physical path as Perl searches for in the script, alter the script to search for the Access database where it is located on your drive. This is done in the connection string after the Data Source statement.

The Common Scripts are commented on in the code, and may require you to install certain modules. For that information, follow the instructions provided as comments in the code. Enjoy the scripts!

User Assistance and Information

The software accompanying this book is being provided as is without warranty or support of any kind. Should you require basic installation assistance, or if your media is defective, please call our product support number at (212) 850-6194 weekdays between 9 A.M. and 4 P.M. Eastern Standard Time. Or, we can be reached via e-mail at wprtusw@wiley.com.

To place additional orders or to request information about other Wiley products, please call (800) 879-4539.

The HTTP Status Description

The status property of the ASP Response object can be used to set the value of the status line returned to the client by the server. This status line is contained within the HTTP headers and consists of a three-digit code that indicates the status and a string that describes the status. All HTTP status codes can be found in the official HTTP specification, which is available on the Internet.

Table C.1 A Few HTTP Status Codes

STATUS CODE	STATUS DESCRIPTION
100	Continue
101	Switching protocols
200	OK
201	Created
202	Accepted
203	Nonauthoritative information
204	No content
300	Multiple choices
301	Moved permanently
303	Move temporarily

Continues

Table C.1   A Few HTTP Status Codes   *(Continued)*

STATUS CODE	STATUS DESCRIPTION
304	Not modified
400	Bad request
401	Unauthorized
403	Forbidden
500	Internal server error
501	Not implemented
503	Service unavailable
505	HTTP version not supported

Content Types

The ASP Response object's ContentType property can be set to tell the browser what type of content is being sent.

Table D.1   A Few Content Types

CONTENT TYPE
text/HTML
text/XML
image/GIF
image/JPEG
text/plain

ActivePerl Activity on the Web

The following is a compilation of the best resources available on the Web.

PerlScript Mailing List

A PerlScript mailing list is available at www.asplists.com/asplists/aspperlscript.asp. It is a very good moderated list that is focused on its topic. You are guaranteed answers on this list.

PerlScript Community

A PerlScript community that you can join is online at www.deja.com/~perlscript. This community includes discussions on PerlScript with ASP and ADO, a chat, and everything else that belongs to a community.

ActivePerl Mailing Lists

ActiveState hosts a number of mailing lists at www.activestate.com/support/mailing lists.htm. The mailing lists deal with a variety of topics such as XML, OLE, COM, database programming, and systems administration with Perl. Although their mailing list on Perl for the Web includes PerlScript, the PerlScript mailing list at asplists.com is the spot where the majority of questions and answers on PerlScript surface.

Active Server Pages (ASP)   A server-side technology created by Microsoft that embeds a server-side scripting language with already-existing markup languages in the one and same document.

ActiveX   A word whose definition has often changed, ActiveX enables interaction between COM components as a technology built on top of the Component Object Model.

ActiveX Data Objects (ADO)   A COM-based application-level programming interface that provides an easy-to-use method of accessing and working with data exposed through an OLE DB data provider.

ActiveX Scripting Engine   A working scripting language implementation that enables the engine to be run in an ActiveX scripting host. To implement an existing scripting language, the programmer follows a specification on how the language should be implemented in order to work with an ActiveX scripting host.

ActiveX Scripting Host   The ActiveX Scripting Host hosts any ActiveX Scripting Engine, and it allows the ActiveX Scripting Engine to run scripts within itself.

ADO   See *ActiveX Data Objects*.

API   See *Application Programming Interface*.

Application Programming Interface (API)   A specification and set of exposed routines that a programmer can use to create software.

ASCII   (American Standard Code for Information Interchange) A 7-bit character set used to display the characters found on most standard U.S. keyboards.

ASP   See *Active Server Pages*.

C   A programming language used for developing high-performance applications.

Cache   A local and temporary storage of data, used by separate applications in order to improve the performance of an application's running instance by accessing commonly used data instead of regenerating or requesting it from another instance.

CGI   See *Common Gateway Interface*.

Class   In object-oriented programming, contains the methods and properties that define an object.

Client   In ASP contexts, the user of the services made available by a Web server.

Collection   A group of related data items that can be accessed through the object by either an index number or key name for the specific item of the collection that you want returned.

COM   See *Component Object Model*.

Command line   In the context of this book, the position of the cursor on a new and empty line in a command prompt window where a command such as running the Perl interpreter can be executed.

Common Gateway Interface (CGI)   An interface of a Web server that allows external programs such as Perl scripts or C/C++ compiled executables to be processed on request of the client and return data from the server to the client, thus enabling capabilities beyond those of a markup language.

Component   A unit of code that exposes a defined set of data and code that can be accessed by the data consumer of the component.

Component Object Model (COM)   A specification and implementation from Microsoft that allows components to interact with each other as long as they follow the written Component Object Model specification. As a binary standard, it makes the programming language the component was written in and the platform it runs on irrelevant for a component's ability to communicate and interact with other components.

C++   An object-oriented language built on the C programming language. C++ is in many terms compatible with C, so many C programs can be compiled as C++ programs. However, there are a number of important differences between the two.

Cursor   In ADO, the software device that returns rows of data and knows the current position in the data plus the next position in the rows of data.

Database   A structured collection of data and metadata where the data is of use for the owner of the database and the metadata describes how the data is structured.

Database Management System (DBMS)   The software used to define the structure and content of databases plus administrate and process databases.

Data Consumer An application that directly uses the services of a data provider. An example of a data consumer is ActiveX Data Objects (ADO), which uses the services provided by the OLE DB data provider.

Data Control Language (DCL) In SQL, the language is used to set the permissions and protect the database.

Data Definition Language (DDL) The statements of SQL that define, modify, and delete database structures.

Data Manipulation Language (DML) The statements in SQL that manipulate data in the database.

Data Provider Entity that provides data and code for a data consumer. An example of a data provider is the OLE DB provider for access to Microsoft Jet databases.

Data Store A place where data is stored—for example, databases and files.

DBMS See *Database Management System*.

DCL See *Data Control Language*.

DDL See *Data Definition Language*.

Delphi A Rapid Application Development environment for Windows, developed by Inprise (formerly Borland) and based on the programming language Object Pascal.

DML See *Data Manipulation Language*.

Extensible Markup Language (XML) A markup language that, contrary to HTML, permits more flexibility than existing markup languages.

Field In ADO, an object that represents a column in a row such as the data returned from a database column after a query.

HTML See *Hypertext Markup Language*.

HTTP See *Hypertext Transfer Protocol*.

Hypertext Markup Language (HTML) A markup language that provides a set of predefined tags that can be used to present documents on the Internet.

Hypertext Transfer Protocol (HTTP) The protocol that allows client and server communication on the World Wide Web.

IIS See *Internet Information Services*.

Instance The embodiment of an object. An instance of a class is created when memory on the machine is allocated to allow room for the object.

Internet Information Services (IIS) A Microsoft Web server that supports Active Server Pages.

MDAC See *Microsoft Data Access Components*.

Method   A method belongs to a class and is normally used to perform an operation on data that is within the class.

Microsoft Data Access Components (MDAC)   A set of components that implement Universal Data Access.

Microsoft Script Control   An ActiveX control that extends a preexisting application such as Microsoft Word by allowing the developer to embed scripts within it.

Object   An object is used to call the methods and properties of an instantiated class.

Object Linking and Embedding (OLE)   An object-based technology from Microsoft that enables sharing of services and information between applications.

Object Linking and Embedding Database (OLE DB)   A COM application-level programming interface that is used as a data provider to give data access to relational and nonrelational data stores.

ODBC   See *Open Database Connectivity.*

OLE   See *Object Linking and Embedding.*

OLE DB   See *Object Linking and Embedding Database.*

Open Database Connectivity (ODBC)   A standard application-programming interface that can be used by an application to gain access to a relational database.

Perl   (Practical Extraction and Report Language) A powerful and popular scripting language that was first developed on UNIX and then became fully adapted to Windows.

PerlScript   An ActiveX Scripting Engine implementation of PERL.

Property   Data that is associated with a object and in good terms of object-oriented programming. Defines the object that is instantiated from the class.

Query   A request formulated by the Structured Query Language that is made about the data in the database.

Record   In ADO, a number of fields that represent a returned row from a database; in a database, a row of columns with populated data.

Server   The machine that receives and processes requests from the client and then returns the result to the client.

Server-side includes (SSI)   A server-side way of including files external from the current document in the current document by using a markup tag.

SQL   See *Structured Query Language.*

SSI   See *Server-side includes.*

Structured Query Language (SQL)   A standard language used to control, manipulate, and access data in relational databases.

Syntax   The rules of a programming language and how it is "spoken."

Table   In general, a database object containing a set of records and defining the columns of those records.

Universal Data Access (UDA)   Microsoft's strategy for providing a common data access method for all types of data available in all locations. It is implemented by Microsoft Data Access Components.

Windows Script Host   A host that allows an ActiveX Scripting Engine to run scripts either on the desktop or from a command prompt. It is not necessary for Perl since Perl can already run its scripts from the command prompt.

XML   See *Extensible Markup Language*.

A

AbsolutePosition property, invalidating, 180
ActiveConnection property, 131, 194–195, 228, 236
ActivePerl:
  components of, 20–29
  documentation, 20–23
  standard modules, 27–29
  Web resources for, 271
ActivePerl package, 8
Active Server Pages (ASP), 1
  applications in, 70–71
  versus CGI, 1
  executing, 264
  versus HTML, 1
  installing, 7
  and object-oriented programming, 13
  state, maintaining with, 3
Active Server Pages engine, 2
ActiveState repository, 23
ActiveX Data Objects (ADO), 118
  accessing, from Perl, 186–188
  components required for, 127–130
  data access with, 115–116
  data provider, 128
  data store access, 127–128
  for disconnected recordsets, 194–199
  spreadsheets, reading with, 255–256
ActiveX Scripting Engine:
  capabilities of, 2
  objects, access to, 4
AddNew() method, 185–186
adExecuteNoRecords constant, 147
ADO object model, 134–136
Advanced Data Tablegram (ADTG) format, 201
adXactAbortRetaining, 159
Aggregate functions, 212, 214

ALL predicate, 125
Alter command, 126
Anchors, 53, 55
AND operator, 122
APPEND command, 205
Append() method, 231
Application, definition of, 4, 70
Application object, 4–5, 69–72, 78
  cleaning up, 75
  locking, 74
Application_OnEnd event, 73
Application_OnStart event, 72
Arrays:
  accessing elements in, 35
  associative, 39
  creating, 42–43
  data storage in, 88
  functions related to, 36–38
  for scalar variables, 35–38
  sorting, 38
ASP documents:
  content of, 1–2
  ending processing, 104
  scripting languages in, multiple, 9–10
ASPError object, 5, 107, 112
  properties of, 113
asp extension, 11
ASP ObjectContext object, 1–3, 107
  events of, 113
  methods of, 111, 113
ASP pages, external, 108
asXactCommitRetaining, 159
At (@) sign:
  for arrays, 35
  as identifier, 30
Attributes, class, 63–64
Attributes property, 129, 159
Authentication, digital certificates, 99–101

B

Backslash:
  for escaping characters, 32
  for prototypes, 61
  for references, 40
Barr, Graham, 251, 253
Batch updates, 195–197
BeginTrans() method, 159
BETWEEN predicate, 123
Blocks, syntax of, 29
Bonds, Steve, 256
Boutell, Thomas, 254
Buffering, 83–84, 103
  turning on and off, 104

C

CacheSize property, 180–181
Caching, 104
  expiration settings, 104
CALC function, 212
Calculations, in subroutines, 58–59
Cancel() method, 247
CD-ROM (accompanying):
  executing scripts, 264–265
  hardware requirements, 263
  installing, 263–264
  scripts on, 263
CGI, maintaining state with, 3
Chapter alias, 205
Character classes, predefined, 53–54
Characters, encoding, 109
Charts, drawing, 256–261
chomp() function, 35
chop() function, 35
chr() function, 35
Christiansen, Tom, 43–44
Classes:
  inheritance characteristics, 64–65
  instances of, 14, 63
  in OOP, 63–64
Client certificates, 99–100
  ignoring, 100–101
Clients:
  Application objects for, 70
  communicating with, 87
  concurrency issues, 73–75
  connection status, 104
  responding to, 97

session data of, 76
  Session objects for, 7, 70
Client state, maintaining, 69, 87
Code reuse, and modules, 56
Collections, 14–17
  counting items in, 16
  iterating through, 16–17
  removing items from, 17
  retrieving values from, 15
Columns:
  separating, 173–174
  in tables, 119
COM components:
  context information about, 103
  functionality of, 4
  instances of, 108
  proprietary, support for, 7
  uses of, 187
COM developers, accessing built-in objects,
    102–105
Command line options, 22
Command object, 136, 227
  collections of, 233
  fast queries with, 227–232
  methods of, 233
  with parameters, 229–232
  properties of, 233
  Recordset returned from, 169
Commands:
  adExecuteNoRecords constant with,
    147
  describing, 149
CommandText property, 228–229
CommandType property, 147–148, 228
Comments, syntax of, 29
CommitTrans method, 159
Common Gateway Interface, 3
Comparison operators, 122–125
COMPUTE statement, 212–214
Concurrency, of client requests, 73–75
Conditional control statements, 47–49
Connection object, 135, 139
  collections of, 160
  DNS-less connection, 141–142
  Errors collection in, 143–144
  methods of, 160
  OpenSchema() method, 150
  properties of, 160–161

Provider property, 238
Recordset returned from, 169
syntax of, 139–140
Connections, *see also* Connection object
DNS-less, 133–134, 141–142
making, 141–142
as transactions, 159
ConnectionString property, 131
Connection strings, 131, 140
copying between files, 264–265
Constructors, 64
Contents collection, 72
adding items to, 73–75
adding Session objects to, 77
removing items from, 73
Content type:
describing, 104
header for, 104
ContentType property, 269
Control characters, escaping, 32
Control structures, 47–51
Cookies:
applications of, 83–84
attributes for, 84
creating, 84
guidelines for, 83
indexes, iterating by, 86
minimizing, 76
properties of, 86
reading, 85
storage of, 83
subkeys, 85
subkeys, iterating, 85–86
variable storage in, 88–90
writing and reading, 82
CopyRecord() method, 240
Count property, 16–17
of cookies, 86
Create clause, 157
Create command, 126
CreateObject() method, 108, 139
for Recordset creation, 163–164
Curly braces:
for references, 40–41
syntax of, 29
Cursor:
definition of, 164
and disconnected recordsets, 195

selection of, 165–166
types of, 165
CursorLocation property, client-side setting, 195–197
CursorType property, 164–166

D

Data:
client to server, 82
in-memory storage of, 88–90
inserting, 156–157
outputting, 101–102
in relational databases, 118–119
from Response object, 6
from Request object, 6
retrieving, 180–181
security for, 99
server to client, 82
sharing on Web, 72–75
universal access to, 115. *See also* Universal Data Access (UDA)
Database queries, 136
Databases:
ADO access to, 127
changes to, 159
connecting to, 130
nonrelational, 117
object definition, 126
ODBC support, 117
relational, 115–116, 118–120
Structured Query Language for, 120–127
structure of, 150–156
virtual, 135
Database tables, *see* Tables
Data consumer, 134
Data Control Language (DCL), 120, 127
Data Definition Language (DDL), 120, 126
Data dictionary, 119
Data Manipulation Language (DML), 120–126
comparison operators, 122–123
comparison predicates, 122–125
logical operators, 122
Select clause, 120–123
Where clause, 122
Data provider, 128
Data shaping, 203

Data source:
  connection with, 135
  disconnecting from, 195–197
  native provider for, 131–132, 141
  for OLE DB, 130–134
  updating, 185–186
Data source name (DSN), 132–133
  DNS-less connections, 133–134
Data stores:
  ADO access to, 127–128
  database structure in, 150–156
  interface for, *see* Universal Data Access
    (UDA)
Data structures, nested, 43
Data type identifiers, 30
  in double-quoted strings, 32
Data types, generic values of, 158
Data validation, 94–97
  failed, 97
Debugging, and Error object, 143
Delete() method, 39, 184–185
DeleteRecord() method, 241
Destructors, 64
Device drivers, ODBC support, 116
Digital certificates, 99
  obtaining, 100
Direction property, 231
Directories, application root, 4
Directory tree, 235
Disk, recordsets storage on, 199–200
DISTINCT predicate, 125
DNS-less connections, 133–134
Dollar ($) sign, 31
  as identifier, 30
Dominus, Mark-Jason, 43
Dot operator, for concatenating strings,
    32–33
Drop command, 126, 159
Dynamic properties, 129–130

E
each() function, 39
Else statements, 48
Elsif statements, 48
E-mail:
  retrieving, 253
  sending, 251–253
E-mail directories, ADO access to, 128

Equal sign, syntax of, 29
Error object, 136, 143–145
  properties of, 144
Errors:
  ASPError objects for, 5, 112
  custom, 11
  detecting, 143
  error messages, 109
  examining, 145–147
Errors collection, 143, 145, 147
  clearing, 143
Events, 14, 71–72
Execute() method, 108, 149
exists() function, 39
Extensible Markup Language (XML),
    200–201
Extensions:
  asp, 11
  inc, 11
  mdb, 264
  pl, 264
  pm, 23
  for regular expressions, 53, 55

F
Field object, 136
  appending, 197
  columns represented as, 167–168
  data types for, 198
  methods of, 169
  properties of, 168
Fields collection, 167–168
  for Record objects, 239
File data source name, 133
File handles, 43–44
  opening, 44
File names, relative, 12
Files:
  ADO access to, 128
  external, accessing, 108
  paths to, mapping, 109–111
  printing, 51
  virtual, 12
Filter property, 181, 183
Find() method, 181
Foreach loop, 50
Foreign key, 120, 125
For loops, 16, 50

Form collection, 98–99
Forms:
  required fields in, 95–96
  sending data from, 87–88
  submitting with GET, 87
FORM tag, 87

G
GD graphics library, 26
  installing, 254
GetLastError() method, 109
GET method:
  security of, 88
  submitting forms with, 87–88
GetRows() method, 174–175
GetString() method, 173
Global.asa file:
  Application events in, 72–73
  Session objects in, 76
  Session Scoped objects in, 75
  variable declarations in, 71–72
Global variables, state maintenance, 69
Graphics:
  GD module for, 26
  script for, 254–255

H
Hash, 39
  data storage in, 88
HasKeys property, 85
Headers:
  adding, 103
  character set name in, 104
  content of, 81–82
hex() function, 34
Hierarchies, 203
  computed, 211–215
  disconnected, 215–224
  grouped, 211–215
  relation-based, 204–211
  reshaping, 224
HKEY_LOCAL_MACHINE registry, navigating to, 10
HREF links, 88
HTMLEncode() method, 109
HTML forms, *see also* Forms
  script for, 251–253
HTML output, clearing, 104

HTTP body:
  bytes in, 105
  form elements in, 105
HTTP header, cookies in, 105
HTTP protocol, 81
HTTP query strings, 87–88
  variables in, 105
HTTP requests, 81–82
HTTP status codes, 267–268
Hypertext Markup Language (HTML), versus ASP, 1

I
If statements, 47–48
IIS ObjectContext objects, 1–3
Images:
  dimensions of, 255
  drawing, 254–255
Image::Size module, 255
inc extension, 11
index() function, 33–34
IN predicate, 124
Instances, 63. *See also* Objects
Internet Information Services (IIS):
  applications, 4, 70–71
  ASP installation with, 7
  Document Security tab, 100
Internet Services Manager:
  script time-out definition in, 108
  session state, disabling from, 78
IScriptingContext interface, 103
item() method, 15–16, 95
Items:
  removing, 17
  subitems of, 15–16

J
Jet Expression Service, 212
join() function, 38
Joins, 125–126

K
Keys, primary and foreign, 120, 125
keys() function, 39
Knowles, Alex, 255

L
Labels, 51
last() function, 51

lcfirst() function, 34
lc() function, 34
length() function, 34
Libnet, 26
 for e-mail functions, 251–253
 installing, 251
LIKE predicate, 123–124
List values, accessing, 41
local() function, 30
Lock() method, 73
Locks, types of, 166–167
LockType property, 166–167
Logical operators, 49, 122
Loop control statements, 49–51
loops, 171
LWP module, 26

M

Mailing lists, for ActivePerl and PerlScript,
 271
Maintaining state, 69, 87
 with query strings, 87–88
 with Transfer() method, 111
map() function, 37–38
MapPath() method, 109–111
Mathematical operators, 48
mdb file extension, 264
Message folders, 235
Metacharacters, for regular expressions,
 52–53
Metadata, in relational databases, 118–
 120
Methods, 13–14
 class, 63–64
 versus properties, 14
Microsoft Access, 137
Microsoft Cursor Service for OLE DB,
 129–130
Microsoft Data Access Components
 (MDAC), 115, 118
 Advanced Data Tablegram format in, 201
 components of, 115–116
 installing, 137
Mode parameter, 236
Modifiers, for pattern matching, 52
Modular programming, 56
 modules, 63
 object-oriented, 63–66
 packages, 56

 subroutines, 56–61
 symbol tables, 61–62
Modules, 56, 63
 characteristics of, 23
 examples of, 26–27
 importing, 63
 installing, 23–26
 naming, 63
 standard, 27–29
MoveRecord() method, 241
MSDASQL, 131–132
MSDatashape, 203
my() function, 30

N

Name property, 129
Names, formatting, 96
Navigation, through records, 164–166
Net::POP3 module, 253
Net::SMTP module, 251
next() function, 51
NOT operator, 122
NOT predicate, 124
NT Option Pack, 7
NULL predicate, 124
Null values, scalar variables as, 31

O

ObjectContext object, 5–6
Object-oriented programming (OOP), 13
 Perl support for, 63–66
Objects, 63
 built-in, 4, 102–105
 collections of, 14–17
 events of, 14
 external, returning, 139
 life cycles of, 71
 methods, 13–14
 properties of, 14
 static, 72
<OBJECT> tag, 72, 75
ODBC drivers, 116–117
OLE DB, 117
 ADO interface for, 118
 data access with, 115
 data consumer, 134
 data source for, 130–134
 service components, 128
 uses of, 117–118

OLE DB provider, 128
  for Internet publishing, 235–239
  invoking for data shaping, 205
  Record objects, accessing, 235–236
  version numbers for, 131
Open Database Connectivity (ODBC):
  data access with, 116
  limitation of, 116
Open() method:
  for connections, 139–141
  CreateOptions parameter, 237–238
  for file handles, 43
  Mode parameter, 236
  Options parameter, 237
  for Record objects, 235–236
  for Recordset, 164
  for Stream objects, 245–246
OpenSchema() method, 150–156
  constraints on, 156
ord() function, 34
OR operator, 122

P

Packages, 56
  installing, 24–25
  outside, accessing, 56
  searching for, 24–25
  symbol table for, 61–62
Page commands, 9
PageCount value, 180
PageSize property, 180
Paging:
  in Perl environment, 188–194
  properties, 174–181
Parameter object, 136
  collection of, 232
  creating, 229–232
  direction constants, 231
  method of, 232
  properties of, 232
Parameters, 229
  appending, 231–232
  for subroutines, 57–60
Parameters collection, 136, 234
Parameters function, aggregate functions
    of, 212, 214
Parent classes, thing descriptor for, 66
Parent record set, setting, 205
Paths, mapping, 109–111

Pattern binding operators, 51–52
Pattern matching, 52–54
Pattern quantifiers, 53
Peer Web Services, 7
Percent (%) sign:
  for associative arrays, 39
  as identifier, 30
Performance, Web server:
  and process launches, 3
  tweaking, 147–149
Perl:
  ADO, accessing from, 187–188
  ADO for, 186
  for CGI, 2–3
  control structures, 47–51
  executing scripts in, 264
  free-form approach to, 19
  logical operators in, 49
  mathematical operators in, 48
  modular programming in, 56–66
  object-oriented, 63–66
  PerlScript, conversion from, 187
  questions about, 21–22
  recordsets, splitting with, 188–194
  syntax of, 29
Perldoc tool, 21–22
Perl documentation, 20–23
  naming conventions in, 22
Perl for Windows applications, 249
PerlIS.dll, 3
Perl Package Manager (PPM), 23–27
  commands for, 24, 26
  customizing, 25
  module installation, 23–26
PerlScript, 2, 8
  for ASP, 2–3
  installing, 8
  Perl conversion to, 187
  setting as default language, 9
  troubleshooting, 8
PerlScript community, 271
PerlScript mailing list, 271
Persistence, 199–201
Personal Web Server (PWS), 7
Plain Old Documentation (POD), 29
pl file extension, 264
pm file extension, 23
PNG format, for images, 254
PNGraph, 256

pop( ) function, 36
POST method, 98
Practical Extraction and Report Language,
  see Perl
Prepared property, 228
Primary key, 120, 125
Print function, 44
Process launches, 3
Properties, 14
  built-in, 130
  dynamic, 129–130
  setting, 14
Properties collection:
  iterating, 129
  Transaction DDL property in, 159
Property object, 136
  properties of, 129
Prototypes, 61
Provider property, MSDatashape setting,
  203–204
Public-key cryptography, 99
push( ) function, 36

Q
Queries:
  execution of, 227
  fast, 227–232
QueryString collection, 88, 90
QueryString environment variable, 88
  validating data, 94–97
Query strings, 87–88
Quotation marks, for strings, 31–32
qw function, 36

R
Ray, Randy J., 255
Record object, 136, 235
  collections of, 242
  copying, 240
  creating, 237–238
  deleting, 241
  methods of, 242
  moving, 241
  opening, 236–237
  properties of, 243
  synchronous and asynchronous manipu-
    lation, 240
Records:
  adding, 185–186

caching, 180–181
comparison operators, 122–123
comparison predicates for, 122–125
Data Manipulation Language management of, 120–126
deleting, 184–185
displaying, 172–174
finding, 183
logical operators, 122
navigation of, 164–166
properties and methods of, 167
retrieving, 120–121
searching for, 181
separating, 173–174
sorting, 184
in tables, 119
updating, 167
Recordset object, 135, 144, 163
  child, dropping, 205
  child, initializing, 216–220
  collections of, 221
  creating, 169, 171–172
  creating, programmatically, 197–199
  CursorType property, 164–166
  default, 169–171
  disconnected, 194–199
  disconnected hierarchical, 215–224
  file format definition, 201
  filtering, 181
  grouped hierarchies in, 211–215
  hierarchical, 201, 203, 208–211
  hierarchical, reshaping, 224
  LockType property, 166–167
  looping, 169–172
  methods of, 221–223
  name of, 224
  navigating, 169–170
  Open( ) method parameters, 164
  paging through, 174–181
  parameterized hierarchical, 211
  parent and child, 205–211
  persisting, 199–201
  preventing, 147–149
  printing to screen, 202–203
  properties of, 223–224
  reading from file, 202
  read-only, 201
  Record object for, 235
  records display, 172–174

relational, 205–206
row sets in, 145, 147
saving as a file, 199–200
saving to ASP Response object, 202–203
splitting, 188–194
RecordType property, 239
Redirect() method, 97
redo() function, 51
References, 39–43
blessed, 64
dereferencing, 40–41
in subroutines, 60–61
ref() function, 41–42
Regular expressions, 51–55
substitution, 54–55
translation of, 55
RELATE statement, 205, 208
Relational databases, 115–116, 118–120
Remote Data Services (RDS), Advanced
Data Tablegram format in, 201
RemoveAll() method, 17, 72, 77
Remove() method, 17, 72, 77
REQUEST_METHOD variable, 101
Request object, 6, 82
collections of, 82, 105
methods of, 105
property of, 105
Requests, simple, 6
Response object, 6, 82
Buffer property, 83–84
collections of, 82, 103–104
ContentType property, 269
methods of, 103–104
properties of, 104
repeated calls to, 102
status property, 267
Return values, for subroutines, 60–61
reverse() function, 37
rindex() function, 34
RollbackTrans method, 159
Root binder, 236
Root node, Recordset returns from,
237–238
Roth, Dave, 256
Rows, adding, 156–157
Rowsets, 144–145, 147, 163
adding records to, 185–186
columns in, 167
deleting records from, 184–185

filtering, 183
flat, 235
sorting, 184
supported functionality, 182–183

S
Save() method, 199, 202
Scalar variables, 29–35
accessing, with references, 41
in arrays, 35–38
defining as, 31
double-quoted, 32
writing to output, 104
Schemas:
printing to screen, 153–156
querying, 150–153
types of, 154–155
Scopes, 30–31
Script commands, 6
special notation (% %), 9
Scripting host, 2
Scripting language:
default, 9–11
multiple, 9–10
Scripts:
on CD-ROM, 263–265
for e-mail, retrieving, 253
for e-mail, sending, 251–253
for graphics, 254–255
for image dimensions, 255
for spreadsheets, 255–256
for system resources statistics, 256–
261
time limits on, 107–108
ScriptTimeout property, 108
Script time-outs, setting, 11
Secure Sockets Layer (SSL), 6
Security, for data, 99–101
Select Clause, 120–123
Semicolon:
for prototypes, 61
syntax of, 29
Server log, appending messages to, 104
Server object, 6, 107
methods of, 112
property of, 107–108, 112
utility methods, 108–111
Servers:
data retrieval from, 180

Servers *(Continued)*:
  default scripting language settings, 10–11
  digital certificates for, 99
Server-side includes (SSIs), 11–13
  loading time, reducing, 142
Server variables, 101–102
  dumping to screen, 101–102
Service components, 128
Session IDs, 76
Session object, 7, 69–70, 75–79
  events of, 76
  process of, 76–78
  for state maintenance, 3
Session_OnEnd event, 76
Session_OnStart event, 76
Sessions, starting, 76
Set command, options for, 25
Set method, 66
SetProperty() method, 84
SHAPE command, 204–205, 220
  error checking, 216
  inline, 208–211
  NEW keyword with, 215
  parameterized, 211
SHAPE language, 163, 203–215
shift() function, 36–37
Software reuse, 64–65
sort() function, 38
Sort property, 184
Source property, 236
splice() function, 37
split() function, 38
Spreadsheets, ADO access to, 127, 255–256
SQL queries:
  error checking, 145–147
  Recordset returns of, 147
  results of, 144
  schema queries, 150–156
SQL (Structured Query Language), 120–127
  DCL in, 127
  DDL in, 126
  DML in, 120–126
  Drop clause, 159
  Insert clause, 156–157
Standard output, writing data to, 104
State:
  maintaining, 3–4, 69, 111
  two-letter, 96

Stateless protocols, 69
Statements:
  compound, 29
  simple, 29
StaticObjects collection, 72
Status, 104
Status codes, 267–268
Status headers, sending, 97
STDERR handle, 43
STDIN handle, 43
STDOUT handle, 43
Stein, Lincoln D., 254
Stream object, 136, 245
  initializing, 245
  methods of, 247–248
  opening, 245–247
  properties of, 248
Streams, 245
Strings:
  concatenating, 32–33
  connection strings, 131
  double-quoted, 31–33
  encoding, 111
  formatting, 173
  functions for, 33–35
  joining, 38
  locations in, matching, 53
  pattern matching, 52–54
  single-quoted, 31–32
  splitting, 38
Structured Query Language, *see* SQL
    (Structured Query Language)
Subroutines, 56–61
  parameters of, 57–60
  prototypes, 61
  return values of, 60–61
Substitution, of regular expressions, 54–55
substr() function, 33
Supports() method, 182
Symbol table, for packages, 61–62
System administration, with Perl, 256
System data source name, 133
System resources, charting, 256–261

T

Tables:
  altering, 126
  creating, 126, 157–158

in databases, 119
deleting, 159
dropping, 126
joining, 125–126
rows, adding, 156–157
Text, regular expressions and, 51–55
Thing description, 66
Time-outs, for scripts, 108
Tong, Andrew, 255
Torkington, Nathan, 44
Transactions, 5
database connections as, 159
nested, 159
running, 111
types of, 112
Transfer( ) method, 109, 111
Translation operator, 55
Typeglobs, 62
Type property, 129

U
ucfirst( ) function, 33
uc( ) function, 33
UDL files, 132
Unique identifiers, 119–120
Universal Data Access (UDA), 115, 117
Universal data link, 132
Unless statements, 49
Unlock( ) method, 73
unshift( ) function, 37
Until loops, 51
UpdateBatch( ) method, 197
Update( ) method, 185–186
URLEncode( ) method, 111
URLs:
appending data to, 87–88
as connection strings, 236
encoding strings for, 111
User sessions, information about, 101

V
Value property, 129, 186
values( ) function, 39
Variables:
$_, 37
adding to Contents collection, 73–75
context of, 30
declaring, 30

dynamically scoped, 30
event-level, 71–72
global, 69
lexical, 30–31, 62
locating, with references, 40
names of, 31
in packages, 56
scalar, *see* Scalar variables
scopes of, 30
special, 44–47
typeglobs for, 62
VBScript, as default, 9
Verbruggen, Martin, 256
Virtual files, 12
Virtual paths, 12

W
Wall, Larry, 43
Web:
LWP interface for, 26
sharing data on, 72–75
Web browsers:
cookies, denial of, 83
redirecting, 97, 104
requests from, 81–82
Web Distributed Authoring and Versioning
protocol, 236
Web Extender Client, 236
Web pages:
remote, fetching, 98–99
session state, disabling, 77–78
transaction directives for, 111
Web servers, API of, 4
Web services, control centers, 4
Where clause, 122
While loops, 50–51
Win32::AdminMisc module, 256
Windows 95/98:
ASP installation with, 7
default scripting language, setting, 10
Windows NT/2000:
ADO, 137
ASP installation with, 7
default scripting language, setting, 11
Win32::GUI module, 27
Win32 modules, 27
Win32::NetAdmin module, 27
Win32::OLE, 27, 187–188

CUSTOMER NOTE: IF THIS BOOK IS ACCOMPANIED BY SOFTWARE, PLEASE READ THE FOLLOWING BEFORE OPENING THE PACKAGE.

This software contains files to help you utilize the models described in the accompanying book. By opening the package, you are agreeing to be bound by the following agreement:

To use this CD-ROM, your system must meet the following requirements:

Platform/Processor/Operating System. Windows 95/98, and Windows NT 4.0/2000

RAM. 8 MB minimum for Windows 95/98, 16 MB recommended. 16 MB minimum for Windows NT 4.0, 32 recommended. 32 MB for Windows 2000, 64 MB recommended.

Hard Drive Space. 250 KB for scripts, 20 MB for ActivePerl

Peripherals. DWS or U.S. Web server, and Microsoft Data Access Components